Teacher-made Aids for Elementary School Mathematics

Volume 2

Readings from the *Arithmetic Teacher*

edited by

Carole J. Reesink

**Bemidji State University
Bemidji, Minnesota**

National Council of Teachers of Mathematics

Library of Congress Cataloging in Publication Data:
(Revised for vol. 2)

Smith, Seaton E., comp.
  Teacher-made aids for elementary school mathematics.

  Vol. 2 edited by Carole J. Reesink.
  Includes bibliographical references.
  1. Mathematics—Study and teaching (Elementary)
  2. Teaching—Aids and devices. I. Backman, Carl A.,
joint comp. II. Reesink, Carole J. III. The
Arithmetic teacher. IV. Title.
  QA135.5.S56   1974   372.7'028   73-21581
  ISBN 0-87353-225-2

Printed in the United States

Contents

2. Geometry

3. Measurement

4. Graphs and Charts

5. Probability and Statistics

6. Problem Solving

7. Everyday Applications

8. Multipurpose Aids

Introduction

*T*he rationale for publishing a second in the series of *Teacher-made Aids for Elementary School Mathematics: Readings from the Arithmetic Teacher* was really quite simple. It had been ten years since the first monograph was published, and there was a new crop of valuable, if not classic, ideas in subsequent *Arithmetic Teacher*s for use in the K–8 classroom. As an education instructor, I found that my own student teachers and classroom teachers made extensive use of the first edition—to the point that my copy was literally falling apart and I had to buy a new one. Students were also searching out articles from the last ten years of the *Arithmetic Teacher* and were wearing out my copies of these journals. The convenience of having these last ten years' activities in a single volume for easy use and reference was another important consideration.

Selecting articles for this edition was a difficult task, since there were so many good ones to choose from. The guidelines for this collection, like the first, called for the articles to (1) have a clear purpose and be related to a contemporary topic in the elementary school mathematics curriculum; (2) provide sufficient information and specifications to enable teachers to construct the aid; and (3) include directions or examples relating the aid to classroom instruction.

The volume contains manipulative aids and activities. Games and puzzles have been omitted because of length considerations. However, this book goes a step further than the first in that the manipulative aids include easily obtained materials that can be purchased as well as those to be constructed by the teacher. One example of this is soda crackers for teaching tiling patterns and area.

This book is organized around the ten basic skill areas proposed by the National Council of Supervisors of Mathematics, endorsed by the NCTM, and published in the October 1977 *Arithmetic Teacher*. For your convenience, this list is reprinted in this book on the inside front cover. Materials were found for all ten areas except *estimation, computer literacy,* and *reasonableness of results*. Representation in some of the other areas is rather sparse, however. This may mean that teachers should actively try to find more activities in these areas.

It is hoped that this book will be a valuable resource to you and your fellow teachers. I know it will be of help in my own classes now that our favorite articles are all compiled under one cover.

Computational Skills

Paper Dot Plates Give Numbers Meaning

By **Charles S. Thompson,** *University of Louisville, Louisville, Kentucky, and* **John Van de Walle,** *Virginia Commonwealth University, Richmond, Virginia*

When children are learning early number concepts, teachers want them to learn a variety of subconcepts. For example, when a child is learning about five, teachers want that child to come to knowing, without counting, that there are five dots in this pattern:

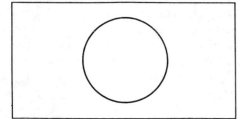

and to learn that—

- five is one more than four;
- a set of five objects can be separated into a set of three objects and a set of two objects;

- five counters, no matter how rearranged, still retain the same numerical quantity;
- the associated oral name for a set of five things is "five"; and finally
- that the numeral corresponding to a set of five objects is "5."

These subconcepts, when taken as a whole, provide a child with a broadly developed concept of the number five.

Paper dot plates are materials that can be used by teachers in developing early number concepts with children. Each plate has a dot pattern drawn on it for one of the numbers from zero through ten. The plates are inexpensive and durable; they can be stacked easily by small children and they hold counters well. Because of their low cost and versatility, several sets of dot plates can

be made for use by small groups of children in a whole-class activity or by individual children in a small group session.

The activities described in this article place a heavy emphasis on matching and ordering sets, on developing mental images of sets, and on perceiving sets of a certain size as being composed of smaller subsets. Subsequent activities involving numerals are suggested for use only after children have a solid understanding of the other subconcepts pertaining to number.

Making the Plates

Luncheon paper plates are a good size for children to use. A large dot pattern is drawn on each plate with a felt tip

Looking for the right dot plate.   Counting to be sure.   Putting up one that shows

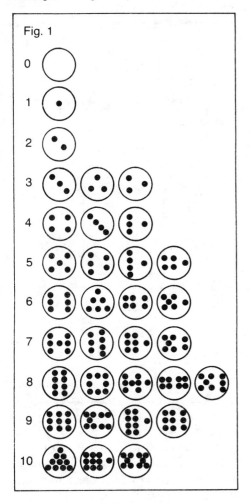

marker. The dots are made large enough that they can be easily seen from across the classroom. A teacher set can be made from dinner-sized paper plates.

There are several groups of dot patterns to be made. One group emphasizes the "one more than" property of the counting numbers. Another group makes use of the familiar domino patterns. Each dot pattern uses dots in rows of four or fewer—children can readily identify these sets by sight, without counting. It is important that several dot patterns for a single number be made whenever possible, so that children do not associate only one pattern with a number. A random dot pattern for each number greater than three should also be made.

The dot patterns shown in figure 1 will be referred to in subsequent activities.

Matching Activities

Counter match

Have a child select counters, one at a time, from a pile and place them directly on top of the dots on a given plate (one counter per dot). Ask the child how the number of dots compares with the number of counters on the plate. Then dump the counters onto a plate with no dots. Again ask the questions comparing the number of counters with the number of dots on the original plate.

Double counter match

Set out two empty plates, one on each side of a given dot plate. Have a child make an equivalent set, using counters,

on one of the empty plates. Then have the same child make another equivalent set, but using a different type of counter, on the other plate. Ask the child how the numbers of counters on the two outside plates compare to one another.

Beanstick match

Beansticks are Popsicle sticks that have beans glued onto them. A beanstick is made for each number from zero through ten. For example, a five-beanstick looks like this:

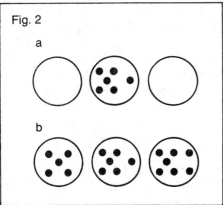

In this activity the child takes a dot plate and places on the plate a beanstick containing a set of beans that he or she thinks is equivalent to the dot set.

Clothespin match

Have a child select a plate with dots and then attach an equivalent set of clothespins around the outside edge of the plate. This one-to-one matching exercise is more difficult than "counter match," since the clothespins often cannot be arranged in the same geometric orientation as the dots on the plate.

One less, one more

Place an empty plate on each side of a dot plate that has one dot separated from the other dots (fig. 2a). On the empty plate to the left, have the child use counters to construct a set contain-

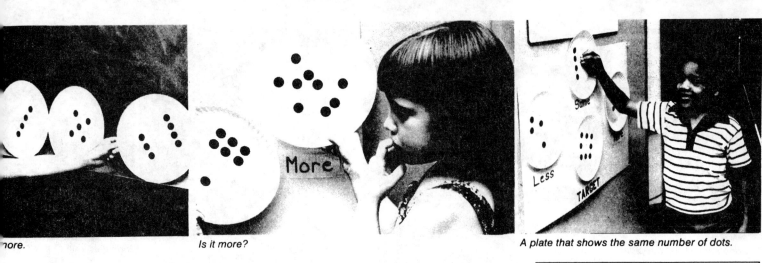

...ore.   *Is it more?*   A plate that shows the same number of dots.

ing *one less* counter than the set on the given dot plate. On the empty plate to the right, have the child construct a set containing *one more* counter than the set on the given dot plate (fig. 2b). Ask the child how the two new sets compare in terms of quantity. This activity emphasizes those dot plates that show one dot separated from the other dots.

Repeat this activity later, but have the child construct sets having *two* less and *two* more counters than the set on a given plate. The given set can be any set. Another variation of this activity is to have the child select from the dot plates those that have one less dot and those that have one more dot than a given dot plate.

A similar learning-center activity can be made by using a sheet of poster board and an arrangement like the one shown in figure 3a. A dot plate is selected and placed in the space marked TARGET. Then the child sorts the remainder of the dot plates and places them in the proper spaces on the poster board, depending on whether the plates have fewer, the same number, or more dots than the target plate (fig. 3b).

Sequencing dot plates

Have a child place a random collection of dot plates in order, beginning with the plate having the fewest dots and ending with the plate having the most dots.

Combination match

Have a child find a pair of plates that together have as many dots as some given dot plate. The emphasis in this activity is to have the child mentally separate a dot set into two subsets and then find the dot sets corresponding to those two subsets.

Paper-and-pencil dot plates

Many of the foregoing activities can be modified only slightly and then be done by individual children in a whole-class session. For example, in the activity, "One less, one more," pictures of plates can be drawn on paper and duplicated by the teacher. The children then can be asked to draw in dot sets that are one less and one more than the sets the teacher has drawn, as in figure 4.

Oral Numbers and Dot Plates

These activities can be interspersed with the matching activities just described if the children are ready to attach oral names with sets. Generally speaking, children are ready to use oral numbers if they know that rearranging a set does not alter the number of objects in the set. The activities described here are especially appropriate for a small group of children sitting around a collection of dot plates that have been spread on the floor.

Plates and number names

The teacher holds up several fingers, say three, and asks the children to hold up just as many fingers. The teacher then asks the children how many fingers each has held up. After it is decided, preferably without counting, that three fingers were held up, the children are directed to find a plate with that many dots on it. To check,

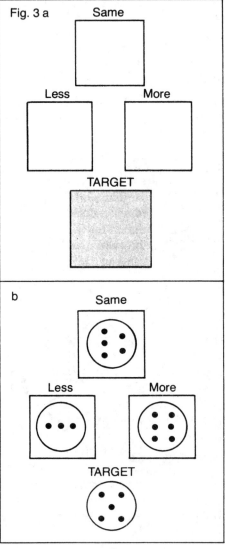

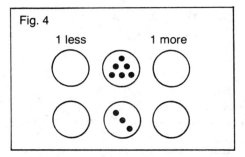

the children can match their fingers with the dots.

The teacher again holds up three fingers and then raises one more finger, which emphasizes the "one more" concept. The children hold up three fingers and then one more, and the group decides that each child has four fingers raised. Then they find a plate with that many dots on it.

The activity continues with other numbers. The teacher emphasizes that each successive number (and dot plate) is one more than the previous number (dot plate). This activity is repeated with other numbers over a period of time until all of the numbers from zero to ten have been introduced.

Oral number practice

The teacher says a number and the children find a dot plate corresponding to the number the teacher has said.

Name the plate

The teacher shows a dot plate for one or two seconds. The children call out the corresponding number. The emphasis should be on quick responses so that children develop mental images of the dot patterns and can identify the patterns *without* counting the dots.

Oral number sequencing

The teacher holds up a dot plate and the children respond orally with the number that is *one more* than the number of dots shown on the plate. The teacher repeats the process, but this time has the children give orally the number that is *one less* than the number of dots shown. Again the emphasis is on speed of response so that children break the habit of recounting from one to determine what number comes before (or after) a given number.

Using Numerals with Dot Plates

The use of numerals with dot patterns should occur only after children have made solid connections between the oral names for numbers and sets of objects. Obviously this cannot be a hard and fast rule. In general, however, children connect oral names with concepts

Showing the same number, less, and more dots.

before they connect written words with concepts. The same principle is applicable to number concepts. That is, children should learn the oral name for a number of objects in a set before they attempt to connect the numeral with that set. In fact, it may be noted that premature use of the activities that follow cannot contribute to the development of number concepts if the oral names for numbers are not a *meaningful* part of the child's vocabulary.

The activities in this section make use of "numeral cards." These are simply small index cards (approximately 8 cm by 12 cm) upon which the numerals 0, 1, 2, . . . , 10 have been written (one per card) in large print with a felt-tip marker. The cards may be used by individual children or by several children in a small group. As a prerequisite, children should be able to read numerals when they are given in a random order.

Numeral and dot pattern match

The numeral cards are spread out in front of a child in numerical order and the dot plates are placed in a stack in random order. The child is asked to find the numeral card that matches the top dot plate and to place it on the plate. The top plate is then set aside and the process is repeated with the next plate. The matching continues until all matches have been made. As this activity is repeated, speed should be emphasized, again so that children do

not revert to counting the dots on the plates.

Make a set

The teacher holds up a numeral card and the child places counters on an empty plate to construct a set having the number of objects indicated by the numeral shown. This activity should also be used in a slightly altered form in which the child constructs a set (or finds a dot plate) having one less or one more counter (or dot) than indicated by the numeral shown.

Pick a pair

The teacher holds up a numeral card and the child's task is to find a pair of dot plates that together have the total number of dots named by the numeral on the card. Then the teacher should ask the child to find another pair of dot plates that also solve the problem. This activity is an especially good one to use as a prerequisite for subsequent work with written addition and subtraction sentences.

Addition Sentences and Missing Addends

Combination match revisited

The child selects a combination of two dot plates that together have the same number of dots as a target plate selected by the teacher and arranges

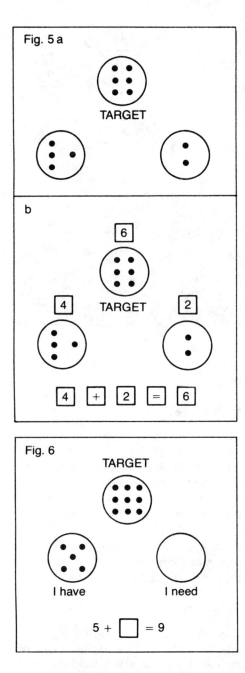

Fig. 5 a

TARGET

b

6

4   TARGET   2

4 + 2 = 6

Fig. 6

TARGET

I have   I need

5 + ☐ = 9

them in the triangle form shown in figures 5a. Then the child places the correct numeral card on each of the three plates. The principal task in this activity is for the child to construct the appropriate addition sentence (fig. 5b). This could be done by using the numeral cards along with two additional cards, one having the word *and*, and the other the word *make* written on them. Later, children can use the reverse sides of these cards, which have the symbols + and = written on them.

I wish I had (adding on)

The teacher holds up a dot plate, for example a four-plate, and says, "I wish I had seven." The child's task is to find

a plate that could be placed with the four-plate to make a total of seven. Initially numerals and number sentences should not be used, but they can be incorporated into the activity *after* the child has a solid understanding of the task and especially of number sentences.

Missing addends with paper and pencil

On a worksheet the teacher draws three dot plates in a triangular arrangement, as shown in figure 5. Two of the dot patterns are filled in. The task for the student is to draw enough dots in the third plate so that the sum of the dots in the two lower plates equals the number of dots in the top plate. The student then fills in the corresponding missing addend number sentence.

Using Dot Patterns with an Overhead Projector

An overhead projector can be very helpful as a demonstration device and as a practice device in working with dot patterns. The projector enables the teacher to conduct a whole-class activity with the dot patterns and insures that each child will be able to see the patterns being discussed and the teacher's work with the patterns. To use an overhead projector, a teacher makes transparencies of the dot patterns. The patterns need to be small enough so that three of them could fit on the overhead at the same time in the triangle arrangement shown in figure 6. Transparencies of numeral cards would also be useful for several of the following activities.

Comparing dot patterns

The teacher shows two dot patterns on the overhead projector and asks the children if the number of dots in one pattern is more, less, or the same as the number of dots in the other pattern. To decide, the teacher places a counter on each dot of one dot pattern and then asks a student to move the counters, one at a time, to the dots on the other pattern. If all counters are used and all dots are covered, then the two dot patterns have the same number of dots. If dots or counters remain, the first set

has fewer or more dots, respectively. The students can use counters with their own dot plates as the teacher demonstrates with the overhead patterns.

Flash practice

With the overhead-projector light turned off, the teacher places a dot pattern on the overhead, then flips the light on for only an instant. The children choose from their spread-out numeral cards the one that tells how many dots were flashed onto the screen and hold the cards up for the teacher to see. At a glance the teacher can identify patterns for which the children have not formed mental images and, thus, can set those aside for further work. The teacher can simultaneously determine which children are having difficulty in forming mental images of specific dot patterns.

Forming sums

The teacher places two random sets of counters on the overhead projector and asks the children to find a dot plate containing the total number of counters shown. When one is suggested, the teacher places the transparent copy of that dot plate on the overhead and then asks which numeral cards go with the three sets. The numeral cards are then placed beside the sets. To determine if the dot pattern is a correct one, the teacher transfers the two random sets of counters, one by one, onto the dot pattern. As a final activity, the children are asked to state orally the number sentence describing the relationship between the three sets.

Conclusion

The activities described in this article are meant to be suggestive rather than prescriptive or restrictive. As written, they have been used successfully with five-, six-, and seven-year-old children and with older children in remedial settings. Children enjoy using the dot plates and quickly learn to form mental images of the dot patterns. Possession of those mental images enables the children to work successfully later with number sentences when the dot patterns or counters are not used. ▉

Teaching Basic Concepts with Slides

By **Stephanie Salem Gibson**

Teaching grades one through three in a Title I mathematics laboratory setting posed problems and situations that I had not encountered in my previous teaching experience. Specifically, I found that I was unable to teach my first graders some of the most basic concepts, even though I had access to a multitude of manipulative materials and teaching aids. It was immediately evident that a nontextbook approach was required and that certain pre-number concepts had to be mastered before I could expect my students to recognize numerals and count rationally.

Since most of my students had had no preschool or kindergarten experience before entering the first grade, I began the year by looking through kindergarten materials and readiness activities. After several weeks of instruction with beginning notions such as big and little, top and bottom, right and left, and so on, I became totally frustrated in my attempts to teach these concepts. Even with the use of concrete manipulative materials and games, I was unable to hold the attention of my students. I also found that they could not relate to the readiness material long enough to adequately develop the ideas ordinarily contained in such material.

In searching for additional materials or approaches, I decided to try using an automatic slide projector. My second and third graders had been highly motivated to learn number facts when they were allowed to use the projector for basic-fact development. Initially, I made a set of slides involving numeral

At the time this article was written, Stephanie Gibson was an elementary remedial mathematics teacher in the Dougherty County (Georgia) School's Title I Program. Her previous experience included teaching in the Tallahassee and Orlando schools.

recognition, 1 through 10. I used bright colored transparency pens and sheets of acetate to make slides. (Fig. 1) This also allowed me to emphasize color recognition.

Fig. 1

The children enjoyed using the projector, but they still had difficulty with many of the prenumber and readiness skills. They were unable to identify with the objects on the slides. After a period of five weeks, a comprehension level of only about 20 percent had been attained.

The consultants to the Title I program from Georgia State University stopped by my class periodically to offer suggestions and take pictures of the children engaged in a variety of learning situations. The children liked the picture and constantly asked to have their pictures taken. It was at this point that I decided to use the children themselves to illustrate the concepts that I was trying to teach.

The automatic slide projector made it possible to use a series of slides to demonstrate concepts like the following: above and below, big and little,

short and tall, up and down, small and large, few and many, numeral recognition (1 through 10), and ordinal numbers (first, second, . . . , fifth). The slides were a simple way to use the students themselves and their classroom environment to help them internalize these concepts. For instance, I found that the cardinal number 5 could be taught effectively by showing the numeral 5 together with five students. (Fig. 2) The cardinal numbers from 1 through 10 were all demonstrated in this way. Figure 3 shows two students posing for a slide that was used to teach the concepts of above and below.

After the slides were prepared, they were used in a large group setting for eight to ten minutes each day at the beginning of each class period. This was done for approximately three weeks. By that time, 80 percent of the students demonstrated mastery of all

Fig. 2

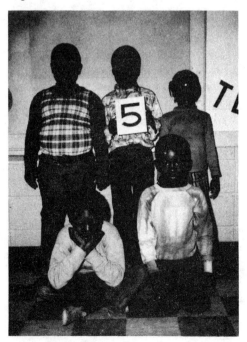

concepts taught. Students who needed additional reinforcement were periodically scheduled, individually or in small groups, to use the projector. Within about two weeks more, even these students had mastered the concepts.

Fig. 3

Because the children enjoyed using the automatic slide projector and it was easy to operate, I tried to make certain that each student had the opportunity to "man the machine" at least once. As an incentive, I chose a different student each day to be responsible for its use. (Fig. 4)

After having used slides with my students, I would make the following suggestions. First, avoid using the slides to teach the concept of left and right. A slide will show the two reversed if the child who is demonstrating the concept faces the camera. Second, when teaching ordinal numbers, it is essential to indicate the starting point to aid the children in determining the beginning and the end. Finally, when making slides showing the cardinality of sets like the one in figure 2, do not use students who are wearing jerseys or shirts with numerals on them. Numerals on jerseys tend to cause a great deal of trouble for the youngsters when they have to differentiate between the nu-

meral on the card naming the set and the jersey numeral.

Overall, the automatic projector and slides can be a valuable aid to the teacher in introducing and teaching basic concepts. Students are motivated by the use of familiar surroundings to rapidly increase their retention and comprehension levels. □

Fig. 4

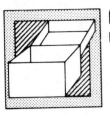

From the File

Numbers

GETTING TO KNOW FIVE

1. Give each child five (and only five) toothpicks and a small piece of construction paper. Ask the children to use the toothpicks to create a design on the construction paper. Have them glue their designs to their pieces of paper. The designs are then examined and discussed: How are the designs different? What is the same about all the designs? The results are then displayed on a bulletin board. The display is given a title. (One class came up with, "Five, You Are Different.")

2. Give five different geometric shapes to some children. Have other children cut from magazine advertisements pictures of five different colored objects, for example, fruit. Give others five sugar lumps. Have the children make and mount on paper the designs, arrangements, or buildings (with the sugar lumps). Make a display and give the display a title. (One class's title, "Five, You Are Beautiful.")

   Similar activities can be used with other numbers to help make them come alive for children.

From the file of Werner Liedtke, University of Victoria, British Columbia.

AT-3-81

Miscellaneous

WALK ON OVER

   Children in kindergarten and first grade get a good feeling about how to use a number line when they can move along one themselves.

   Use masking tape and large numerals, from 0 to 10 or 0 to 20, to make a number line for your classroom floor. I usually have some toy, plastic kangaroos or rabbits the children can hold as they "jump" from one number to another. Use directed activities such as the following: "If you take two jumps and then one more, where will you be? Try it." "If you take five jumps forward and then one back, where will you be? Try it."

   Make the number line as permanent as possible. Experimenting during free play is also very important.

From the file of
Rose Marie Iovino, mathematics laboratory teacher, Plainedge School District, Massapequa, Long Island, New York.

AT-11-81

Let's Do It

Give Bean Sticks a New Look

By **John Van de Walle,** *Virginia Commonwealth University, Richmond, Virginia*
and **Charles S. Thompson,** *University of Louisville, Louisville, Kentucky*

Good manipulative materials need not be commercially made, expensive, or in short supply in your classroom. Some of the very best teaching aids are made by teachers and their students. We would like to use this article to encourage you to take a fresh look at a manipulative that has been around for years, is easily and cheaply made in your classroom, and can be produced in sufficient quantities for all of your children. Most importantly, it is quite useful in teaching the major topics, number, place value, and computation.

Bean Sticks

Bean sticks are nothing more than dried beans glued to tongue depressors or ice cream sticks. We have found that small dried limas and junior size tongue depressors work best. Apply white glue *liberally* to the stick, place th᠎ beans in the glue, and follow with a final gluing over the tops of the beans and in between. This final gluing is essential to make the bean sticks last and to prevent the beans from cracking off the stick. Let the glue dry for twenty-four hours before using the bean sticks.

"Fewer than ten" sticks

For early number activities in kindergarten and first grade, bean sticks can be made for each of the numbers 0 through 10. To make these bean sticks, glue only the correct number of beans to the tongue depressor and always start at the end of the stick. Use the same spacing between beans on all bean sticks so that sticks for two different numbers can be compared by placing the sticks side by side (see fig. 1). On the reverse side of each stick use a felt tip pen with permanent ink to write the numeral for that stick. The zero stick of course has no beans.

These "fewer than ten" sticks probably should be made by the teacher. The spacing of the beans is very important. In one evening it would not be too difficult to make thirty or forty sets. If only a few sets are made, you will not be able to work with a full class or a large group. Spend a little extra time and create materials you can *really* use.

The following are simple ideas for using the less-than-ten sticks.

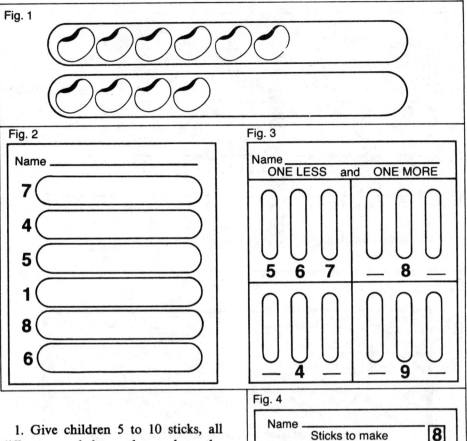

1. Give children 5 to 10 sticks, all different, and have them place the sticks in order from least beans to most beans. This seriation task need not be done with consecutive numbers.

2. Use the sticks for counting and number recognition. "Find a stick with seven beans. Point to each bean as we count. Write the number 7 on your paper. Does it look like the 7 on the back of your stick?"

3. Write several numerals down the side of a worksheet. Next to each, trace around a blank bean stick (fig. 2). Give the worksheets to the children; let them find the corresponding bean stick and draw the beans with a crayon. See if this can be done without looking at the backs of the sticks. This activity involves matching, counting, and numeral recognition. It is also self-correcting.

4. Emphasize the one-more-than and one-less-than relations between numbers. "Find a stick with six beans. What stick has one more bean? Find it and count the beans." Do this with *one less* and with *two more* and *two less*. This activity can also be done with a worksheet as in figure 3.

5. Use the sticks to determine "greater than" and "less than" rela-

tions. Given two numbers, children can find the corresponding sticks, place the sticks side by side and determine which number is greater (or less). This could be done as a class activity or also as a worksheet similar to the one in figure 3.

6. Have the children find two sticks which together have a specified number of beans. For example, a 3-stick and a 5-stick or two 4-sticks can be used to make eight. (Note that children would need two of each stick.) Figure 4 shows how a worksheet might be made. Or, again, this is an activity that could be done with a large group. Later have children try to find three sticks for a given number.

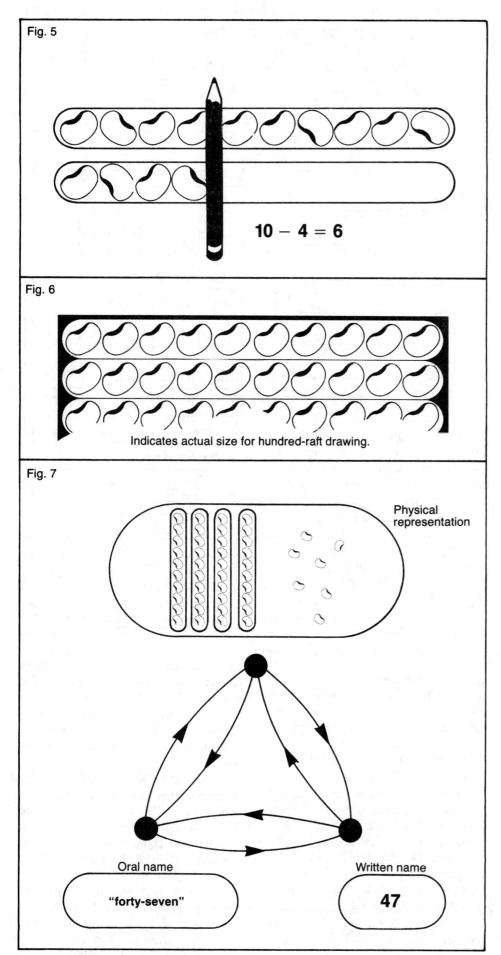

Fig. 5

$$10 - 4 = 6$$

Fig. 6

Indicates actual size for hundred-raft drawing.

Fig. 7

Physical representation

Oral name

"forty-seven"

Written name

47

7. Show the children how to select two sticks at random and write an addition fact to go with them. They do not need to find the stick with the total because this would restrict the sums to ten or less.

8. Subtraction facts can be written using the sticks in a similar manner. Select two sticks at random and place one above the other. A pencil or thin stick can be placed as in figure 5 to "take away" the smaller number from the larger number.

Place-value bean sticks

A more traditional use of bean sticks is to model tens and ones. For this purpose, loose beans are used as ONES and ten beans are glued to a stick for TENS.

By second grade (or even earlier), there should also be a good representation for one hundred. A hundred-piece can be made by forming a "raft" of ten ten-sticks placed side-by-side and held together by cross-strips glued across the back. Make only one or two of these rafts for demonstration. For additional rafts, use drawings. Make a spirit master with pictures of four rafts (use figure 6 as a guide for size). Duplicate these, mount them on posterboard, and cut them apart. Children readily accept these pictures of rafts in lieu of one hundred real beans.

A bean-stick factory

Before discussing specific activities, we would like to suggest one method for getting a large quantity of bean sticks in your classroom. Create a "bean-stick factory" by simply providing a work table together with an ample supply of beans, tongue depressors, and glue in plastic squeeze bottles. At the factory, have your children make ten-sticks by gluing ten beans on a stick as described earlier. Show the class the process of spreading glue on the stick, putting on ten beans, and then spreading on more glue. Since this is a case where "more is better," you need not worry about the children using too much glue.

You may wish to add signs or other factory pictures to your table. Assign children to specific tasks in the bean-stick factory. "Susan, before lunch please make seven bean sticks in the bean-stick factory." Or, "I want Ray and Bob to spend fifteen minutes working in the bean-stick factory."

You could, of course, make your own ten-sticks, but there are distinct advantages to letting the children make them. Besides saving you time, it helps reinforce the idea of the tenness of a ten-bean stick. We believe, however, that you should make the raft picture cards.

After the bean sticks are made, make up bean-stick kits in large resealable plastic bags. A bag for one or two children should have about twenty tens and twenty ones (loose beans). Later, when work with hundreds begins, eight to ten tagboard hundreds-rafts should be added to the bag. It is reasonable, with some effort, to have a "kit" for every child (or every two children). The kits can be easily collected and distributed for full-class activities, as well as for independent work at a learning station.

Place-value activities

A proper development of place-value concepts is one of the most important topics in elementary school mathematics. The activities that follow can all be done using bean sticks or any other place-value materials that physically show ones, tens, and hundreds. Payne and Rathmell (1975), in their discussion of place-value development, note that numbers greater than 10 can be represented in three ways: physically (as with bean sticks), orally, and in the form of a written numeral. A child must develop an understanding of each of these forms and be able to translate readily from one form to another. Figure 7 provides a diagram of these connections. Activities directed toward these objectives follow.

1. Count by tens (physical ↔ oral). Work on the names *twenty*, *thirty*, *forty*, . . . , *ninety*. "Get six bean sticks. Let's count the beans by tens." Also, "If I want seventy beans, how can I get them easily?" (Pick up seven sticks). When each child has her or his own bean-stick kit, these oral exercises can be done with a full class.

2. Count by tens and ones (physical ↔ oral). "Set aside four bean sticks

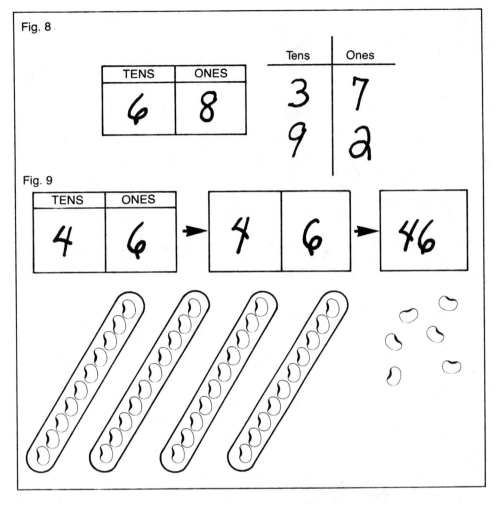

Fig. 8.

Fig. 9

and 7 beans. Let's find out how many beans. Count ten, twenty, thirty, forty, forty-one, forty-two, . . . , forty-seven." Here you started with the physical representation and developed the oral name. This is reversed by asking for a specified number of beans. "Take out eighty-three beans. How many sticks will you need? (eight) And how many single beans? (three)"

In exercises like 1 and 2, stop occasionally and let the children count all the beans in a set by ones. This seems to be important in convincing children that three sticks and six beans really are thirty-six beans.

After the hundred raft is introduced, repeat activities 1 and 2 with three-digit numbers. First count by hundreds (rafts), then hundreds and tens, and finally hundreds, tens, and ones. For example, counting two hundred thirty-two beans would proceed like this: one hundred, two hundred, two hundred ten, two hundred twenty, two hundred thirty, two hundred thirty-one, two hundred thirty-two. Notice that these

activities stress only spoken number names. Children should be comfortable with and understand the oral names for numbers before they learn to read and write numbers.

3. Writing numerals (physical ↔ written). When teaching the meanings of written numerals, begin with labeled columns. These could be on worksheets, the chalkboard, or overhead projector (fig. 8). Instruct the children to display a certain number of beans by saying the oral number name. Be sure they have the correct number of sticks and loose beans. Explain how this can be recorded in the labeled boxes for tens and ones. The reverse activity is to display a numeral in the labeled boxes and have the children find that many beans. After sufficient experience of this nature, have children record the numbers in unlabeled boxes and finally in a single box (fig. 9).

Again, similar activities should be conducted for three-digit numerals using the posterboard rafts.

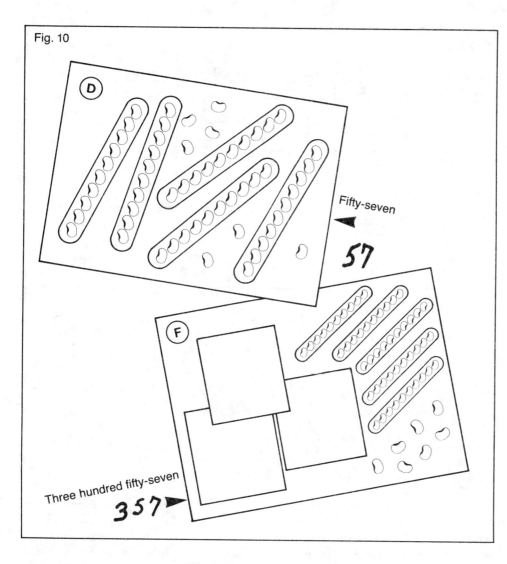

Fig. 10

D

Fifty-seven

57

F

Three hundred fifty-seven

357

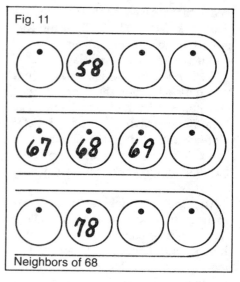

Fig. 11

58

67 68 69

78

Neighbors of 68

Once the connections between bean sticks (physical) and the written numerals are firm, you can begin to stress the connections between the written numerals and oral names for numbers. Then the objectives indicated in figure 7 will be complete.

These simple activities can be varied somewhat by teaching the children how to make drawings of their bean sticks and beans. Drawings allow the children to record their work on paper for you to check later. They also permit you to create activities that use pictures of bean sticks instead of the actual materials. For example, a set of flash cards, each showing some bean sticks and beans, can be made on large index cards. Children can say or write the appropriate number. If letter codes are written in the corner of each card, independent self-checking activities can be developed. An answer sheet of numerals or number names is keyed to the letters on the cards (fig. 10).

A super-raft

A super-raft, which is really just a hundreds board drawn on a piece of plywood that is about 70 cm square, is an extension of the bean raft idea. With a felt-tip marker draw ten large, blank bean sticks horizontally on the board. On each "stick," near the top edge, drive in ten nails on which to hang the "beans." Make all the nails equally spaced and aligned vertically and horizontally so that when all one hundred "beans" are hung on the board, they will form a neat square array of ten rows and ten columns. The "beans" are best made from the round key tags with a metal rim that can be purchased in dime stores or stationery shops. On each tag is written a numeral, from 1 to 100. When all the tags are hung in order on the super-raft, the top "bean stick" has the tags 1 through 10 in order left to right, the next stick has the tags 11 through 20 in order, and so on.

Super-rafts can be used in different ways.

1. In this activity the focus is on neighboring numbers. Place all the tags so that the numeral side faces the board. Turn over one tag and ask the children to name orally or write the names of the neighboring tags, to the right and left, above and below. The neighbors are then turned over for verification (fig. 11). Vary the activity by asking for the neighbors located between two tags on the same "stick" (for example, between 32 and 37). Another version would be to ask for the neighbors between two tags in the same column (for example between 26 and 76).

2. The super-raft can also serve to model the tens and ones for each number through one hundred. With numerals not showing, point to a tag and have the class name it. Turn the tag over for verification. Now let the children use their bean sticks to represent that number. Note that the number of rows above a "stick" on the super-raft is the number of full bean sticks required. For example, there are two complete rows of tags above the tag with 27 on it.

Many worthwhile activities for hundreds boards or hundreds charts have been developed. The article by Volpel (1959) and the resource book by Judd (1975) are among many useful references you might want to examine. Perhaps the best source of good activities for your super-raft is *you*.

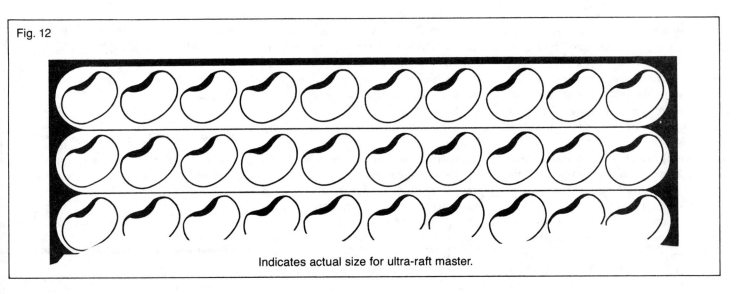

Fig. 12

Indicates actual size for ultra-raft master.

The ultra-raft

Hundreds rafts, *tens* sticks, and loose beans permit modeling of numbers up to 999. Children also need to have some reference for or real experiences with larger numbers. An ultra-raft provides a nice visual image of 10 000 "beans." The beans on the ultra-raft are ordered. That is, there is a procedure that can be used to uniquely locate the 5268th bean, for example.

The ultra-raft may take a bit of time and effort, but it is a teaching aid well worth the time invested. Get a colleague to help you make it and then share the raft when you are finished. To make the raft you will need to make a duplicating master of a bean raft. Figure 12 will give you an idea of the actual size to draw the raft for the best results—a bean raft should be about 16 cm by 16 cm. From the master make one hundred copies and cut them out carefully, making sure that each is a square.

The ultra-raft is a large chart (about 1.7 m square) with ten rows of ten copies of the bean raft. Although a number of assembly alternatives are available, an excellent ultra-raft chart can be formed by sandwiching the one hundred squares between clear Contact paper. About 15 meters (approximately 16 yards) of Contact paper are required.

Cut the Contact paper into lengths of 1.8 m (long enough to take ten bean rafts plus a margin.). Peal the backing from one strip, leaving the adhesive side up, and lay it on a large, clean table. The squares of one hundred beans are then placed in rows of ten, face down, on this strip. Each square is placed so that the bean sticks are horizontal. A straight border of construction paper about 4 cm wide is very helpful. Place each square exactly next to its neighbor, leaving no gaps.

After two rows of squares have been positioned, a second strip of Contact paper is overlapped about 1 cm with the first so that the third, fourth, and fifth rows of squares can be positioned. Complete the remaining five rows by adding two more strips of Contact paper. Complete the border of construction paper around the entire raft.

Next use the remaining four strips of Contact paper to cover the back side of the ultra-raft. Place these strips perpendicular to the other strips. Trim the edges and round off the corners. Along the top edge of the ultra-raft, reinforce five places with poster board squares of about 3 cm by 3 cm. Punch holes through these squares for hanging the chart.

To use the ultra-raft, display it so that all can see. Count by hundreds across the top row of hundreds to one thousand. The second thousand is the second row, and so forth. Within each square of 100 beans, order the beans as on the super-raft. Thus to find the 3624th bean, count 3 rows of squares, 6 rafts, 2 rows of ten, and find the 4th bean in the next row of ten.

With the raft you can again think of the connections between physical (the ultra-raft), oral, and written names,

now extended to any four-digit number.

1. Show a numeral, find the bean.

2. Point to a bean, say the number.

3. Point to a bean, write the number.

4. Say a number, find the bean.

5. Work on names of numbers that include zeroes in their written form (3008 or 6010 or 4702, and so on).

6. Develop number names such as thirty-four hundred for 3400.

7. How many ultra-rafts would you need to make a million? How big would it be?

An alternative to the ultra-raft would be to make super-bean-sticks for formed from a row of ten copies of the large bean rafts. Each super-bean-stick would model numbers to 1000. Ten such super-sticks would permit counting to 10 000 in a similar manner.

Trading Games and Addition and Subtraction Algorithms

The bean sticks we have been discussing form a basic set of place-value materials. No single journal article could include all of the important uses of place-value materials in the development of whole number and decimal arithmetic. We would be remiss, however, if we did not at least encourage you to use your bean sticks to teach the process of regrouping or trading of ten ones for one ten and one ten for ten ones.

If a posterboard place-value mat (columns for ones, tens, and hundreds) is used along with the bean sticks, children can learn to trade ten beans in the ones column for one stick in the tens column. Similarly, they can learn to trade ten bean sticks for one raft in the hundreds column. The reverse trades (borrowing) can also be modeled. Once these operations are developed, addition and subtraction with regrouping is an easy next step.

These trading games and the development of the addition and subtraction algorithms are explained in the "Let's Do It" articles of the December 1980 and January 1981 issues. Another excellent reference is the chapter by Merseth in the 1978 NCTM Yearbook, *Developing Computational Skills.*

Conclusion

In the March 1978 *Arithmetic Teacher,* Anderson asks why there is a continued resistance to the use of place-value materials in first-grade classrooms. He reports research strongly supporting the use of materials to teach place-value concepts.

We strongly support the use of any materials that show one ten physically as ten ones (and hundreds as ten tens). We have suggested that bean sticks provide readily available sets of such materials for a very reasonable investment of time and money. We have included some activities that precede place value as well as some that are extensions beyond simple tens and ones, but we have not been able to discuss all the possible activities. We, like Anderson, are somewhat amazed that so many teachers are not using place-value materials in their instruction. If you are currently using place-value pieces of some sort—congratulations! Perhaps we have been able to add to your current ideas. If you are not using place-value pieces, we hope this article will make it more difficult for you to find an excuse. Perhaps it's time for a change.

References

Anderson, Alfred L. "Why the Continuing Resistance to the Use of Counting Sticks?" *Arithmetic Teacher* 25 (March 1978).

Judd, Wallace P. *Patterns to Play on a Hundred Chart.* Palo Alto, Calif.: Creative Publications, Inc., 1975.

Payne, Joseph, and Edward C. Rathmell. "Numeration." In *Mathematics Learning in Early Childhood.* Thirty-seventh Yearbook of the National Council of Teachers of Mathematics. Reston, Va.: The Council, 1975.

Merseth, Katherine K. "Using Materials and Activities in Teaching Addition and Subtraction Algorithms." In *Developing Computational Skills.* 1978 Yearbook of the National Council of Teachers of Mathematics. Reston, Va.: The Council, 1978.

Volpel, Marvin C. "The Hundred-Board." *Teacher-made Aids for Elementary School Mathematics, Readings from the Arithmetic Teacher.* Reston, Va.: National Council of Teachers of Mathematics, 1974. ❥

Mr. Ten, You're Too Tall!

by **Alison D. House Brennan**

Teachers are often confronted with children who are unable to make the transition from the conceptual stage of mathematical thought to the computational stage in base-ten operations. One of the major areas of difficulty occurs when the children begin working with place value. They are unable to conceptualize and therein comprehend the base-ten place-value system. With most children, paper-and-pencil activities are not enough to lead them to successful independent computation. One way to overcome this difficulty is to demonstrate visually the processes of addition, subtraction, regrouping, and so on. A simple, yet effective, manipulative device that meets the needs of children encountering such difficulties can easily be constructed from the following materials:

One large piece of light poster board
A black felt-tip marker
Several sheets of large-grid graph paper
Three sheets of light cardboard
Clear contact paper (optional).

With the black marker, separate the poster board into three sections, heading each section, from left to right, *Hundreds, Tens,* and *Ones.* Next, draw a dotted line across the bottom of the chart, below which the numerical answer can be written in with a washable marker (fig. 1). To make it more durable, the chart can be covered with clear contact paper.

Next, cut out single blocks from the graph paper (ones), rows of ten blocks each (tens), and ten-by-ten blocks (hundreds). The blocks of graph paper also may be coated with clear contact paper.

From the cardboard, cut out three houses, graduated in size. These are the

---

Alison House Brennan is currently teaching educable mentally retarded children in the Jefferson County school system in Louisville, Kentucky. Formerly, as a staff member for the Learning Improvement Center, School of Education, University of Louisville, she diagnosed and prescribed corrective programs for children in mathematics and reading.

Fig. 1

Hundreds	Tens	Ones

Fig. 2

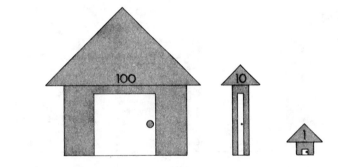

Fig. 3

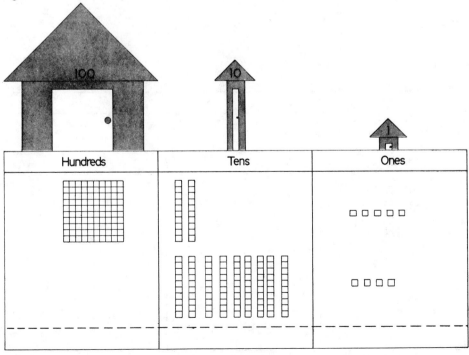

Fig. 4

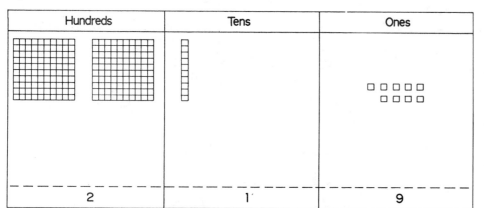

Hundreds	Tens	Ones
		☐ ☐ ☐ ☐ ☐ ☐ ☐ ☐ ☐
2	1	9

Fig. 5

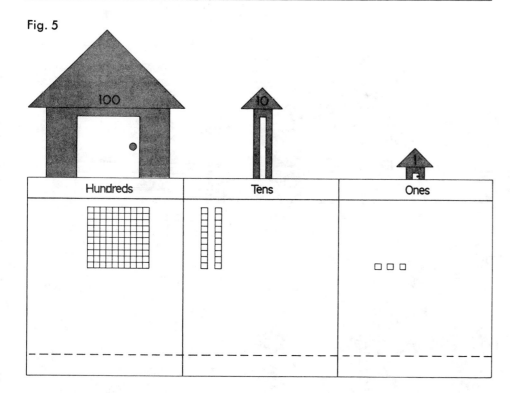

Hundreds	Tens	Ones
		☐ ☐ ☐

Fig. 6

Hundreds	Tens	Ones
		☐ ☐ ☐ ☐ ☐ ☐
1	0	6

houses of Ones, Tens, and Hundreds in place value. Using the one-block region of graph paper as a guide to size, cut a one-block door in the smallest house. Similarly, use a row of ten blocks to determine the size of the door for the middle-sized house, and a ten-by-ten block for the door of the largest house. Care must be taken to make the doors the same size as the graph paper cut-outs (fig. 2).

From the cardboard, cut one large structure to represent the Bank. The cutouts of graph paper blocks not in use will be placed on the Bank. Cover the houses and the Bank with contact paper.

Place the houses at the top of the appropriate column on your chart. The Bank will be positioned alongside the chart. For the purpose of demonstrating how the chart is used, take the following addition problem:

$$125 \\ + \underline{\ 94}$$

First place graph-paper blocks on the chart to represent the problem (fig. 3). From this point on, it is a simple matter to explain why there are too many tens for Tens' house, since the house is only big enough for nine tens, and that tens would be lost in the Hundreds' house. The solution is a visit to the Bank to exchange 10 tens for 1 hundred. The children should lay the 10 tens on the hundred block in order to reinforce visually the equality between 10 tens and 1 hundred. When the exchange of 10 tens for 1 hundred is completed, the resulting collection of cutouts is 2 hundreds, 1 ten, and 9 ones, or 219, as recorded in figure 4.

A subtraction problem can be demonstrated in a similar way. Take the following problem, which can be represented as shown in figure 5.

$$123 \\ - \underline{\ 17}$$

The first question is, "Can we take away seven ones when we only have three ones in Ones' house?" Since the answer is no, we must borrow from our neighbor, Mr. Ten. Mr. Ten of course, is far too tall to enter into Ones' house, so we must visit the Bank to exchange 1 ten for 10 ones. From that point on, the answer is easily demonstrated. The result is shown in figure 6.

After the children become accustomed to the chart, it is more beneficial to leave the marked side of the house face down so as to gradually decrease the visual clues. For the purpose of reinforcement, the problem in numerical form should be displayed to the side of the chart. This assists in the teaching of the operational signs.

To stress the idea that each house is limited to just nine occupants, it may be helpful to draw nine beds of the appropriate size in each house. Drawing the beds is a problem because of their size, but, dependent on the needs of your children, the visual reinforcement that seeing the beds provides may make it well worth the effort.

The use of the place-value chart has never failed to stimulate interest among the students I have worked with. The students generally become excited as they tell the place-value stories, matching the blocks to the appropriate houses and, to the teacher's delight, their imagination is captivated by mathematics. □

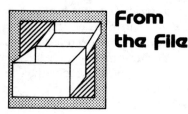

From the File

Computation

EVERY-PUPIL PLACE VALUE

Make a pocket holder for each child by folding up the bottom of a tagboard strip and stapling four places. Laminate the entire holder, then with a sharp point carefully cut open the "pockets." Using a different color for each pocket, make three sets of digit cards.

hundreds	tens	ones

Example:

hundreds	pink	0, 1, 2, 3, ⋯ 9
tens	yellow	0, 1, 2, 3, ⋯ 9
ones	blue	0, 1, 2, 3, ⋯ 9

Children can respond to the teacher's questions or directions by holding up their pocket holders. Activities like the following can be used:

For numbers 0–99
(1) Naming tens and ones
(2) Answering questions, What comes next? and What comes before?
(3) Two-digit addition and subtraction

For numbers 0–999
(1) Naming hundreds, tens, and ones
(2) What comes next? What comes before?
(3) Three-digit addition and subtraction, with three-digit answers.

Variation: Separate the class into two teams. Then the first team with all members having the correct answer gets a point.

From the file of
Beth Heckert, Westminster, Maryland

AT-12-81

Basic Facts

AN ANSWER PIG

To construct an answer pig, you need a half-gallon, plastic bleach bottle, four egg-carton pockets, and a magic marker. With a razor, cut a slit approximately one centimeter wide through the top half of the bottle, 3 or 4 centimeters from the neck of the bottle. Glue the egg-carton pockets to the bottom of the container to form the pig's feet. Draw the pig's face with the magic marker.

Make the basic fact cards on 5-by-8 note cards, with the answers at the center of the bottom portion of the card. Put the fact cards in the slit in the bottle. Individual children can check their answers for the basic facts by unscrewing the bottle cap and looking in the pig's mouth.

From the file of Robert Sovchik, college instructor, and Debbie Lowers, student, University of Akron, Akron, OH 44325.

AT-10-77

Editor's note: This aid is a definite asset in the classroom. My student teachers have decorated the pig to look like Miss Piggy, and children loved her. The pig can be used for any kind of drill-and-practice activity whether it is math related or not. It has been used in my classroom for multiplication, division, subtraction, addition, numeration, geometric shapes, telling time, fractions, decimals, color identification, and so forth. It could also be used for vocabulary words.

Doubles Up—Easy!

By Carol A. Thornton

Easy facts first, then harder ones! This is the natural route to take in the mastery of basic addition facts, and addition doubles are certainly among those "easy" facts. Using objects to help children "picture" each double makes learning the doubles even easier and a lot of fun. That at least has been the experience of children enrolled in the Illinois State University Mathematics Learning Clinic for area children with learning difficulties in mathematics.

Look, Touch, Feel, and Match

Objects used to picture the doubles include the following:

for 1 + 1, eyes, hands, knees (a body part that comes in pairs)—two in all;

for 2 + 2, car (2 front tires and 2 back tires), dog or other animal, or chair (2 front legs and 2 back legs)—four in all;

for 3 + 3, grasshopper or other insect (3 legs on each side)—six legs in all;

for 4 + 4, rubber spider (4 legs on each side) or 8-carton

Carol Thornton is an associate professor of mathematics at Illinois State University. She teaches preservice and inservice mathematics education courses and directs a clinic for children with learning difficulties in mathematics. During the current academic year, she is visiting lecturer at Kelvin Grove College of Advanced Education, Brisbane, Australia.

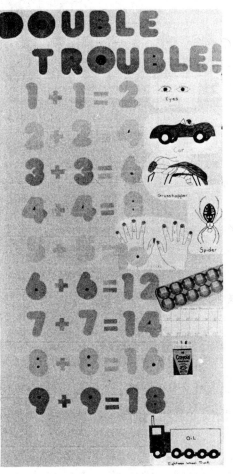

soft-drink pack—eight in all;

for 5 + 5, child's two hands (5 fingers on each hand)—ten in all;

for 6 + 6, egg carton (6 cups in each row)—twelve in all;

for 7 + 7, two calendar weeks or two touchdowns with extra point good each time—fourteen in all;

for 8 + 8, box of crayons (8 in each row)—sixteen in all;

for 9 + 9, eighteen wheeler semi (9 wheels on each side) or two baseball teams on the field (9 on each team)—eighteen in all.

Interns at the clinic bring in *real objects* and invite children to look, touch, and feel. An example is the "calendar number," 7 + 7—an otherwise difficult double. In this instance, children would actually mark off two weeks on the calendar, noting that there are seven days in each week. The fact itself is then matched to or written on the calendar sheet. Other matching exercises follow. Children match flash cards of doubles facts first to the objects and then to pictures of the objects. Motivational practice exercises and speed drills follow, and auditory cues like "Remember, that's the calendar number" are used whenever a child hesitates.

Interns typically pretest the children individually to determine which doubles facts are not mastered. Then *two* unknown facts are presented in the manner just outlined. When these two facts are mastered, other facts are introduced, one at a time. To check for mastery, each doubles fact is presented in a mixed review with other easy facts. A criterion of three correct responses in successive presentations of a fact is set.

For children needing help with addition facts, an average of 18 minutes each clinic day is devoted to the topic. This is sometimes broken into a longer 10- or 12-minute period and a shorter review period toward the end of the 45-minute clinic session. Under these conditions, the average time to mastery of all doubles facts, according to data accumulated over the past four years, is two and one-half days. Retention generally remains stable over the 6-week clinic period.

Several area teachers have tried this picture-verbal reinforcement approach to doubles. The photograph in figure 1 is that made by a student teacher and displayed in a first-grade classroom. Even at this level, the reported success rate is striking. ♥

The multiplication family

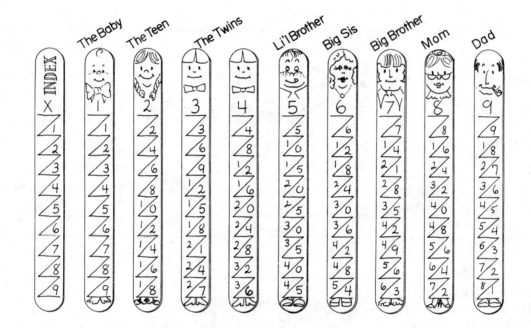

The "multiplication family" is a variation of Napier's bones. While providing practice with multiplication facts, the activity also shows the relationship between factors and common products. The materials are inexpensive, and the aid is so easy to make that children will enjoy making a multiplication family for their individual use.

Popsicle sticks or tongue depressors make sturdy, easy-to-manipulate family members. Crayons or felt pens can be used to draw the pictures of the family members on the sticks, but the sharper point of a pencil makes it the better tool for writing the products. The sticks can be covered with strips of adhesive, clear plastic to avoid smearing of the numerals.

The first stick is the index and contains a vertical listing of all the factors. An index factor is also written at the top of each stick. Each individual family member then has the products of the two index factors listed vertically on it. The products are divided by a horizontal line. The ones and tens of each product are separated by a diagonal line. A multiplication family that contains the one through nine members is shown here.

PATRICIA MALAVOLTI
Susick Elementary School
Troy, Michigan

> **Editor's note:** Using two different colors for the numbers might help eliminate confusion. The index numbers at the top of each stick could be, say, red, and the rest of the numbers, the multiples, could be black. Some of my student teachers have constructed a pocket holder with enough slots for each member of the family. Storing the sticks this way helps prevent losing them.

A Pocket Multiplier

By **Julia Grove**

Coordinating rectangular arrays, repeated addition, skip counting, and multiplication can be confusing tasks for teachers, not to mention for children. Here is a simple, child-made device which can establish a basis for understanding the relationships involved and which, at the same time, can help to fix multiplication facts in mind.

Take a strip of oaktag about eight centimeters wide. The length of the strip will depend on the number of sections desired. Beginning at one end, fold over a small (four-centimeter) flap. Continue folding over and over to the end and snip off the excess. (Fig. 1) Crease well.

Unfold once, and on the exposed section draw a row of dots (three, for example). Unfold again, and on the next section draw another row of the same number of dots. (Fig. 2) Continue in this way to the end, but draw nothing on the last section.

Refold the strip; then open, showing one section. There will be three dots—one set of three—so write 1 × 3. (Fig. 3) Unfold once more. Now two sets of three dots are exposed. Write 2 × 3 (Fig. 4) Continue to the end. (Fig. 5) Now fold up the multiplier. It's ready to use.

- Open, one section at a time. What do you see?

    (3 + 3 + 3 + 3 + 3 . . .)

- Refold. Now open, one section at a time, and count all of the dots each time.

    (3, 6, 9, 12, 15, . . .)

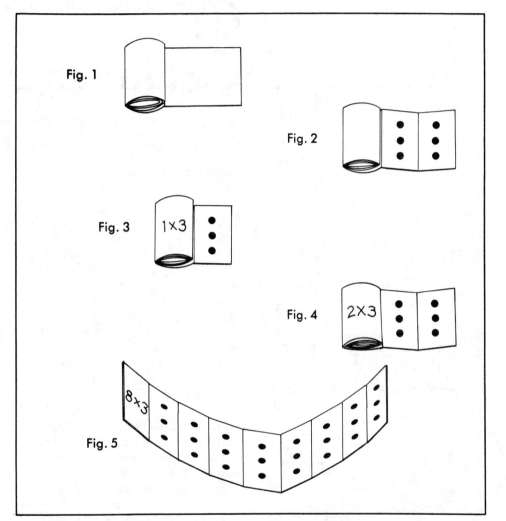

Fig. 1

Fig. 2

Fig. 3 1×3

Fig. 4 2×3

Fig. 5 8×3

- Count as you fold it up again.
    (. . . 15, 12, 9, 6, 3)

- Unfold until you see four sets of three. How many dots? (4 × 3 = ?) Make the multiplier show 5 × 3.

- Open the multiplier until you see a rectangle of dots, three wide and five long. What is written there? How many dots?

- Unfold two times. (2 × 3) Unfold four more times. (4 × 3 more dots) What is (2 × 3) + (4 × 3)? Try to show (5 × 3) − (2 × 3).

Having used the multiplier yourself you may recognize its strong kinesthetic as well as visual appeal. One *feels* 6 × 3 while physically unfolding six times, then sees it as six sets of three.

Children can make the multipliers easily, perhaps inventing their own symbols in lieu of dots, or using rubber stamps or inked corks. A new multiplier can be made for each set of multiplication facts. Finished strips can be secured with a rubber band and kept for future use, but don't be surprised if they become pocket treasures to be taken home and shared with family and friends. □

As a mathematics specialist at the Durham Child Development Center in Philadelphia, Julia Grove has worked with children in a mathematics laboratory and in classrooms. She is currently advising and conducting workshops for teachers at the Learning Centers Project's Teacher-Parent Center, one of Durham's components.

Cal the Calculator Can Help Parents Become Involved

By **Robert J. Sovchik**

Classroom teachers have known for a long time that a child's parents are an important determinant of success in school. In a paper "Improving Mathematics Education in Disadvantaged Areas," which he presented at the 52nd Annual Meeting of the NCTM, Atlantic City, 1974, Williams stated that programs designed to improve mathematics achievement in disadvantaged areas must involve meaningful relationships between parents and teachers. Getting parents to make and use inexpensive mathematics games and activities with their children may be one way to help bridge the gap between home and school. This article describes one device that some parents have found enjoyable to make and use with their children. Cal the Calculator is an inexpensive, easy-to-make device that can help children practice basic skills in an enjoyable fashion.

Robert Sovchik is an assistant professor in the Department of Elementary Education, College of Education at the University of Akron in Akron, Ohio. He teaches mathematics methods and content courses for prospective elementary school teachers.

Directions for Making Cal

1. Get a 1/2-gallon milk carton, some tagboard, scissors, a ruler, and tape or glue.

2. Open the top of the milk carton and cut the sides to the first fold line. The bottom of the carton will be the top of Cal the Calculator. (Fig. 1)

3. Cut two rectangular openings, one about 4 cm from the top and the other one about 4 cm from the bottom. The opening should be as wide as the milk carton and each should have a height of about 1 cm. (Fig. 1)

4. Cut a piece of tagboard about 10 cm long and a little less wide than the width of the top opening. Crease this about 3 cm from the end. Insert the longer end of the tagboard into the upper opening of the carton and glue or tape the remaining 3 cm to the outside of the carton. (Fig. 2)

5. Cut another piece of tagboard about 25 cm long and a little less wide than the width of the bottom opening. Crease this about 4 cm from the end. Insert the tagboard through the bottom opening and push it until it forms an arc inside the carton. Tape or glue the

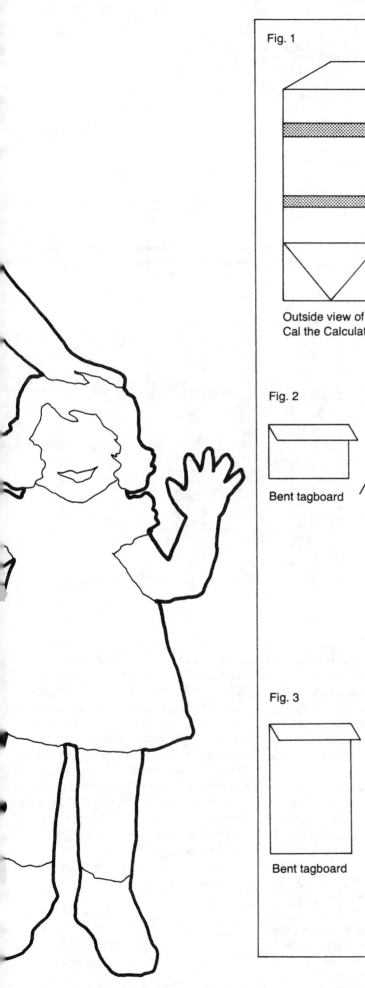

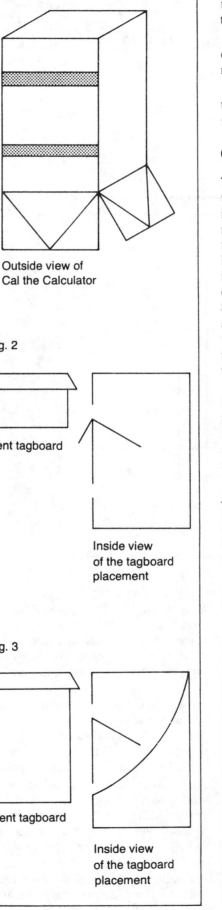

Fig. 1

Outside view of
Cal the Calculator

Fig. 2

Bent tagboard

Inside view
of the tagboard
placement

Fig. 3

Bent tagboard

Inside view
of the tagboard
placement

short end of the tagboard to the outside of the carton. (Fig. 3) The portion of the tagboard inside the carton is not taped or glued.

6. Fold in and tape down the sections of the bottom of Cal (what was originally the top of the milk carton).

7. Cover the carton with construction paper and draw a face on it. (Fig. 4) Cal is now ready to calculate.

Calculating with Cal

To be of maximum value, the facts that the child needs to practice should be identified. The facts that the child needs to master may then be put on fact cards and used with Cal the Calculator. If families of facts are being studied, then Cal the Calculator can help to develop a family like $4 + 8$, $8 + 4$, $12 - 8$. The fact cards are made of tagboard and are about 8 cm by 8 cm. The fact is written on one side of the square and the answer is written, upside down, on the other.

A fact card is fed into the top opening of Cal the Calculator, with the fact showing—for example, $4 + 8$. The card turns over as it goes through Cal and slides out at the bottom, with the answer, 12, showing.

Making Cal the Calculator is an enjoyable activity for parents. They can practice basic skills with their children at home and thus feel that they are an important part of their child's mathematics program.

By the way, having Cal the Calculator in your classroom is not a bad idea.□

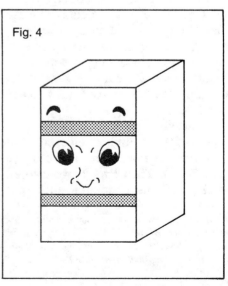

Fig. 4

More Popsicle-Stick Multiplication

By Andrejs Dunkels

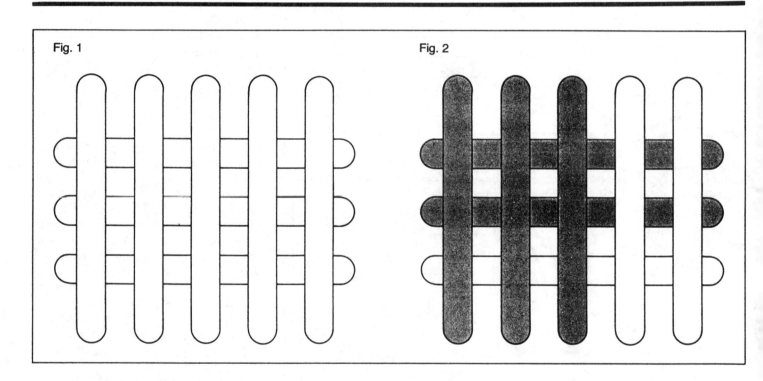

Fig. 1 Fig. 2

After reading the article, "Fractions and Popsicle Sticks," by Carlisle (*Arithmetic Teacher*, February 1980), I decided to tell my students about the idea. I did not have an adequate supply of Popsicle sticks, but I was able to purchase some tongue depressors at a drug store. I painted some of the tongue depressors red (any color would do).

I started by showing my students a model of the multiplication exercise, 3 × 5, the way it was done in the article (see fig. 1). Then I took two colored sticks and one uncolored stick, put

Andrejs Dunkels is an associate professor of mathematics at the University of Leleå in northern Sweden. He devotes one half of his time to teaching civil engineering students and the other half to teaching student teachers in the primary grades.

them on the table, and asked what number the sticks represented. The students suggested 21—some said 12. I was about to turn the suggestions down and tell them the "right answer," 2/3, but then changed my mind. I decided to see what could be done with the idea of the sticks representing 21.

I next showed three colored sticks and two uncolored sticks, which we agreed represented 32. I then put the sticks representing 32 across the sticks representing 21, as we had done earlier with the uncolored sticks (see fig. 2). We agreed that we had obtained a model for the multiplication 21 × 32.

Analyzing the situation, we found that there were two intersections of uncolored sticks, each of which repre-

sented 1 × 1 or 1. There were four intersections of a horizontal colored stick and a vertical uncolored stick. Since each colored stick was equivalent to ten uncolored sticks, each of these four intersections represented 1 × 10 or 10. Then we had three intersections of a horizontal uncolored stick and a vertical colored stick and each of these intersections represented 10 × 1 or 10. Finally, there were six intersections of colored sticks, each intersection representing 10 × 10 or 100 (see fig. 3).

From our model we had thus found the following:

$$2 \times 1 = 2$$
$$4 \times 10 = 40$$
$$3 \times 10 = 30$$
$$6 \times 100 = \underline{600}$$
$$\text{Total } 672$$

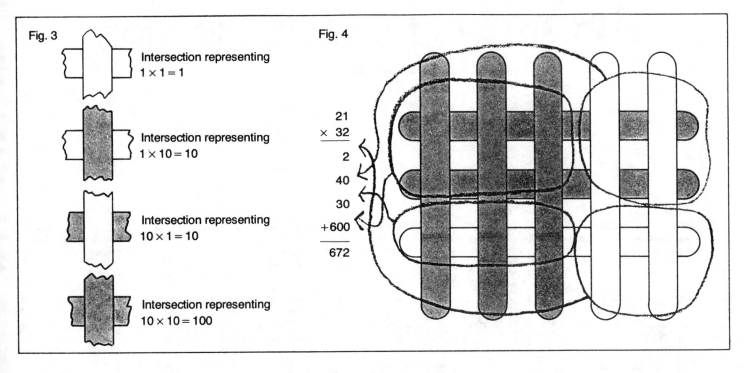

Fig. 3

Intersection representing
$1 \times 1 = 1$

Intersection representing
$1 \times 10 = 10$

Intersection representing
$10 \times 1 = 10$

Intersection representing
$10 \times 10 = 100$

Fig. 4

$$\begin{array}{r} 21 \\ \times\ 32 \\ \hline 2 \\ 40 \\ 30 \\ +600 \\ \hline 672 \end{array}$$

At this stage it was obvious to my students how the Popsicle-stick model could be used to reach the paper-and-pencil stage. The record keeping could be organized and explained as shown in figure 4.

We then discussed the possibility of painting some of the sticks another color and tried them out with a multiplication exercise involving three-digit numbers. We also talked about division, and found our digression very

inspiring.

The use of a variety of models helps to build a concept of multiplication, and I believe the Popsicle-stick (or tongue-depressor) model is really worth trying. ♦

Grid Arrays for Multiplication

By **Alice I. Robold**

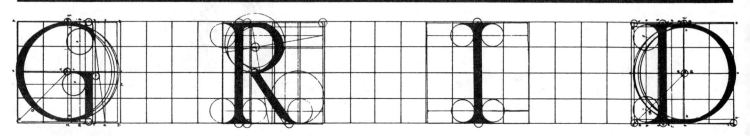

Arrays are often used as excellent models for beginning multiplication examples, but sometimes are put aside when they become unwieldy for greater factors. Learners, therefore, may be deprived of the benefits of array models just when they need help with more challenging examples. The use of grid arrays, made from paper marked in squares, allows the learner to continue to benefit from array models and to follow a logical sequence of multiplication experiences.

In the early stages of the multiplication learning sequence, concrete arrays are most desirable. After manipulating the concrete materials, children can make pictures of their concrete arrays. For example, when children use bottle caps to represent "two times three," the picture of the array would show two rows of three bottle caps (fig. 1). When wooden cubes are used to represent "three times two," the corresponding picture would show three rows of two cubes

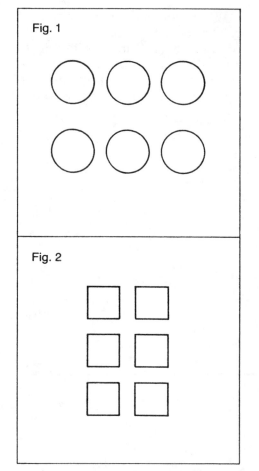

Fig. 1

Fig. 2

(fig. 2). After children experience many examples with concrete objects and pictures, they can move to a more abstract level, matching their pictures with equations. Then the bottle cap array pictured in figure 1 is represent-

ed by the equation, $2 \times 3 = 6$, and the array of cubes pictured in figure 2 is represented by the equation, $3 \times 2 = 6$. This sequence of experiences—allowing the students to move from concrete to pictorial to abstract levels—promotes the learning of multiplication.

The children can use geoboard arrays after they have gained experience and skill in using arrays of objects to represent many examples with small factors. They use rubber bands to outline arrays of squares. For example, to represent $2 \times 3 = 6$, the students enclose two rows of three squares within a rubber-band boundary, and then count the number of squares in the rectangular region (fig. 3). Geoboard arrays are efficient models for factors up to ten.

Pictures of the geoboard arrays are made on grid paper containing 1-cm or 2-cm squares. The children may color in the squares in the rectangular region, or they may draw the boundary, representing the rubber band, around the array (fig. 4).

As children progress to greater factors, they may use paper with smaller squares. Special attention should be given to arrays that represent $10 \times 10 = 100$, so that students notice the "box" of 100 squares in each of these arrays (fig. 5).

Sturdy grid models are prepared for

Alice Robold is a professor of mathematical sciences at Ball State University in Muncie, Indiana. She teaches mathematics content and methods courses to preservice and inservice elementary school teachers.

introducing multiplication examples with factors greater than ten. The students glue sheets of grid paper containing 1-cm squares to corrugated cardboard. The teacher cuts the grids to form many 10-by-10 arrays ("boxes"), 1-by-10 arrays ("strips"), and single squares ("singles"). (Commercially available base-ten blocks called "flats," "longs," and "cubes" may be used also for array models.)

The children use "strips" to make models for "ones times tens." To show 4 × 20 (4 times 2 tens), the students arrange four rows of two "strips" as shown in figure 6. The model clearly shows the "8 tens." Thus students find that "4 times 2 tens is 8 tens," or 4 × 20 = 80.

The children manipulate the 10-by-10 arrays to represent examples whose factors are multiples of ten. To represent 20 × 30, the students show 20 rows of 30 squares by making an array of 2 rows of three "boxes" (fig. 7). If we think about 20 rows with 30 in each row as making 6 of the "boxes," we see that 2 tens × 3 tens = 6 hundreds. By testing other examples with multiples of ten as factors, the students can generalize that whenever "tens" are multiplied by "tens" the product is "hundreds." At first, the array can be represented with sentences containing both numerals and words:

4 tens × 2 tens = 8 hundreds, and
3 tens × 5 tens = 15 hundreds.

Then the matching number sentences or equations can be used:

40 × 20 = 800
30 × 50 = 1500

The teacher will recognize the necessity of having children understand place-value concepts before they deal with multiplication examples whose factors or products are greater than nine.

Both "strips" and "singles" are used for examples with one factor less than ten and the other factor greater than a multiple of ten. The model for 3 × 24 is shown in figure 8. The children find that they use six "strips" and twelve "singles" to make the 3-by-24 array. The two partial products (60

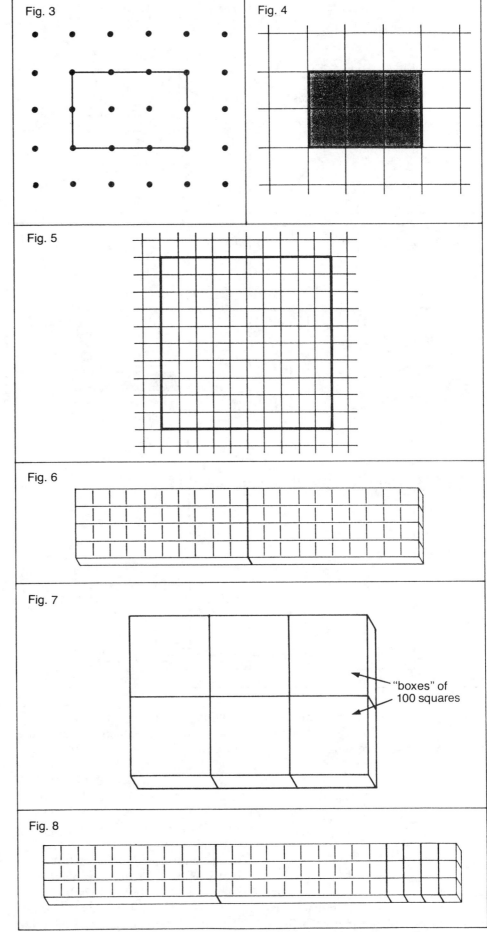

Fig. 3

Fig. 4

Fig. 5

Fig. 6

Fig. 7

"boxes" of 100 squares

Fig. 8

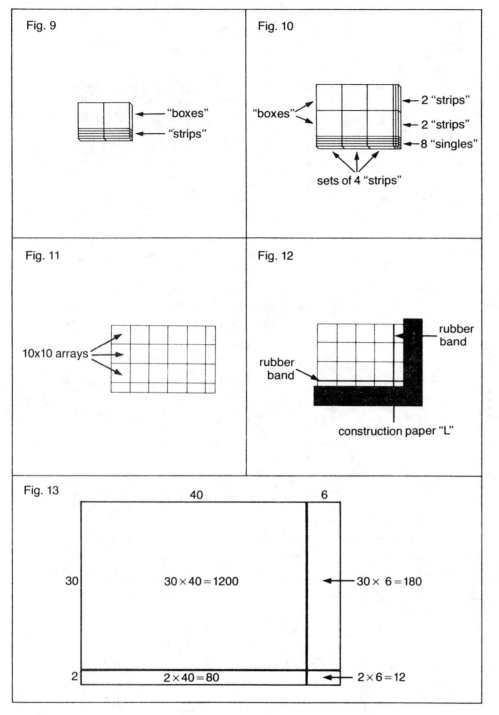

Fig. 9

"boxes"
"strips"

Fig. 10

"boxes"
2 "strips"
2 "strips"
8 "singles"

sets of 4 "strips"

Fig. 11

10x10 arrays

Fig. 12

rubber band

rubber band

construction paper "L"

Fig. 13

	40	6
30	30 × 40 = 1200	30 × 6 = 180
2	2 × 40 = 80	2 × 6 = 12

them together to find that there are 280 little squares.

A beginning recording method, which can later lead to a more polished algorithm, may look like this:

$$\begin{array}{r} 20 \\ \times\ 14 \\ \hline \end{array}$$

$$\begin{array}{r} 1 \text{ ten} \times 2 \text{ tens} = 200 \\ 4 \times 2 \text{ tens} = 80 \\ \hline 280 \end{array}$$

Notice how clearly the two partial products, the 200 and the 80, are represented in the grid model.

All three grid shapes are needed for examples in which factors are greater than ten, but neither factor is a multiple of ten. To represent 24 times 32, the children form an array with 24 rows of 32 squares. It is best to place the "boxes" in the upper left corner of the array so that the left-to-right arrangement of hundreds, tens, and ones is consistent with place value in the numerals (fig. 10). To find the total number of squares in the array for 24 times 32, it is most efficient to notice four parts of the array: an array of "boxes," two different arrays made of "strips," and a small array of "singles." The children find the number of squares in each part, and then add to find the total number of squares. Their record may look like this:

$$\begin{array}{r} 32 \\ \times\ 24 \\ \hline \end{array}$$

$$\begin{array}{r} 20 \times 30 = 600 \\ 4 \times 30 = 120 \\ 20 \times 2 = 40 \\ 4 \times 2 = 8 \\ \hline 768 \end{array}$$

At this stage, children are most likely to count squares in the largest regions first. The order of the partial products does not matter. Much later, when children work at a more abstract level using more sophisticated algorithms, they may find that it is convenient to use a different order for finding partial products. With the basic understanding built with arrays and less sophisticated algorithms, however, work at more abstract levels will be meaningful and less difficult.

As students progress in their multiplication, they can construct another

and 12) are evident in the array, and the total number of squares are shown in this beginning recording method:

$$\begin{array}{r} 24 \\ \times\ 3 \\ \hline \end{array}$$

$$\begin{array}{r} 3 \times 2 \text{ tens} = 60 \\ 3 \times 4\ \ = 12 \\ \hline 72 \end{array}$$

The next step is to introduce examples having both factors greater than ten, with one of the factors being a

multiple of ten. To represent 14 × 20, for example, the children must build an array with 14 rows of 20 squares. Two "boxes" side by side make 10 rows of 20 squares. Below that, 4 rows, each containing 2 "strips," make 4 rows of 20 squares. Thus, a 14-by-20 array is created (fig. 9). To determine how many little squares are in the entire array, the children see that it is easy to find the number of squares in the "boxes" (200) and the number of squares in the eight "strips" (8 tens or 80), and then add grid model that is efficient for use with larger factors. The following materials are needed for the model:

Grid paper with squares about 0.5 cm on each side

Corrugated cardboard

Glue

Felt-tip pen

Large rubber bands

Construction paper

A sheet of grid paper is glued to a piece of corrugated cardboard. The cardboard is cut along the outside lines of the grid paper and the felt-tip pen is used to outline as many 10-by-10 arrays as possible, beginning in the upper left corner (fig. 11). One rubber band is placed around the cardboard horizontally, and another is placed around it vertically. The construction paper is cut to form a large "L" shape, with each leg of the L 5 cm wide.

To use the new grid model to represent a product like 32×46, the part of the grid that is outside the 32-by-46 array is covered with the paper L. What the student sees, then, is an array containing 32 rows of 46 squares. The rubber bands are placed to mark the 30-by-40 part of the array in the upper left corner. The rubber bands separate the array into the four regions representing the four partial products (fig. 12).

Students may make a diagram of the model before writing an algorithm. The diagram should show a rectangular region to represent the 32-by-46 array, with horizontal and vertical lines to represent the two rubber bands. Numerals and equations indicate factors and partial products (fig. 13).

Then the algorithm that shows what the students found, using the model and diagram, may look like this:

$$
\begin{array}{r}
46 \\
\times\ 32 \\
\hline
\end{array}
$$

$$
\begin{array}{rcr}
30 \times 40 &=& 1200 \\
30 \times 6 &=& 180 \\
2 \times 40 &=& 80 \\
2 \times 6 &=& 12 \\
\hline
& & 1472
\end{array}
$$

Notice how clearly the four partial products are represented in the model, the diagram and the algorithm.

The making of diagrams to match grid-array models prepares students to use diagrams alone for much larger factors. When factors are larger than 100, for example, the model is inappropriate. The experiences with diagrams for smaller factors, however, will provide the basis for devising diagrams for large factors.

The ideas presented here are useful for helping students develop, in a logical sequence, concepts and skills in multiplication. The use of the grid-array models provides a meaningful transition from early concrete and pictorial arrays to more abstract diagrams and algorithms for large factors. ◗

Expanded Division

By **Sarah E. Patrick**

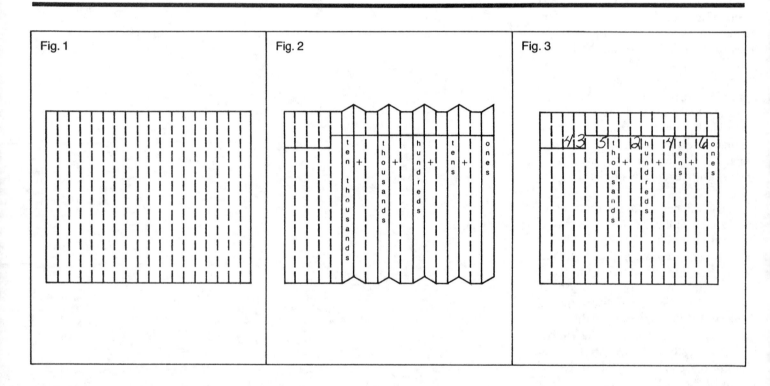

Fig. 1

Fig. 2

Fig. 3

In a discussion on the developmental division algorithms with a class of prospective elementary school teachers, the following question arose: How do you justify the steps of the traditional division algorithm particularly bringing down a number, when presenting the algorithm to students?

When we tried to remember how it had been presented to us, we could recollect no developmental work. We all recalled being told to do it such and such a way, but with no whys. We checked a well-known mathematics series, but found only that the transi-

Sarah Patrick is an assistant professor of mathematics at Troy State University of Dothan/Fort Rucker in Alabama. She teaches both mathematics content and methods courses for prospective elementary school teachers.

tion from developmental algorithms to the traditional algorithm was called a "shortcut." No in-depth explanation was given.

A workshop presented at an NCTM meeting gave me an idea for an aid that would help to explain why we "bring down" a number in division. The aid is based on the idea of an expanding place-value chart that allows you to show a number such as 4321 as any one of the following:

4 thousands + 3 hundreds + 2 tens + 1 one

43 hundreds + 2 tens + 1 one

43 hundreds + 21 ones

432 tens + 1 one

4321 ones.

To make the aid, you can use a file folder or a long sheet of construction paper. First, draw eighteen vertical

bands of equal width, as shown in figure 1. This allows for a divisor of from one to four digits and a dividend of from one to five digits. Fewer bands can be used if your maximum divisors or dividends are smaller numbers.

Draw the division bars as in figure 2, using four bands for the divisor and fourteen bands for the dividend. Be sure to leave space across the top for the quotient. Next, working from left to right, and starting in the sixth column, write in place-value names and plus signs, leaving spaces for numbers, as in figure 2.

The next step is to fold the paper into pleats so that no place-value names or plus signs are visible. The creases will be made on each side of the columns with the place-value names so that the name column is folded onto the plus-sign column. On the right edge, the ones column is folded behind the column where the number of ones is written, as shown in figure 2. Once the folds are well creased, unfold and laminate the aid.

Now the aid is ready to use. As an example, let us divide 5246 by 43. Be sure to use nonpermanent markers when writing on the aid. Fill in the numbers in the appropriate bands, as in figure 3. Fold the aid so that the ten-thousands band is out of sight. The division exercise is then worked, explained, and folded as follows and as illustrated in figures 4 through 9.

(1) We have 5 thousands. We cannot make a group of 43 thousands from this. Thus we refold the aid to show 52 hundreds (fig. 4).

(2) We have 52 hundreds. We can make one group of 43 hundreds from this. Thus we write 1 in the number band for hundreds and subtract 43 hundreds from 52 hundreds (fig. 5).

(3) We now have 9 hundreds + 4 tens + 6 ones. Since we cannot make another group of 43 hundreds from the 9 hundreds, we refold the aid to show 94 tens + 6 ones. The 4 is out of line with the 9 so we "bring it down" to be in line with the 9 for easier reading (fig. 6).

(4) We have 94 tens. We can make two groups of 43 tens from this. Thus we write 2 in the number band for tens and subtract 2 × 43 tens, or 86 tens, from 94 tens (fig. 7).

(5) We now have 8 tens + 6 ones. Since we cannot make another group of 43 tens from the 8 tens, we refold the aid to show 86 ones. The 6 is out of line with the 8 so we "bring it down" to be in line with the 8 for easier reading (fig. 8).

(6) We now have 86 ones. We can make two groups of 43 ones from this. Thus we write 2 in the number band for ones and subtract 2 × 43 ones, or 86 ones, from 86 ones (fig. 9).

The aid emphasizes the place-value aspects involved in the division algorithm. Thus you can see a reason for bringing down numbers when you are using the traditional division algorithm. ☛

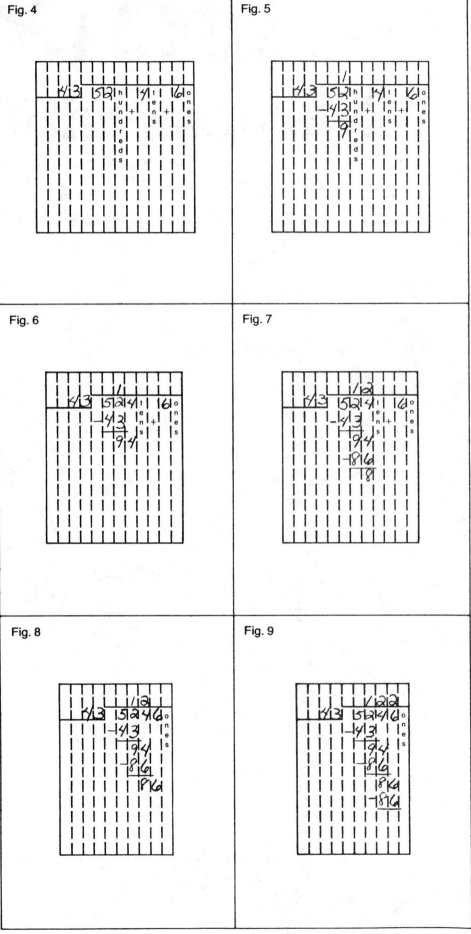

Let's Do It

Fractions with Models

By **Larry P. Leutzinger**
Area Education Agency 7
Cedar Falls, Iowa
and **Glen Nelson**
University of Northern Iowa
Cedar Falls, Iowa

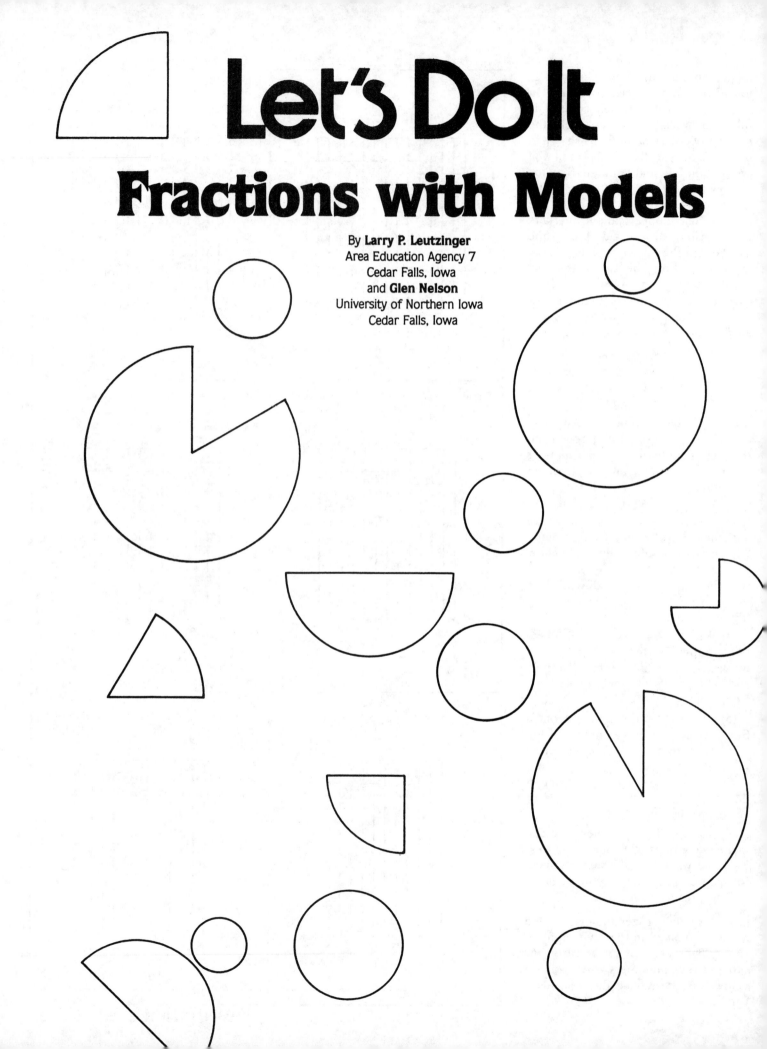

There is still value in learning about common fractions, even with the increased use of the metric system of measurement. In the past, much of the computation with common fractions has resulted from measurement situations with the customary system. In the future, with metric measurements using decimal fractions, there may be less emphasis on computation with fractions and more emphasis on fractions as representations of parts of a whole (One-third of the pie has been eaten.) and comparisons of fractions (Two-thirds of this pizza is less than three-fourths of it.). Students will need to have an even better understanding of the meaning of fractions, as well as greater skill in comparing fractions. To achieve the desired level of understanding, the introduction of fraction concepts should begin in the intermediate grades.

A sound, detailed teaching sequence is proposed by Ellerbruch and Payne in "A Teaching Sequence from Initial Fraction Concepts through the Addition of Unlike Fractions" in the 1978 NCTM Yearbook, *Developing Computational Skills*. They illustrate extensively with the rectangular-region model for a fraction. This model—where

represents one-third, for example—is a good choice for initial work with fractions because it relates well to student experiences and is easy to provide (a piece of paper, folded and marked, will do nicely).

The purpose of this article is to suggest ways you can help your students develop precomputational fraction concepts and skills using a circular-region, or "pie" model. It is hoped that by becoming familiar with the circular region model as well as with the rectangular region model, your students will be better able to generalize and transfer their learnings about fractions.

The circular-region model—where

represents three-fourths for example—has all of the features of the rectangu-

lar region and it is easy to "see" the unit. The figure

is readily associated with one-half, even if the rest of the unit is not indicated. The pie has traditionally served as a real-world referent for this model.

The drawback of the circular model has been the difficulty in providing it in large numbers. It is quite a chore to mark and cut out by hand the quantity of circles needed for a large class. A fairly durable and rather inexpensive circular model for initial work can be made from two paper plates of the same size but contrasting colors. If you can obtain plates of only one color, have students color one of their plates. Eventually you and your students will each need ten paper plates, five of each color.

To make the first model, you will need two paper plates, one of each color, for each student. Place the plates in a stack and push the point of a compass, or other sharp point, through the center of all of the plates. Determine this center carefully. You can take a plate and fold it in half twice and the intersection of the diameters will be the center. (Fig. 1)

Give each student a plate of each color. Have them draw a line segment from the center point to the edge of each plate, then cut along this radius. The cut of one plate is slid into the cut of the other and the two plates are pushed together until they "fit," one in the other. (Fig. 2) Establish that the combination of the two plates is the model that represents one whole and that the front of the plates is the side of the model viewed. (Note that an advantage of this model is that the whole unit is always shown.) Also, determine which of the two different colors is to show the fractional part. Then, by grasping the edge of one plate with one hand and the other plate with the other hand, and rotating the plates in opposite directions, different fractions can be modeled.

You can introduce the use of the model by questions: Can you arrange the model so that one-half is red (or whatever color)? Show me. Now show me what you think one-third looks like. Three fourths? Can you show me a fraction that's less than one-half? More than three-fourths?

Next, represent a fraction with the model that is close to, but obviously not, one-half. Ask some more questions: Is this one-half? Why not? Is that right, that each of the two parts must be the same size? Represent a fraction that is close to, but not, one-fourth, and repeat the process. Determine that when a whole is divided into fractional parts, each of the parts must be the same size as the other parts.

By asking questions such as these about more familiar fractions, you can assess each student's understanding of fractions and the use of this model. Similar questions should also be asked using the rectangular model.

Because the radii are perpendicular

Fig. 1

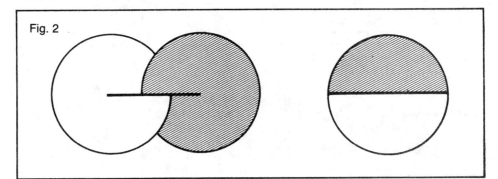

Fig. 2

when one-fourth and three-fourths are represented, these fractions, along with one-half, are easy to model accurately. Discussion about representing other fractions should reveal the need for more precision in representing thirds, sixths, and so on. An accurately marked model is needed for all fractions investigated. A good starter set for each student would include a model for halves, thirds, fourths, sixths, and eighths. This will require two more plates per model for each student. Luckily, each model will represent all proper fractions for the given number of parts. For example, only one model will be required for all of the eighths, not nine separate models.

To mark each model accurately, you can correctly mark one plate, then use it as a guide to mark a stack of plates. Draw lines on the edges of the stack at appropriate intervals and again mark the center. (Fig. 3) Or, if the plates are of that kind, with just the center marked, your students can mark the plates at correct intervals by counting off the correct number of ridges, or indentations, on the plate's edge. For instance, if the plate has eighty ridges, every twentieth would mark it for fourths.

Each of the edge markings is now connected to the center with a line segment, *one* radius is cut, and each pair of plates is assembled as before.

A completed starter set would look like that shown in figure 4. (Only one of the equal parts is represented for each of the models here, but each can be rotated to show all other proper fractions with that denominator.)

Developing Meaning of the Terms

The meaning of the two terms of a fraction (the numerator and the denominator) and equivalence of fractions can now be developed using the models. Model work with oral instructions should precede symbol work with numerals. For the model work, each student and you should have a set of five models.

"This model shows thirds. Can you find your model that shows thirds? Hold it up. Now can you make it show one-third? How many of the equal parts are red? How many equal parts in the whole? Yes, one of the three equal parts is red—it shows one-third."

Ask similar questions for two-thirds, no (or zero)-thirds, three-thirds. Note that three-thirds is the same as one-whole.

Repeat for other fractions.

Again, work with rectangular models should complement the work with circular models.

When your students have a good understanding of the relationship between the model and the oral work, symbolism can then be introduced. The terms of the fraction are related to the model to show the meaning of the top number, or numerator, as the number of shaded or colored parts and the bottom number, or denominator, as the number of equal parts in the whole. Ellerbruch and Payne suggest using an intermediate step first, before transferring to the standard numeral. For example,

would be written first as "5 sixths", then as "5/6".

After they attain familiarity with the numeral, you may give your students either the oral name or the symbol, and have them model it; or you (or a student) may model a fraction and have students say or write its name.

Write "3/8" on the board and ask, "Can you show me this fraction? How do we read this fraction? What does the 3 mean? The 8?"

Display the model showing five-sixths and ask, "Can you tell me what fraction this is?"

Display one-sixth. Ask, "Can you write what fraction this is?"

Activities

There are several good activities that can reinforce this model-symbol relationship.

Make a set of "fraction" cards for each pair of students. Each card should have on it one of the fractions that it is possible to represent with a model. (See fig. 5).

Students can work in pairs, taking turns drawing a fraction card from the face-down deck, saying the fraction, then modeling it. Or one student may model a fraction and the other names it and finds the matching fraction card.

A minideck of five cards, one for each of the different denominators, can be selected by one student and given to

Fig. 3

Fig. 4

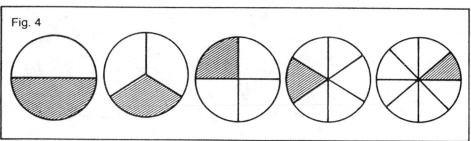

Fig. 5

$\frac{0}{2}$	$\frac{1}{2}$	$\frac{2}{2}$	$\frac{0}{3}$	$\frac{1}{3}$
$\frac{2}{3}$	$\frac{3}{3}$	$\frac{0}{4}$	$\frac{1}{4}$	$\frac{2}{4}$
$\frac{3}{4}$	$\frac{4}{4}$	$\frac{0}{6}$	$\frac{1}{6}$	$\frac{2}{6}$
$\frac{3}{6}$	$\frac{4}{6}$	$\frac{5}{6}$	$\frac{6}{6}$	$\frac{0}{8}$
$\frac{1}{8}$	$\frac{2}{8}$	$\frac{3}{8}$	$\frac{4}{8}$	$\frac{5}{8}$
$\frac{6}{8}$	$\frac{7}{8}$	$\frac{8}{8}$		

another. The second student must model each fraction named and place the card on the matching model. A scoring system of one point for each correct match could be instituted if a more competative situation is desired. This activity could be adapted to an activity center, also.

By making decks of "model" cards (fig. 6) to match the fraction cards, other activities are possible. At this time, activities with equivalent fractions, such as 1/2 and 2/4, should be avoided.

For a concentration-type game, eight fraction cards of nonequivalent fractions (for example, 1/2, 1/3, 2/3, 0/4, 3/4, 5/6, 6/6, 5/8) and their eight matching model cards may be selected. The fraction cards are shuffled and placed face down in a 4-by-2 array, and the model cards are shuffled and placed face down in a 4-by-2 array beside the array of fraction cards. Players take turns turning over two cards, one of each set of cards, and attempting to match a fraction card and a model card. Players get to keep each pair they match.

Comparing and Ordering Fractions

Many students have difficulty comparing fractions such as 1/4 and 1/5 because they have little or no understanding of the terms and make comparisons based only on the sizes of the denominators. Model work is essential in order to overcome this difficulty.

Begin by comparing two models that are obviously not equivalent, giving oral instructions only. For example, show models of one-half and two-thirds and ask, "Which is more? Which has more red (or whatever color) showing? What is the name of the greater fraction? The lesser fraction? Yes, two-thirds is greater than one-half. Show me a fraction greater than two-thirds—there are many. What fraction did you model?"

Symbols for the fraction models are then displayed for convenience, but the comparison is still made using the model.

Special attention should be given to like fractions, those with the same denominators. Begin again with models and oral discussion.

"Pair up with a partner. One of you show two-sixths; the other, three-sixths. Which is greater?" Repeat with other pairs of like fractions, leading to the conclusion that when the whole is divided into the same number of equal parts, the fraction that shows more of these parts is the greater.

The unit fractions, 1/2, 1/3, 1/4, 1/6, and 1/8, can be investigated as a special set of fractions, also.

"Pair up. One partner, show one-fourth; the other, show one-sixth. Which is greater? In the model that shows one-fourth, how many parts are in the whole? How many of those four equal parts are red? In the model that shows one-sixth, how many parts in the whole? How many are red? Which is

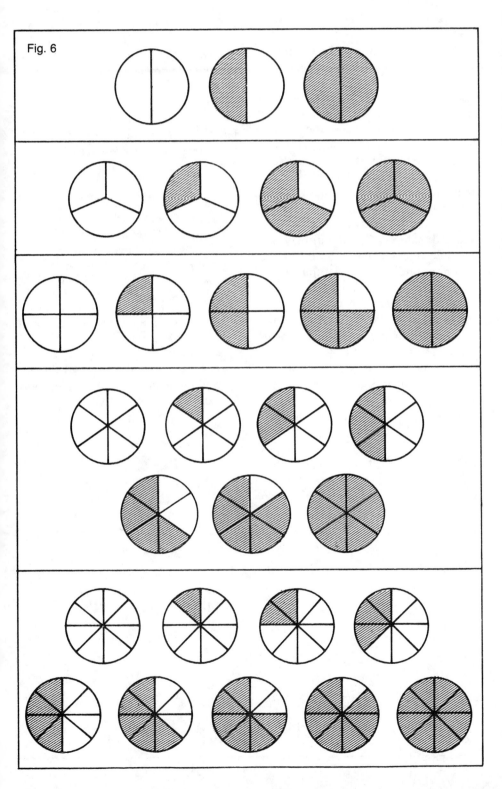

Fig. 6

larger, one of the pieces when the whole has been divided into six equal parts, or one of the pieces when the whole has been divided into four equal parts?" Repeat with other unit fractions, leading to the conclusion that the larger the denominator, the smaller the size of each part.

For comparing two fractions, a "war" type of game can be played by students, in pairs. To begin with, use the dozen model cards for 1/2, 1/3, 2/3, 0/4, 1/4, 3/4, 1/6, 5/6, 6/6, 1/8, 3/8, and 5/8. One player shuffles the cards and deals six to each player, face down. Players stack their cards without looking at them, then turn over the top card. Whoever turns over the card that shows the greater fraction, names both fractions and takes both cards. Play continues as before, with the object being to win the most cards. Close calls can be modeled on the larger paper-plate models and direct comparisons made to determine the greater.

Comparing two fractions can be extended to ordering three (or more) fractions by having students model the fractions and asking, "Which is greatest? least?"

Using a subset of the fraction cards, 1/2, 1/3, 2/3, 0/4, 1/4, 3/4, 1/6, 5/6, 6/6, 1/8, 3/8, 5/8, and 7/8, assign a card to each of several students and have the students model their assigned fractions with their paper plate model. Then have the students come to the front of the room, one at a time, and arrange themselves in order, from least to greatest, according to their models. Once the order is established, have them place their models in the chalk tray and write the fractions above the models.

Equivalent Fractions

Equivalent fractions can be introduced nicely by trying to do the previous comparing (and ordering) activities, but starting with two equivalent fractions.

"Work with a partner. One of you show this fraction, 2/4, the other 1/2. Which is greater? What happened? What did you find out about these two fractions? Yes, they are different names for the same amount. Look at one-half. How many parts in the whole? How many are red? Look at two-fourths. How many parts in the whole? How many are red? Yes, fourths has twice as many parts in the whole (as halves does). And there are twice as many shaded or colored. Can you display two other fractions that show the same amount as one-half and two-fourths?"

Compare one-half and three-sixths. Conclude that there are three times as many sixths as halves in the whole and three times as many are shaded or colored.

Ask students to find other sets of equivalent fractions and to model them.

Activities

By removing the six cards that show 1/6, 5/6, 1/8, 3/8, 5/8, and 7/8 from the deck of model cards, each of the remaining 22 cards will have at least one other equivalent card in the deck. A rummy-type game can be played where players are dealt five cards and attempt to get rid of all the cards in their hands by matching models of equivalent fractions. The matching can be done by either picking up a card from the face-up, discard pile or drawing from the pile of face-down, unplayed cards. Any matching cards may then be laid down and a card discarded.

After working with equivalent fractions at the model level, sets of equivalent fractions can be written and patterns noted. Problems such as

$$\frac{2}{4} = \frac{}{8}$$

should be modeled and reasoned through as, "Twice as many parts in the whole, so need twice as many shaded parts." Such reasoning, backed by the models, adds meaning to the symbolic solution,

$$\frac{2 \times 2}{4 \times 2} = \frac{4}{8}.$$

The fraction cards can now be used as well as the model cards to adapt several of the previous activities.

Fig. 7

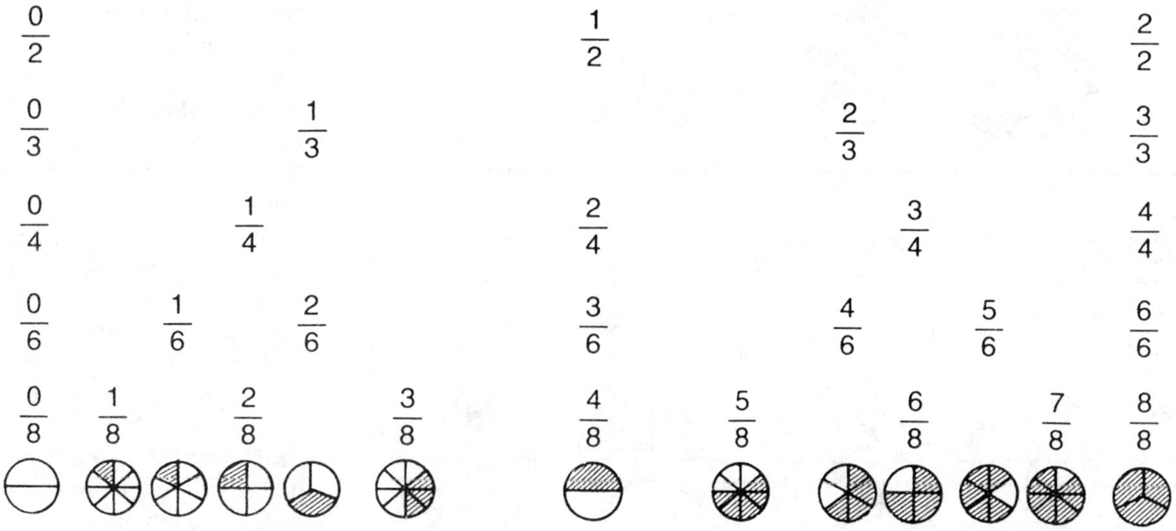

$$\frac{0}{2} \qquad \frac{1}{2} \qquad \frac{2}{2}$$

$$\frac{0}{3} \qquad \frac{1}{3} \qquad \frac{2}{3} \qquad \frac{3}{3}$$

$$\frac{0}{4} \qquad \frac{1}{4} \qquad \frac{2}{4} \qquad \frac{3}{4} \qquad \frac{4}{4}$$

$$\frac{0}{6} \qquad \frac{1}{6} \qquad \frac{2}{6} \qquad \frac{3}{6} \qquad \frac{4}{6} \qquad \frac{5}{6} \qquad \frac{6}{6}$$

$$\frac{0}{8} \quad \frac{1}{8} \quad \frac{2}{8} \quad \frac{3}{8} \quad \frac{4}{8} \quad \frac{5}{8} \quad \frac{6}{8} \quad \frac{7}{8} \quad \frac{8}{8}$$

Students could model each of the 28 different fractions and order them, as before, in the chalk tray. Models for equivalent fractions could be stacked one in front of another and then all names written on the board, above each model or set of equivalent models. (Fig. 7)

The concentration game could match model cards to fraction cards that name the fraction of an equivalent fraction; the model

could match 1/3, for instance.

A variation of the war game could be to include all model cards (or even all model and fraction cards mixed together). The game would be played as before, but if the first two cards turned over are equivalent, then the next two cards are compared. The greater of these wins all four cards.

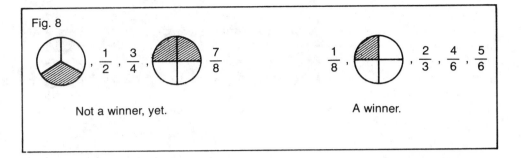

Fig. 8

Not a winner, yet.

A winner.

An ordering activity might be to use all fraction cards and all model cards mixed together. Players are dealt five cards, one at a time, which they must arrange in the order dealt—first card to the left, second card to its right, . . . with the fifth card on the extreme right. The cards should be positioned so that opponents cannot see them. The object is to be the first to get five cards in sequence, least from (on the player's left) to greatest. The order of the five cards cannot be interchanged, but during

each turn one of the five cards in a hand may be replaced by one drawn from the face-up, discard pile or from the face-down deck of unplayed cards. Equivalent fraction cards may be adjacent to one another, but no card naming a lesser fraction may end up to the right of a greater fraction. (Fig. 8)

We hope that the results obtained from increased understanding of fractions by your students will make the time you spent preparing these activities worthwhile. □

Fractions Taught by Folding Paper Strips

By **Wayne R. Scott**

The folding of paper strips into equal segments is an excellent model for conceptualization of operations with fractions, both simple common fractions and mixed numbers. There are several advantages to this model:

1. The relationship to the unit is immediate.

2. Size comparisons are easily made in the ordering of fractions.

3. Common denominators are apparent in addition and subtraction.

4. Equivalent fractions can be easily generated.

5. Multiplication, like subtraction, becomes a fold, label, and count procedure.

6. The arbitrary nature of the choice of the unit becomes apparent.

7. All four of the fundamental operations with fractions can be represented by folding strips.

Furthermore, people are much more accustomed to working with linear measures than with area measures. This makes the strip-folding model more desirable than the area model since it is a more natural model. A fraction represented by a linear unit strip is much more easily compared than a fraction represented by a unit square.

Then why is folding of paper strips not used more frequently? Folding a strip into more than four congruent segments is viewed as difficult. In fact it is not difficult, if the proper technique is used.

Folding Paper Strips

Prior to beginning to fold, it is necessary to locate a supply of strips. These might be obtained as scrap from a print shop. Or strips that fold well can be produced by cutting legal-size note pads into strips length-wise. *Fractions that are being compared must be on strips of equal length.*

Two equal parts

Everyone can do this. Loop the strip, placing the ends together, and crease. Label each part 1/2.

Three equal parts

Most people have done this. Loop the strip one and one-half times, bringing the ends opposite one another, and crease. Label each part 1/3. (See fig. 1)

Wayne Scott is a mathematics specialist with the Michigan Department of Education in Lansing.

Four equal parts

Most people do this by folding in half, creasing, and folding in half again. This is indeed 1/2 of 1/2, or 1/4. There is another technique which is an extension of the three-fold. Loop the strip twice, bringing the ends together, and crease. (See fig. 2) How many equal parts? Four. Label each part 1/4.

There are two hints for making this work well: (1) Keep the loops tight. (2) Squeeze the loops together without creasing to be certain that the ends are at the same place.

Five equal parts

After folding a strip into four equal parts, using the method just described, a five-fold should be easy. Loop the strip two and one-half times before creasing. Be certain that the ends of the strip are at the creases. (See fig. 3) How many equal parts? Five. Label each 1/5. After folding the strip, it is a good plan to "accordion fold" it. This gives you an opportunity to check your accuracy and to mark the folds.

Six equal parts

Of course! There are three ways. You can fold in half and then fold the halves in thirds. Or you can fold into thirds and then fold each third in half. (1/2 of 1/3 = 1/6) You can also use three loops.

Seven equal loops

Use three and one-half loops. Be sure the loops are tight! For more than seven equal parts! You're on your own.

Size Comparisons and Seriation

One very important rule when using fold strips is *fold the portion not used behind—do not cut it off*. With the entire strip left intact, it is possible to make size comparisons with the unit length. Comparison to the unit is not only desirable but necessary when working with fractional manipulatives. When fractions are compared, the units must be the same.

With the possibility of direct comparison offered by paper folding, it is not difficult to determine which is

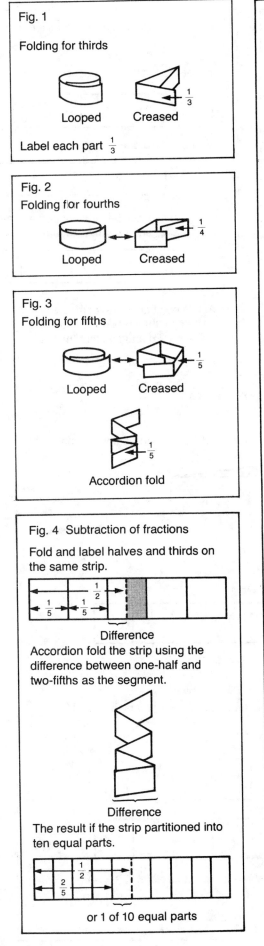

Fig. 1
Folding for thirds
Looped   Creased $\frac{1}{3}$
Label each part $\frac{1}{3}$

Fig. 2
Folding for fourths
Looped   Creased $\frac{1}{4}$

Fig. 3
Folding for fifths
Looped   Creased $\frac{1}{5}$
Accordion fold $\frac{1}{5}$

Fig. 4 Subtraction of fractions
Fold and label halves and thirds on the same strip.
$\frac{1}{2}$ $\frac{1}{5}$ $\frac{1}{5}$
Difference
Accordion fold the strip using the difference between one-half and two-fifths as the segment.
Difference
The result if the strip partitioned into ten equal parts.
$\frac{1}{2}$ $\frac{2}{5}$
or 1 of 10 equal parts

Fig. 5 Addition of fractions

Fold one strip into thirds and label it.

$\frac{1}{3}$

Fold a second strip into fifths and label it.

$\frac{1}{5}$

Unfold the first strip and append one-fifth to one-third. Draw a line at $\frac{1}{3}+\frac{1}{5}$. Label the one-fifth.

$\frac{1}{3}$ $\frac{1}{5}$

$\frac{1}{5}$

There is a small segment between the line drawn and the fold for two-thirds. Beginning with this segment, accordion fold, right side behind the segment, left side in front of the segment. The left section folds evenly. The right section, however, folds two and one-half times. Therefore, crease again to make segments the size of what was left over.

$\frac{1}{2}$ as long as the others

Unfold and count. There are fifteen segments, five of them in the one-third and three in the one-fifth portions.

$$\frac{1}{3}+\frac{1}{5}=\frac{8}{15}$$

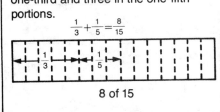

$\frac{1}{3}$ $\frac{1}{5}$

8 of 15

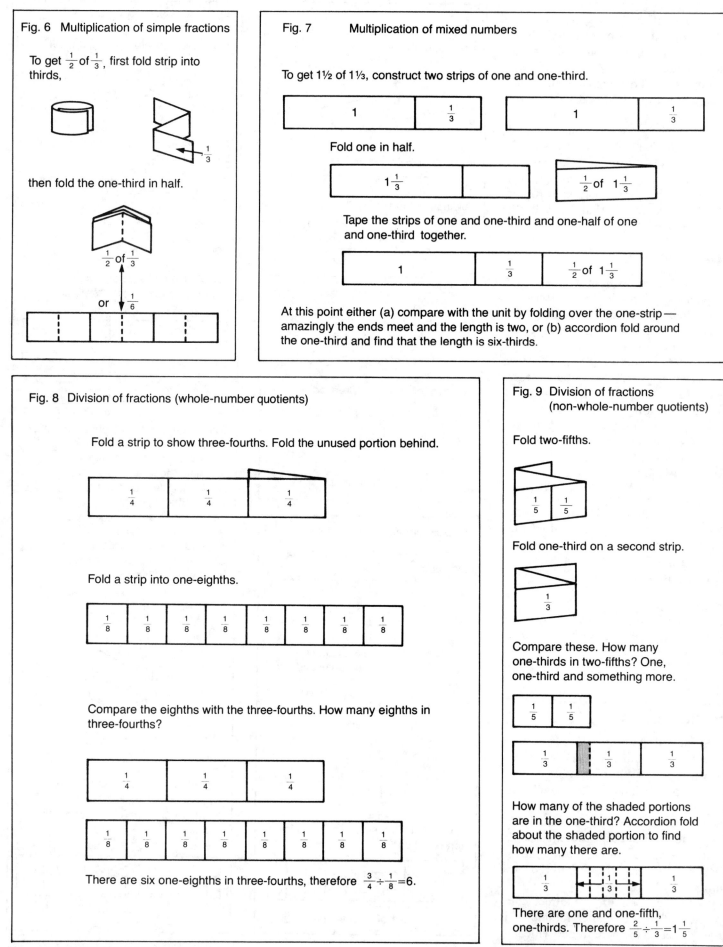

Fig. 6 Multiplication of simple fractions

To get $\frac{1}{2}$ of $\frac{1}{3}$, first fold strip into thirds,

then fold the one-third in half.

$$\frac{1}{2} \text{ of } \frac{1}{3}$$

or $\frac{1}{6}$

Fig. 7   Multiplication of mixed numbers

To get 1½ of 1⅓, construct **two** strips of one and one-third.

| 1 | $\frac{1}{3}$ |
| 1 | $\frac{1}{3}$ |

Fold one in half.

$1\frac{1}{3}$ $\frac{1}{2}$ of $1\frac{1}{3}$

Tape the strips of one and one-third and one-half of one and one-third together.

| 1 | $\frac{1}{3}$ | $\frac{1}{2}$ of $1\frac{1}{3}$ |

At this point either (a) compare with the unit by folding over the one-strip — amazingly the ends meet and the length is two, or (b) accordion fold around the one-third and find that the length is six-thirds.

Fig. 8 Division of fractions (whole-number quotients)

Fold a strip to show three-fourths. Fold the unused portion behind.

| $\frac{1}{4}$ | $\frac{1}{4}$ | $\frac{1}{4}$ |

Fold a strip into one-eighths.

| $\frac{1}{8}$ | $\frac{1}{8}$ | $\frac{1}{8}$ | $\frac{1}{8}$ | $\frac{1}{8}$ | $\frac{1}{8}$ | $\frac{1}{8}$ | $\frac{1}{8}$ |

Compare the eighths with the three-fourths. How many eighths in three-fourths?

| $\frac{1}{4}$ | $\frac{1}{4}$ | $\frac{1}{4}$ |

| $\frac{1}{8}$ | $\frac{1}{8}$ | $\frac{1}{8}$ | $\frac{1}{8}$ | $\frac{1}{8}$ | $\frac{1}{8}$ | $\frac{1}{8}$ | $\frac{1}{8}$ |

There are six one-eighths in three-fourths, therefore $\frac{3}{4} \div \frac{1}{8} = 6$.

Fig. 9 Division of fractions (non-whole-number quotients)

Fold two-fifths.

| $\frac{1}{5}$ | $\frac{1}{5}$ |

Fold one-third on a second strip.

$\frac{1}{3}$

Compare these. How many one-thirds in two-fifths? One, one-third and something more.

| $\frac{1}{5}$ | $\frac{1}{5}$ |

| $\frac{1}{3}$ | | $\frac{1}{3}$ | $\frac{1}{3}$ |

How many of the shaded portions are in the one-third? Accordion fold about the shaded portion to find how many there are.

| $\frac{1}{3}$ | $\frac{1}{3}$ | $\frac{1}{3}$ |

There are one and one-fifth, one-thirds. Therefore $\frac{2}{5} \div \frac{1}{3} = 1\frac{1}{5}$

larger, 2/5 or 1/2. Fifths can be folded on one strip and halves on another. Then a direct comparison of 2/5 and 1/2 can be made. Simply place a 1/2 strip beside a 2/5 strip.

Subtraction of Fractions

If, on the other hand, 1/2 and 2/5 are both folded and labeled on the same strip, the difference between the two fractions can be found. There is a small segment with folds at the 1/2 and 2/5 creases. Using this segment as a width, accordion fold the strip. (See fig. 4) It will fold into ten equal parts, one of which is the difference. Thus we have discovered that

$$\frac{1}{2} - \frac{2}{5} = \frac{1}{10}.$$

(The thrill of discovery comes only by folding. Try it!)

Addition of Fractions

Addition is not as easy as subtraction because one segment must be appended to another. (See fig. 5) The modeling of addition could also be done by taping the 1/5 segment to the 1/3 segment. Taping becomes necessary when the sum is greater than one.

Multiplication of Fractions

Multiplication of fractions using paper strips uses the "of" model. When folding a strip into six equal parts, one way is to fold into thirds and then to fold the thirds in half. This is the multiplication model. (See fig. 6) Multiplication of mixed numbers is fun using the paper-folding technique. This can be demonstrated with the example 1 1/2

× 1 1/3, or one and one-half, one and one-third. (See fig. 7)

Division of Fractions

The paper-folding model is one of the few models that can be used for all four arithmetic operations on fractions. Few people have a good conceptual model of division of fractions. Paper folding provides such a model. The division model follows that of whole numbers very closely. Just as 52 ÷ 13 = ? asks How many 13's are there in 52? in the example 3/4 ÷ 1/8 = ? asks How many one-eighths are there in three fourths? (See fig. 8)

Division problems with quotients that are not whole numbers are only slightly more difficult. The problem 2/5 ÷ 1/3 = ? asks How many one-thirds in two-fifths? (See fig. 9) ◆

Fractions and Popsicle Sticks

By **Earnest Carlisle**

That inexpensive and abundant aid, the Popsicle stick, can provide an excellent "concrete" model for multiplication and division of fractions. To effectively use the sticks in modeling fractions, we need to dye one set of sticks so we have sticks of two different colors.

Prior to using the sticks to model fractional operations, a review of their use in forming arrays to model multiplication of whole numbers may be helpful. For example, consider the model of $3 \times 4 = 12$ shown in figure 1. Three understandings are essential to interpreting this model:

1. The first factor, 3, is represented by the horizontal sticks.

2. The second factor, 4, is represented by the vertical sticks.

3. The array formed by the intersections of the sticks represents the product, 12.

An associate professor of education at Columbus College in Columbus, Georgia, Earnest Carlisle teaches mathematics education courses for elementary education majors at both graduate and undergraduate levels.

To use the Popsicle sticks for modeling multiplication and division of fractions, we must organize our model in a way such that the vertical and horizontal arrangement of sticks may be interpreted as models of fractional numbers. To do this, colored sticks are essential. For purpose of illustration, let's consider the example $2/3 \times 3/4 = N$.

First, we construct models of the fractions, as shown in figure 2. We should observe that the white sticks represent the numerators of our fractions. The denominators of the fractions are represented by the total number of sticks.

Next, place the model of 2/3 over the model of 3/4, as shown in figure 3. Examining this model, we see that two arrays are formed. One array, formed by the intersections of the white sticks, is the product of our numerators (3×2). The other array, formed by the intersections of all the sticks, is the product of the denominators (3×4). Our observations lead us to conclude that $2/3 \times 3/4 = 6/12$.

An understanding of multiplication and division as inverse operations enables us to model the division of fractions with arrays of Popsicle sticks. From a structural point of view, multiplication is finding a product when the factors are known and division is finding a factor when the product and one of the factors are known. Let's consider the example $6/12 \div 2/3 = N$, which can be restated as $2/3 \times N = 6/12$.

First, we construct a model of 2/3, our known factor (fig. 4). Next, we use white sticks until we form an array of white intersections that represent the numerator of the product, namely, 6 (fig. 5). We complete the model by using colored sticks to form an array that has 12 intersections, the number in the denominator of the product (fig. 6). Examining the model, we conclude that $6/12 \div 2/3 = 3/4$.

This simple model works very well when the factors are less than one. In spite of its limitations, the model can help children develop an understanding of multiplication and division of fractions. □

Fig. 1   Fig. 2   Fig. 3

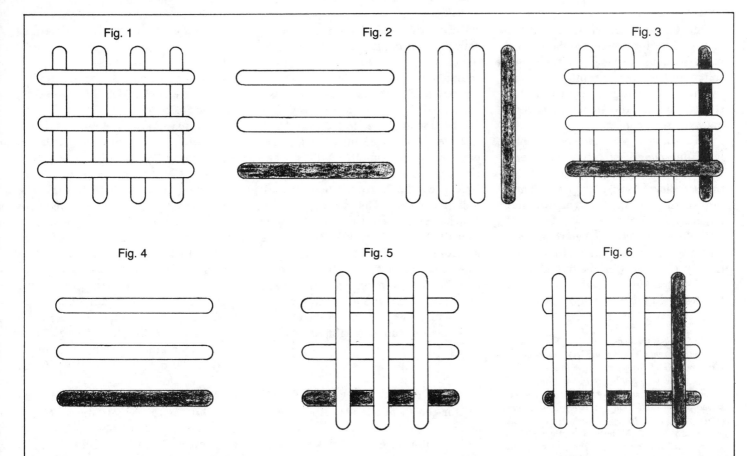

Fig. 4   Fig. 5   Fig. 6

Mathematics and Saltine Crackers

By **Gloria Sanok**

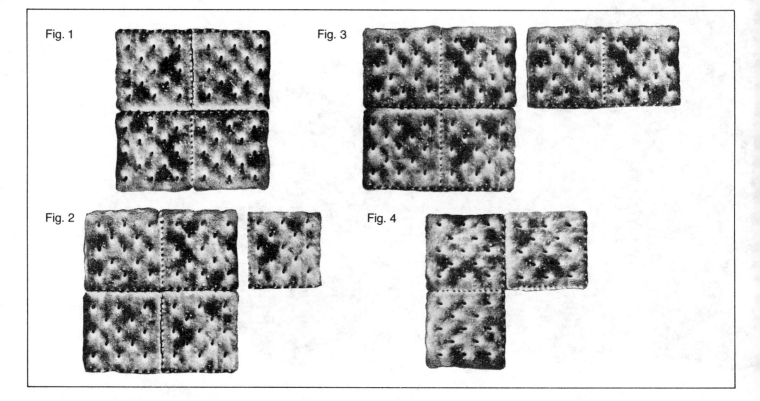

Fig. 1

Fig. 2

Fig. 3

Fig. 4

One saltine cracker can give a student a taste for whole numbers, common fractions, decimal fractions, percents, and money—geometrically and rationally speaking, of course. A saltine cracker can illustrate several mathematical concepts.

To start with, a saltine cracker splits into four *congruent* (same size, same shape) pieces (fig. 1). Each of the smaller pieces is *similar* (same shape, but smaller in size) to the original, larger saltine.

Each individual cracker (one small piece) is one piece out of four pieces (fig. 2). The name for one out of four is one-fourth and the notation is 1/4. The fraction, two-fourths, can be illustrated

Gloria Sanok is a teacher and inservice instructor in the public schools in Wayne, New Jersey. She is also an adjunct instructor at William Paterson College and a mathematics consultant for the New Jersey State Department of Education. She has served on the evaluation and interpretation committee of the New Jersey State Assessment Tests, grades 3, 6, 9, and 11, and is currently a member of the Editorial Panel of the Mathematics Teacher.

by two individual crackers, two of the four pieces (fig. 3). The notation is 2/4, which is equivalent to 1/2. Eating two individual crackers is the same as eating one-half of the larger, original saltine.

The fraction three-fourths can be illustrated with three individual crackers, three of the four pieces (fig. 4). The notation is 3/4. The fraction four-fourths can be illustrated by four individual crackers. The notation is 4/4, which is equivalent to 1 whole. Eating four of the small crackers is the same as eating one whole saltine.

Another name for one-fourth is one-quarter. The word *quarter* lends itself well to the coins in our money system. And with money, the transition to decimal fractions can be taught very easily.

$$\frac{1}{4} + \frac{1}{4} + \frac{1}{4} + \frac{1}{4} = \frac{4}{4}$$

$$= 1 \text{ whole thing}$$

One-fourth of a dollar is one quarter.

One quarter is written as 25¢ or $0.25.

Two quarters can be written as 1/4 + 1/4, 2/4, 1/2, 25¢ + 25¢, 50¢, or $0.50.

Three quarters can be written as 1/4 + 1/4 + 1/4, 3/4, 25¢ + 25¢ + 25¢, 75¢, or $0.75.

Four quarters are 1/4 + 1/4 + 1/4 + 1/4, 4/4, 1 whole thing, 25¢ + 25¢ + 25¢ + 25¢, 100¢, or $1.00.

Lessons can be extended to the introduction of the study of percent. The word *percent* means per hundredth or by the hundredth. One hundred pennies equal one dollar. Therefore, one cent is one out of a hundred and is written as $0.01. One cent is 1/100 or 1% of a dollar. Twenty-five cents (one quarter) is 25/100 or 25% of a dollar. Seventy-five cents (three quarters) is 75 out of 100, $0.75, or 75/100 or 75% of a dollar. One hundred cents (four quarters) is 100 out of 100, or 100/100 or 100% of a dollar.

As part of their schooling and daily life, children can be introduced to concepts dealing with money, decimals, and percent, even through the study of a saltine cracker. ☙

Teaching Division of Fractions with Understanding

By **Charles Thompson**

How did you learn to solve 3/4 ÷ 1/6 = □? Like me, you probably learned the clever rule, invert the second fraction and multiply it by the first fraction. Specifically, 3/4 ÷ 1/6 = 3/4 × 6/1. A logical question arises: Why does that procedure, which seems extremely arbitrary to children, yield the correct answer? An explanation such as the following is often given:

$$\frac{3}{4} \div \frac{1}{6} = \frac{\dfrac{3}{4}}{\dfrac{1}{6}}$$

$$= \frac{\dfrac{3}{4}}{\dfrac{1}{6}} \times \frac{\dfrac{6}{1}}{\dfrac{6}{1}}$$

$$= \frac{\dfrac{3}{4} \times \dfrac{6}{1}}{\dfrac{1}{6} \times \dfrac{6}{1}}$$

$$= \frac{\dfrac{3}{4} \times \dfrac{6}{1}}{1}$$

Although helpful to some children, this seems to many of them to be simply an invention of the teacher to justify the invert and multiply rule. Most children remain unsure about the reasons for inverting and multiplying. I think there are two main reasons for children's insecurity about the rule:

1. They have not been taught an interpretation for division of fractions. What does it mean to divide 3/4 by 1/6?

2. They have not had the opportunity to solve division-of-fraction problems by using concrete objects. How can the problem 3/4 ÷ 1/6 = □ be solved by manipulating concrete representations of fourths and sixths? The

An assistant professor in the early and middle childhood education department at the University of Louisville, Charles Thompson teaches undergraduate and graduate courses in mathematics education, with emphasis on the use of concrete materials to model mathematical concepts.

method for teaching division of fractions that I describe here resolves these two problems and provides a solid foundation for children's understanding of the operation.

The materials I prefer for teaching division of fractions are sections of circular regions which are cut from colored construction paper and have the fraction names written on *one side only*. All fraction sections of the same size should be of the same color. They are easily made by drawing the fraction sections on duplicating masters and feeding construction paper through the duplicating machine just as you would ordinary duplicating paper. The fraction sections that I will refer to are shown in figure 1.

Readiness Activities

These activities will provide a solid basis for understanding what division of fractions means. The activities are done with the fraction sections, *with the numerals face down.*

A.   1. How many browns in a yellow?
   2. How many greens in a blue?
   3. How many purples in a yellow?
B.   4. How many browns in 2 blues?
   5. How many purples in 2 pinks?
   6. How many greens in 3 blues?
C.   7. How many sets of 2 purples are in a yellow?
   8. How many sets of 2 greens are in 2 blues?
   9. How many sets of 3 purples are in 2 yellows?
D. 10. How many sets of 2 purples are in 4 purples?
   11. How many sets of 2 greens are in 6 greens?
   12. How many sets of 3 purples are in 6 purples?
E. 13. How many sets of 2 purples are in 5 purples?
   14. How many sets of 2 greens are in 7 greens?
   15. How many sets of 3 browns are in 7 browns?
F. 16. How many pinks in a yellow?
   17. How many browns in a blue?
   18. How many blues in a pink?

Exercises 1–9 are basically of the same type. Each can be solved by covering the second-named set of fraction sections with as many of the first-named set as possible. (See fig. 2.) Problems 10–15 are slightly different. These may be solved by regrouping the second-named set of fraction sections into smaller sets. (See fig. 3.) Problems 16–18 look similar to 1–3, but they require the children to determine fractional amounts of a given fraction section. (See fig. 4.)

Having children do these readiness problems will practically guarantee the children's subsequent understanding of what division of fractions means and their ability to use fraction sections to solve division problems.

Division of Fractions

Let's first relate the readiness activities to dividing fractions using numerals. In the division problem 28 ÷ 7 = □, what do the numerals 28 and 7 mean? The most common interpretation (and the one we will use for fractions) is, How many 7s are in 28? To do this problem with bottle caps you would take 28 bottle caps and put them into sets of 7. You would find that there are 4 sets of 7 bottle caps in 28 bottle caps. Thus, 28 ÷ 7 = 4.

In general, any division problem of the form ○ ÷ △ = □ can be interpreted as, How many sets of size △ are there in ○ ? Using the same interpretation, the division-of-fractions problem 1/2 ÷ 1/6 = □ means, How many 1/6s are there in 1/2? Consequently, solving 1/2 ÷ 1/6 = □ with the fraction sections is exactly the same as solving the corresponding readiness problem, How many browns (1/6s) are in a yellow (1/2)? The only difference is that the fraction sections are referred to

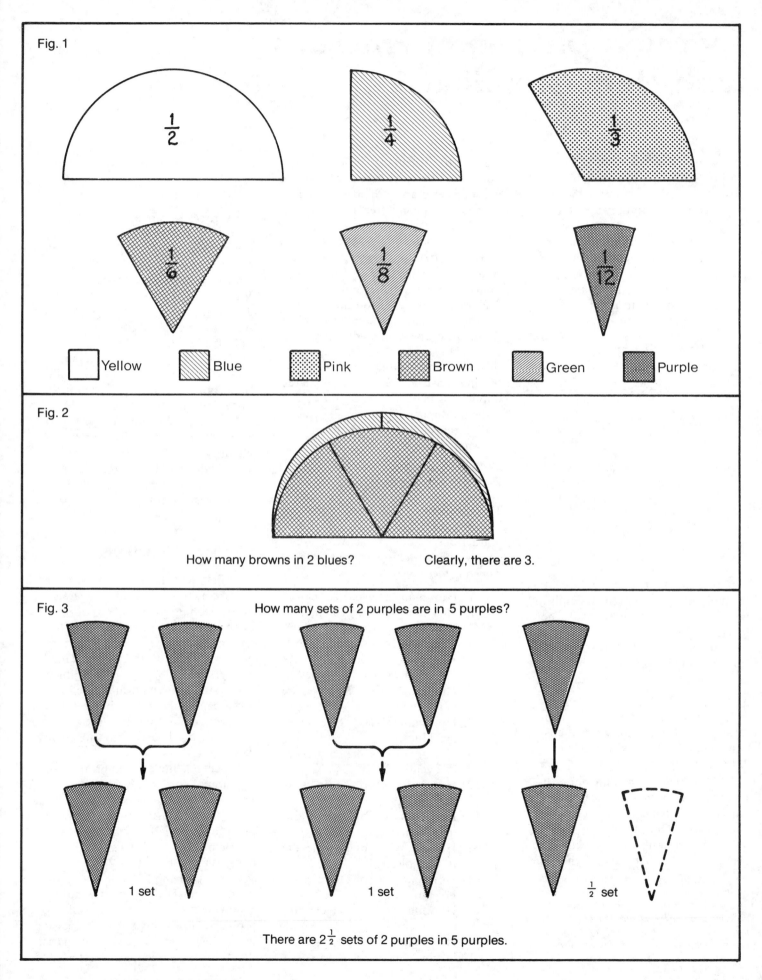

Fig. 1

$\frac{1}{2}$ $\frac{1}{4}$ $\frac{1}{3}$

$\frac{1}{6}$ $\frac{1}{8}$ $\frac{1}{12}$

Yellow   Blue   Pink   Brown   Green   Purple

Fig. 2

How many browns in 2 blues?   Clearly, there are 3.

Fig. 3   How many sets of 2 purples are in 5 purples?

1 set   1 set $\frac{1}{2}$ set

There are $2\frac{1}{2}$ sets of 2 purples in 5 purples.

by numerals rather than colors. (See fig. 5.)

Now that we have seen the relationship between the readiness activities and division of fractions using numerals, let's look at some initial numerical exercises for children.

A. 1. 1/2 ÷ 1/6 = □
    2. 1/4 ÷ 1/8 = □
    3. 1/2 ÷ 1/12 = □
B. 4. 2/4 ÷ 1/6 = □
    5. 2/3 ÷ 1/12 = □
    6. 3/4 ÷ 1/8 = □
C. 7. 1/2 ÷ 2/12 = □
    8. 2/4 ÷ 2/8 = □
    9. 2/2 ÷ 13/12 = □

These nine exercises are simply the numerical translations of the first nine readiness exercises. The students need only to be able to interpret the numerical exercises; working these problems involves exactly the same procedures as the corresponding readiness problems. For example, problem B5, $2/3 \div 1/12 = \square$, when interpreted, becomes the readiness problem B5, How many 1/12s (purples) in two 1/3s (pinks)? (See fig. 6.)

Subsequently, I would have children work the following problems, 10–15. These exercises are the numerical translations of readiness exercises 10–15.

D. 10. 4/12 ÷ 2/12 = □
    11. 6/6 ÷ 2/6 = □
    12. 6/12 ÷ 3/12 = □
E. 13. 5/12 ÷ 2/12 = □
    14. 7/8 ÷ 2/8 = □
    15. 7/6 ÷ 3/6 = □

My goal here would be to have the children generalize from the exercises to obtain a computational procedure. To assist that generalization I would add two more sets of problems having common denominators:

F. 19. 6/12 ÷ 2/12 = □
    20. 6/8 ÷ 2/8 = □
    21. 6/6 ÷ 2/6 = □
G. 22. 5/12 ÷ 3/12 = □
    23. 5/8 ÷ 3/8 = □
    24. 5/6 ÷ 3/6 = □

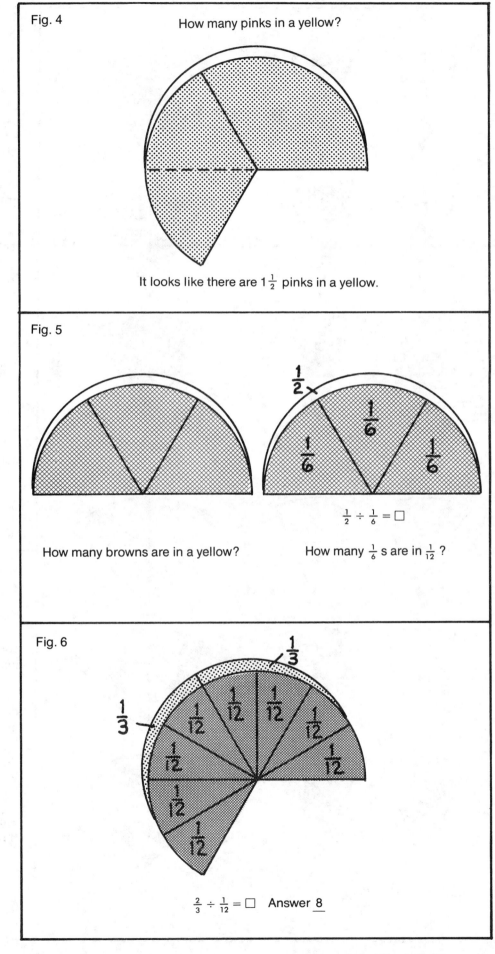

Fig. 4

How many pinks in a yellow?

It looks like there are $1\frac{1}{2}$ pinks in a yellow.

Fig. 5

How many browns are in a yellow?

$\frac{1}{2} \div \frac{1}{6} = \square$

How many $\frac{1}{6}$ s are in $\frac{1}{12}$?

Fig. 6

$\frac{2}{3} \div \frac{1}{12} = \square$ Answer 8

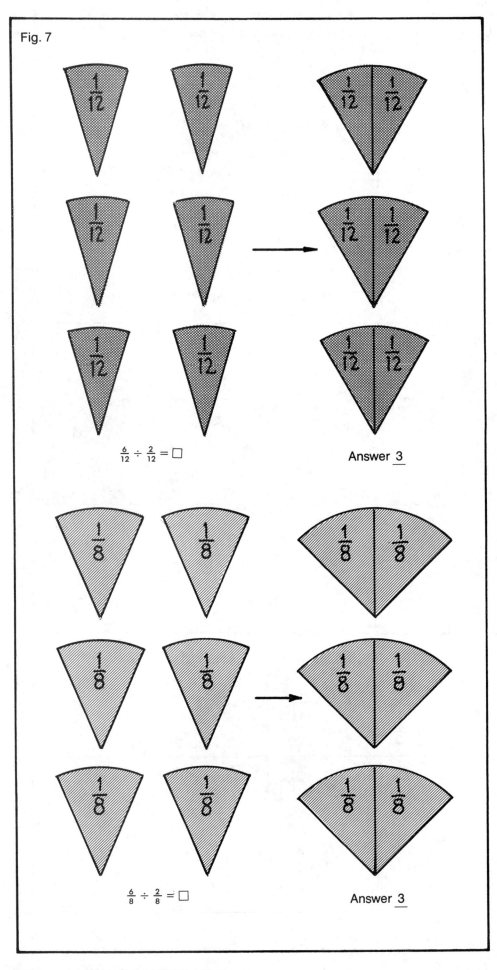

Fig. 7

$\frac{6}{12} \div \frac{2}{12} = \square$

Answer 3

$\frac{6}{8} \div \frac{2}{8} = \square$

Answer 3

In doing problems 19–21, children notice that the procedure is the same for all three problems. (See fig. 7.) In each case they take 6 pieces of the indicated size (twelfths, eighths, or sixths), sort them into groups of 2, and get 3 groups. Each problem is solved like the whole-number problem $6 \div 2 = \square$.

Likewise, problems 22–24 involve a common procedure. In each case 5 pieces of the indicated size are grouped into sets of 3. The result is 1 group of 3 and 2/3 of another group of 3. Each problem is equivalent to the problem $5 \div 3 = \square$.

Then I would seek the general rule by asking the students how to solve a problem like the following:

$$\frac{164}{200} \div \frac{4}{200} = \square .$$

Children readily answer, "You divide 164 by 4."

At this point the children have obtained a computational procedure for the division of like fractions. But what about unlike fractions? Well, since any pair of fractions can be made to have like denominators, the children have a procedure for dividing any pair of fractions—make the fractions have like denominators and divide the numerator of the first by the numerator of the second.

Summary and Conclusion

This method of teaching the division of fractions emphasizes the use of concrete materials and helps children understand what division of fractions means. In the process, the children obtain a computational procedure for dividing fractions—the common denominator method. This computational procedure has a major advantage over the traditional invert and multiply rule; it can be developed by using concrete materials. For this reason I think it leaves children with a better understanding of division of fractions than the overwhelmingly popular invert and multiply rule. □

Editor's note. The techniques described in this article are appropriate only for division exercises in which the divisor is less that the dividend.

Another Look at the Teaching of Percent

By **Jacqueline M. Dewar**

The traditional approach to percents in the elementary school is to separate the problems into three classes depending on what is unknown. Unfortunately, even after students have learned (memorized?) the three "cases," they still have trouble recognizing which case applies to a given problem. College-level mathematics textbooks designed for preservice elementary school teachers do little better. Some offer a translation approach in which students are told to replace "is" by "=," "what" by "y," and "of" by "×." For example:

Jacqueline Dewar is an associate professor of mathematics at Loyola Marymount University in Los Angeles, CA 90045. She teaches a wide variety of undergraduate mathematics courses, including mathematics for future elementary school teachers.

36 = 9% of what? becomes 36 = 9% × y.

Then, after interpreting 9% as 9/100, the student obtains the equation to solve:

$$36 = \frac{9}{100} \times y.$$

Even recent texts claiming to emphasize problem solving offer little to increase students' real understanding of percent problems. No wonder our school children have trouble with percents when both they and their teachers depend on rote techniques for solutions.

Dollins (1981) described a way of unifying percent problems into one class based on ratios. Dollins suggested considering the ratios "a parts out of c" and "b parts out of 100." If a is b percent of c, then the two ratios b/100 and a/c are equal. Thus, if one

of a, b, or c is unknown, the proportion

$$\frac{b}{100} = \frac{a}{c}$$

can be solved to find it.

This is a step in the right direction, since we already teach students at all levels to think of b percent as a ratio of b to 100 or as b parts out of 100 parts. But the use of ratios and proportions in this way is quite abstract. Apparently students still have problems picking out c, since Dollins suggested a mnemonic device for finding c: "the number after the 'of' goes on the bottom."

I would suggest making this proportional approach to percent problems more concrete by using a simple drawing. The technique is best illustrated by an example. I will use the previously discussed problem:

36 is 9% of what?

To explain the solution of this problem I draw a comparison scale (fig. 1) for the percents and the quantities involved. Usually the percent side is the easier one to fill in first (see fig. 2). Then I tell the students that opposite 100% we must place the whole amount, and next to 9% we must place the amount that corresponds to that part of the whole. Students rarely have trouble matching 36 to 9% on the scale and placing *y* next to 100% (see fig. 3). Once the corresponding quantities are matched on the scale (as in fig. 3), the correct proportion is right before the students' eyes:

$$\frac{9}{100} = \frac{36}{y}.$$

At this point the proportion seems to have real meaning for the students, since it came from the scale that they constructed.

This approach solves the other two standard types of percent problems just as easily. Furthermore, the emphasis on *matching* the corresponding quantities and percents on the scale helps students deal with more difficult percent problems.

Consider the following word problem:

Gophers ate 20% of the carrots Jessica planted in her garden. If Jessica harvested 300 carrots, how many did she plant?

Students usually begin by filling in the given percentages on the scale (fig. 4). Then they see that 300 matches neither the 100% nor the 20%, since 300 is the amount *picked* and 20% is the portion *lost* to the gophers. Although not every student obtains the correct figure (fig. 5) without help, almost every student can recognize that figure 6 is incorrect.

I have had considerable success using this approach when discussing percents with preservice elementary teachers. Because of its semiconcrete nature, it should also be suitable for use with elementary school students. The sentiments expressed by Swart (1981) in reference to the teaching of fractions apply equally well to per-

cents: "We need to cut through the symbolism and the formalism of algorithm development and seek models and schemes to reveal the basic nature of elementary school mathematics."

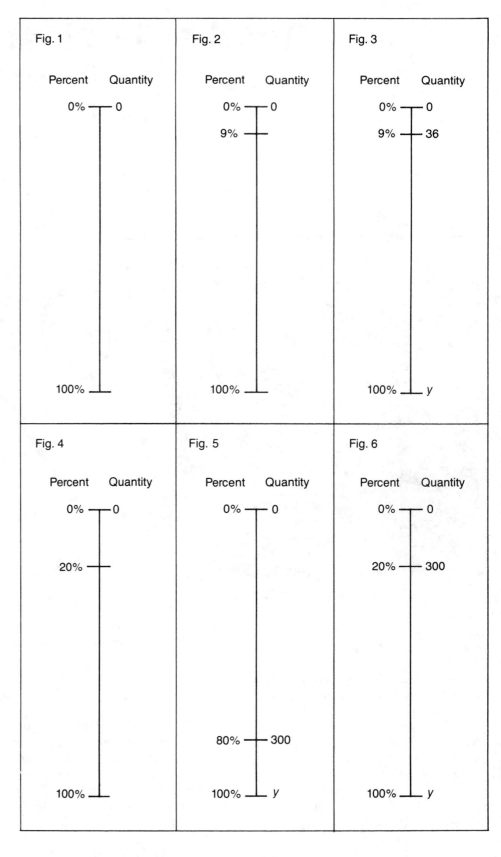

References

Dollins, Anabeth. "How I Teach It: Percent." *Arithmetic Teacher* 29 (October 1981):37.

Swart, William L. "Fractions vs. Decimals— the Wrong Issue." *Arithmetic Teacher* 29 (October 1981):17–18.

The Integer Abacus

By **Michael K. Dirks**

Everyone knows the difficulty that secondary students [and even university students!] have in understanding the algebraic rule of signs—"minus times minus equals plus."

—*Jean Piaget*

The difficulty that many students have with this rule of signs in particular, and with operations using integers in general, is part of the folk wisdom of mathematics education. For anyone who has not taught this topic, a look through back issues of the *Arithmetic Teacher* should be convincing. Peterson's (1972) "Fourteen Different Strategies for Multiplication of Integers or Why $(^-1)(^-1) = {}^+1$" is especially illustrative of the many articles that have sought to offer useful teaching schemes.

Why does subtracting a negative number amount to the same thing as adding a positive one, and why is the product of two negative numbers positive? Results that are so easy to verbalize yet pose such difficulties for meaningful conceptualization by students are a real challenge for the concerned teacher.

Many textbooks use the number line to teach operations with integers. Some authors emphasize rather formal arguments involving the associative, commutative, and distributive properties. Others employ pattern completion, such as $^+3 \times {}^+4 = {}^+12$, $^+2 \times {}^+4 = {}^+8$, $^+1 \times {}^+4 = {}^+4$, $0 \times {}^+4 = 0$, $^-1 \times {}^+4 = ?$, $^-2 \times {}^+4 = ?$, and so on, to suggest the computational rules. Although the various presentations could be profitably analyzed and compared, they are all fairly abstract. Galbraith (1975) and Vaughan (1974) have suggested that the demands for formal thinking made by computations with integers exceed the Piagetian level reached by most students when they encounter these topics in the schools. Dexter (1975) has proposed the use of Cuisenaire rods in teaching operations with integers. Bartolini (1976) has found the use of an abacus, and a pictorial representation of it, useful in his classroom for teaching the addition and subtraction of integers.

In this article I shall explain and extend through multiplication the abacus method for instruction in arithmetic with integers that I have found to be effective with eighth-grade students. Students can perform concrete operations on the abacus that give meaning to their corresponding written arithmetic statements. Moreover, the abacus is straightforward and simple to use and does not require the kind of preliminary instruction needed with the Cuisenaire material.

Materials

A two-loop abacus will be needed for every four or five students. Each loop should contain fifteen or twenty beads. The two sets of beads should be of different colors—red (for negative) and black (for positive) are ideal,

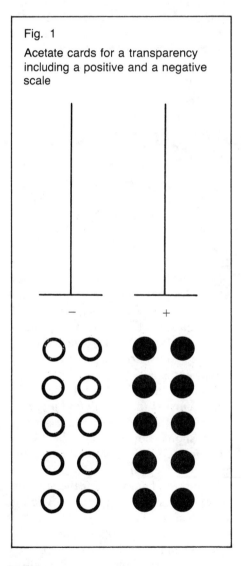

Fig. 1

Acetate cards for a transparency including a positive and a negative scale

although any combination will do. Mark a plus under one loop and a minus under the other at the base of the front of the abacus. Although a large demonstration version can be used by the teacher, an effective alternative is to cut colored circles from an acetate transparency for use with an overhead projector (see fig. 1). The

Michael Dirks teaches at North Central High School, Spokane, WA 99203. He is a doctoral candidate in mathematics education at the University of British Columbia, where he has been a Killam Scholar. He has worked on the Second International Mathematics Study and previously taught at the International School, Bangkok, Thailand.

circles can be moved about using the eraser end of a pencil.

As the teacher represents integers and performs operations at the overhead, the students can carry out similar actions on each abacus.

Representing Integers on the Abacus

Zero can be represented on the abacus whenever the same number of beads is displayed on each scale. Figure 2 shows some representations of 0. Other integers are formed when the numbers of beads on the scales are unequal. The configurations in figure 3 represent $^+2$, and those in figure 4 represent $^-3$.

Addition and Subtraction on the Abacus

On the abacus the action for addition is combining, whereas the action for subtraction is taking away. These operations are natural extensions of the analogous counting-number operations.

To perform $^+2 + ^-3$ on the abacus, start with any representation of 0 and then bring over two beads from the back of the abacus on the positive scale and three on the negative scale. Figure 5 shows one way this problem might appear.

Two observations should be made. First, most students will find it unnecessary to form zero as the first step. They should not be required to do so, and, in fact, the teacher should eliminate this step after a few examples. Second, the final goal for the students is to perform computations without the abacus. Thus, in the first few examples the students will add on the abacus and merely make verbalizations, for example, "form positive two, add negative three, result negative one." Quite early on, however, it is crucial that they write the addition equation—here, $^+2 + ^-3 = ^-1$. To further cement the relationship between concrete action and symbolization, the teacher can perform an operation silently and have the students write the appropriate arithmetic equa-

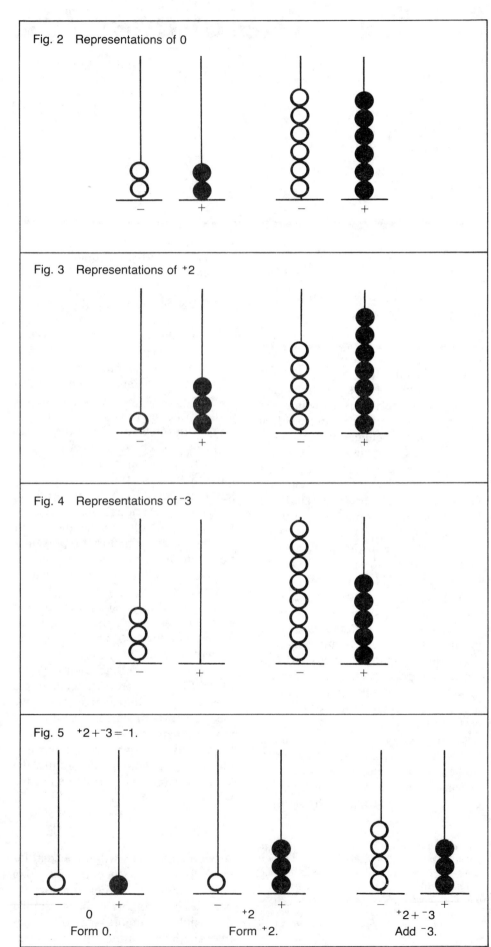

Fig. 2   Representations of 0

Fig. 3   Representations of $^+2$

Fig. 4   Representations of $^-3$

Fig. 5 $^+2 + ^-3 = ^-1$.

0
Form 0.

$^+2$
Form $^+2$.

$^+2 + ^-3$
Add $^-3$.

tion. The eventual need strongly to connect manipulative materials and symbolization cannot be overestimated.

The action required for $^-3 - {}^-1$ is shown in figure 6. A student may have to add beads to both scales so that there will be enough beads to subtract. More beads than are needed can be added so that no mental calculation is required—one of the advantages of the nonunique representation of integers on the abacus.

Suppose the operation to be performed is $^-2 - {}^+3$. Even though $^-2$ has been formed in figure 7(a), the subtraction is not possible because three beads cannot be taken away from the positive scale. A new version of $^-2$ has been created in figure 7(b) and the operation performed.

The equivalence of subtracting $^-2$ and adding $^+2$

The abacus enables students to see that although subtracting a number involves a different physical operation than adding its opposite, the result is the same. Performing a number of such equivalent operations side by side while writing down the equations will give meaning to this relationship. Consider the actions required for $^+3 - {}^-2$ and $^+3 + {}^+2$ as shown in figures 8 and 9.

Multiplication on the Integer Abacus

A "letter carrier" model is one approach to teaching the multiplication of integers. When the carrier brings two checks for $5 each (making you $10 richer), the equation $^+2 \times {}^+5 = {}^+10$ is modeled. If the carrier takes away two misdelivered bills for $5 each, you are also $10 richer. This time the equation is $^-2 \times {}^-5 = {}^+10$. The first factor in a multiplication problem is an operator; so in our examples $^+2$ means "bring two," whereas $^-2$ means "take two away." Explanations of this type are usually helpful to a few students, but the mental gymnastics involved are beyond the capabilities of many. The abacus uses the operator approach, but the physical action is much more

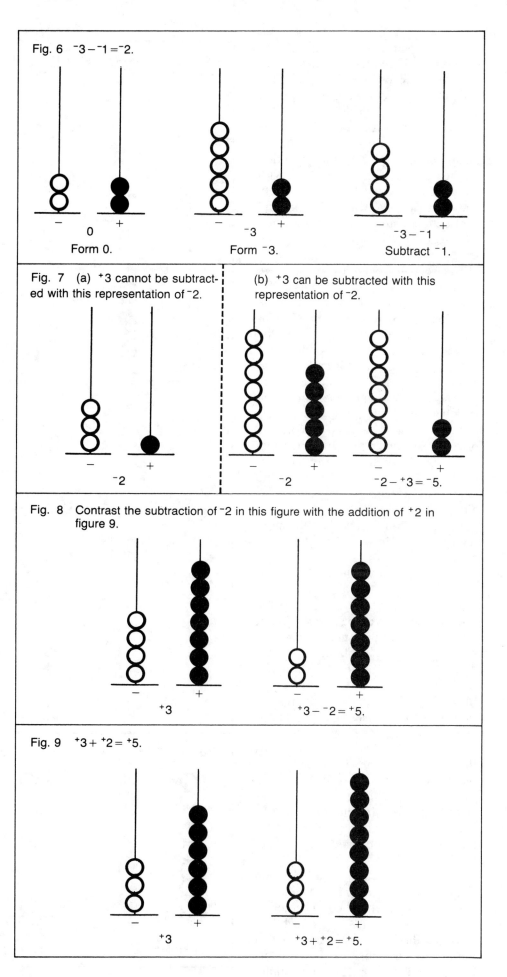

Fig. 6 $^-3 - {}^-1 = {}^-2$.

Form 0. Form $^-3$. Subtract $^-1$.

Fig. 7 (a) $^+3$ cannot be subtracted with this representation of $^-2$.

(b) $^+3$ can be subtracted with this representation of $^-2$.

$^-2$ $^-2$ $^-2 - {}^+3 = {}^-5$.

Fig. 8 Contrast the subtraction of $^-2$ in this figure with the addition of $^+2$ in figure 9.

$^+3$ $^+3 - {}^-2 = {}^+5$.

Fig. 9 $^+3 + {}^+2 = {}^+5$.

$^+3$ $^+3 + {}^+2 = {}^+5$.

easily grasped than the mental one required by the letter-carrier model.

To use the abacus for multiplication, begin by reviewing the meaning of a statement such as $3 \times 4 = 12$. Three groups of four things are to be added; the result is twelve things. Next perform this repeated addition on the abacus (see fig. 10). Work with multiplication should begin concretely and verbally, as with addition and subtraction, but a written equation should soon accompany each problem.

The repeated addition of negative numbers can be handled just as easily and naturally on the abacus as the addition of positive numbers. Consider the multiplication $^+2 \times {}^-3$ displayed in figure 11. (A preliminary sketch showing 0, in this example two beads on each scale, would be helpful for the first few multiplications, just as it was for the first few additions.)

Now, what if the first factor, the operator, is negative? Interpret this problem as calling for repeated subtraction! This situation is just like the letter carrier taking away checks or bills, but the physical manipulation is much more convincing than the mental argument for an eighth-grade student.

Figure 12 shows how $^-2 \times {}^+3$, requiring two subtractions of $^+3$, looks. It is a good idea to keep the operator small in case students do not initially see that they must begin with sufficient beads to subtract. Some students will probably move all the beads to the front of the abacus at first, but they will soon begin use of multiplication facts to increase their efficiency.

Students can investigate operation pairs like $^+2 \times {}^-3$ and $^-2 \times {}^+3$, just as they compared the different actions but identical results of subtracting a number and adding its opposite. Again, the relationship of different actions but identical results will be more meaningful through physical activity.

Finally, the action required when both factors of a multiplication are negative can be handled. The action on the abacus is just as straightforward in this circumstance as when both factors are positive. In considering $^-3 \times {}^-2$ (see fig. 13), for example,

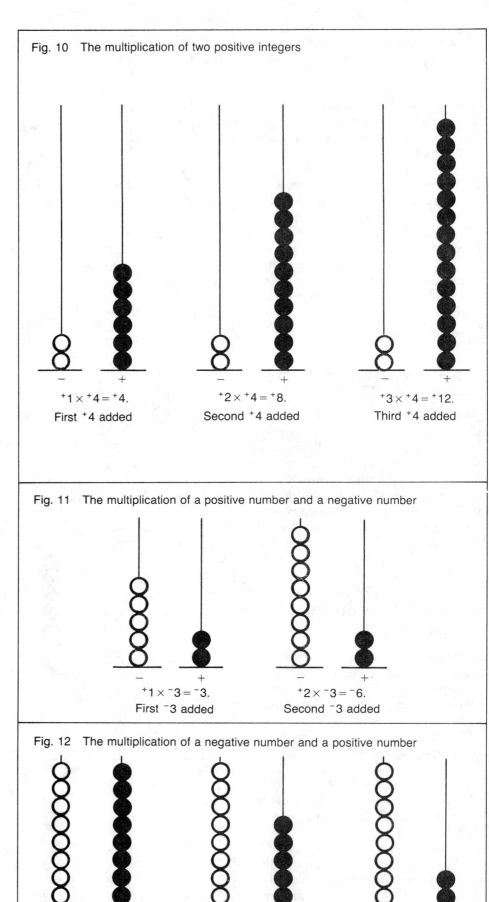

Fig. 10 The multiplication of two positive integers

$^+1 \times {}^+4 = {}^+4$.
First $^+4$ added

$^+2 \times {}^+4 = {}^+8$.
Second $^+4$ added

$^+3 \times {}^+4 = {}^+12$.
Third $^+4$ added

Fig. 11 The multiplication of a positive number and a negative number

$^+1 \times {}^-3 = {}^-3$.
First $^-3$ added

$^+2 \times {}^-3 = {}^-6$.
Second $^-3$ added

Fig. 12 The multiplication of a negative number and a positive number

0
0 formed

$^-1 \times {}^+3 = {}^-3$.
First $^+3$ subtracted

$^-2 \times {}^+3 = {}^-6$.
Second $^+3$ subtracted

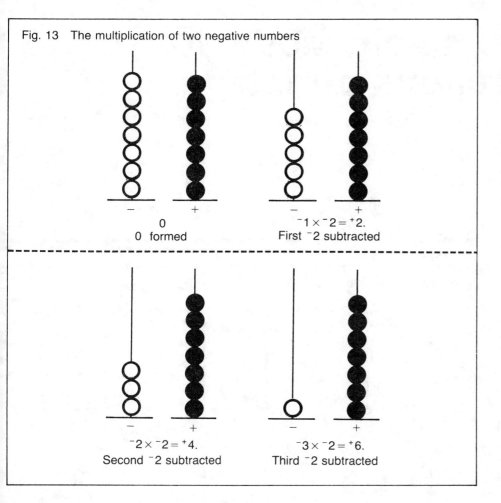

Fig. 13   The multiplication of two negative numbers

0
0 formed

$^-1 \times ^-2 = ^+2$.
First $^-2$ subtracted

$^-2 \times ^-2 = ^+4$.
Second $^-2$ subtracted

$^-3 \times ^-2 = ^+6$.
Third $^-2$ subtracted

many students who recognize that $^-2$ must be subtracted three times will not, at first, be able to form the result through mental action alone. The physical use of the abacus will be needed at this initial stage.

After they carry out a number of physically performed operations, simultaneously writing the appropriate equations, students *will* anticipate the result and the abacus will be out of a job.

References

Bartolini, Pietro. "Addition and Subtraction of Directed Numbers." *Mathematics Teaching* 74 (March 1976):34–35.

Dexter, John Harry. "The Development of a Product for the Concrete Manipulation of Negative Numbers." Ph.D. dissertation, Columbia University, 1975.

Galbraith, Mary J. "Smith and Jones: Children's Thinking about Some Problems Involving Displacements along the Number Line." *International Journal of Mathematical Education in Science and Technology* 6 (1975):287–302.

Peterson, John C. "Fourteen Different Strategies for Multiplication of Integers or Why $(^-1)(^-1) = ^+1$." *Arithmetic Teacher* 19 (May 1972):396–403.

Vaughan, B. W. "The Only Thing We Can Be Sure of—Is Change." *Mathematics in School* 3 (November 1974):16–21. ◥

A Complete Model for Operations on Integers

By **Michael T. Battista**

Teaching students the four basic operations on the set of integers in a meaningful way is a difficult task. The task could be made easier, however, if there was a single physical model for the integers in which all four basic operations could be represented. The number-line model, though useful, has serious shortcomings and is incomplete. As an alternative, some authors have suggested the "positive-negative charge" model (Frand and Granville 1978, Grady 1978), but they used this model only for representing addition and subtraction. In this article I will describe the "charge" model and demonstrate how it can be extended to all four operations on the set of integers.

Integers as Collections of Charges

To use the model you will need a small set of transparent jars of the same size and a good supply of two colors of poker chips or counters. Let us assume that the chips are red and white. On each white chip paste or use a magic marker to write a "+" sign. These are the positive "charges." On each red chip put a "−" sign. These are the negative "charges."

We will be concerned, not with individual charges, but with collections of charges in jars. When we speak of the *charge on a jar*, we will be referring to the integer represented by the collection of charges inside it. So, if a jar is empty or contains an equal number of positive and negative charges, it has charge zero. (In the latter case, every positive charge "cancels" exactly one negative charge.) If a jar contains five positive charges, it has charge $^+5$. If it contains three negative charges, it has charge $^-3$. If a jar contains five positive charges and three negative charges, the charge on the jar is $^+2$. (Three positive charges cancel three negative charges and we find the charge on the remaining collection.) See figure 1.

Thus, in this model, *integers are represented by collections of charges*. Every jar of charges represents an integer, and every integer can be represented by a jar of charges. Note though, that although a jar of charges represents a unique integer, an integer can be represented in an infinite number of ways. See figure 2.

It should be stressed at this point that before proceeding to operations on integers, students must have a firm understanding of how integers are represented in the model. Teachers introducing the model should emphasize from the outset that integers have multiple representations. Students should be able not only to recognize what integer is represented by a given jar of charges, but also to construct multiple jar representations for any given integer.

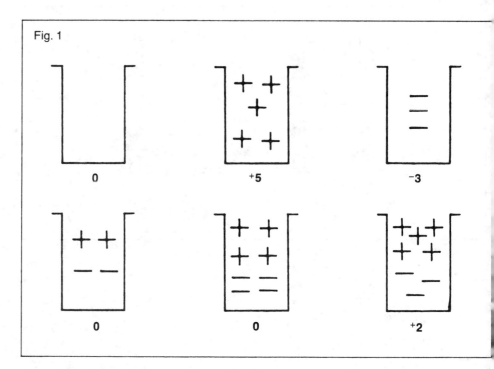
Fig. 1

Michael Battista is presently an assistant professor of elementary and secondary education at Kent State University in Ohio. He teaches graduate courses in mathematics and computer education, and mathematics methods courses for preservice elementary and secondary school teachers.

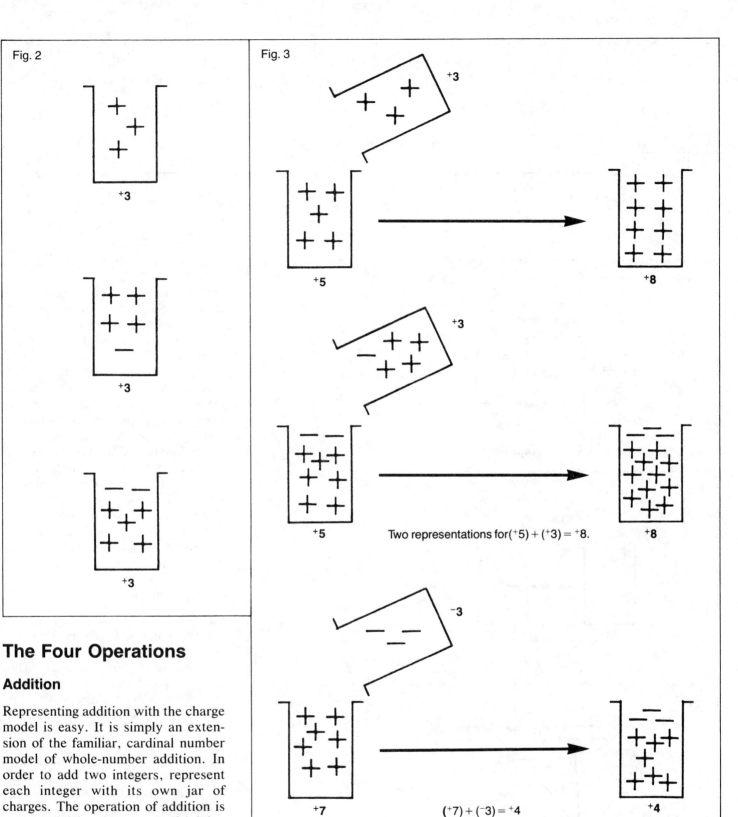

Fig. 2

Fig. 3

Two representations for $(^+5) + (^+3) = ^+8$.

$(^+7) + (^-3) = ^+4$

The Four Operations

Addition

Representing addition with the charge model is easy. It is simply an extension of the familiar, cardinal number model of whole-number addition. In order to add two integers, represent each integer with its own jar of charges. The operation of addition is represented by the *action* of joining the contents of the two jars. So pour the contents of one jar into the other and find the charge on the latter jar. This is the sum. See figure 3. Note that an addition problem can be represented in more than one way.

You should also note that we are making an important convention here. For the problem $a + b = $ _____, we pour the contents of the jar representing b into the jar representing a. Thus $(^+5) + (^+3)$ and $(^+3) + (^+5)$ have different physical representations. This point should be stressed to students because it is essential for later understanding of the commutative property of addition.

Subtraction

Just as addition is represented by a "joining" action, subtraction is represented by a "take away" action. To subtract one integer from another, represent the first integer (the minuend) with a jar of charges. Then re-

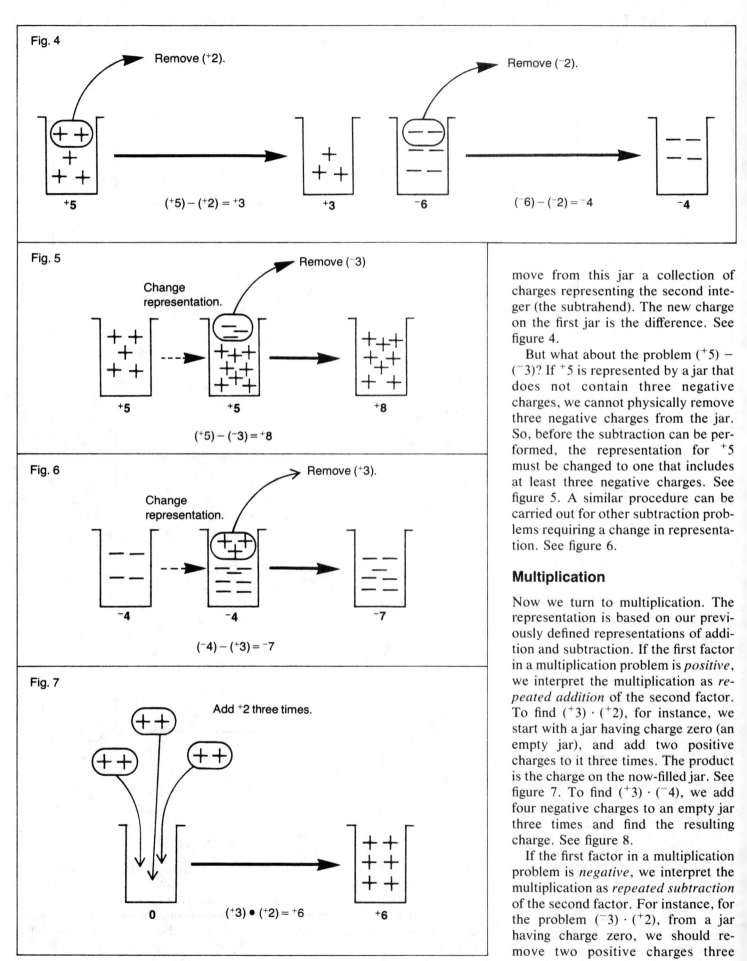

Fig. 4

Remove (⁺2).

$$(\text{}^+5) - (\text{}^+2) = \text{}^+3$$

⁺5   ⁺3

Remove (⁻2).

$$(\text{}^-6) - (\text{}^-2) = \text{}^-4$$

⁻6   ⁻4

Fig. 5

Change representation.

Remove (⁻3)

$$(\text{}^+5) - (\text{}^-3) = \text{}^+8$$

⁺5   ⁺5   ⁺8

Fig. 6

Change representation.

Remove (⁺3).

$$(\text{}^-4) - (\text{}^+3) = \text{}^-7$$

⁻4   ⁻4   ⁻7

Fig. 7

Add ⁺2 three times.

$$(\text{}^+3) \bullet (\text{}^+2) = \text{}^+6$$

0   ⁺6

move from this jar a collection of charges representing the second integer (the subtrahend). The new charge on the first jar is the difference. See figure 4.

But what about the problem (⁺5) − (⁻3)? If ⁺5 is represented by a jar that does not contain three negative charges, we cannot physically remove three negative charges from the jar. So, before the subtraction can be performed, the representation for ⁺5 must be changed to one that includes at least three negative charges. See figure 5. A similar procedure can be carried out for other subtraction problems requiring a change in representation. See figure 6.

Multiplication

Now we turn to multiplication. The representation is based on our previously defined representations of addition and subtraction. If the first factor in a multiplication problem is *positive*, we interpret the multiplication as *repeated addition* of the second factor. To find (⁺3) · (⁺2), for instance, we start with a jar having charge zero (an empty jar), and add two positive charges to it three times. The product is the charge on the now-filled jar. See figure 7. To find (⁺3) · (⁻4), we add four negative charges to an empty jar three times and find the resulting charge. See figure 8.

If the first factor in a multiplication problem is *negative*, we interpret the multiplication as *repeated subtraction* of the second factor. For instance, for the problem (⁻3) · (⁺2), from a jar having charge zero, we should remove two positive charges three

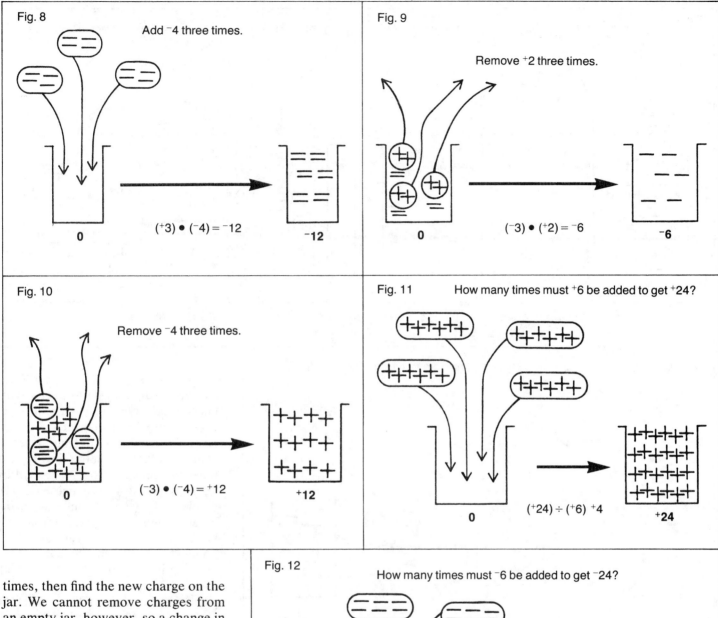

Fig. 8

Add ⁻4 three times.

$(^+3) \bullet (^-4) = {}^-12$

0   ⁻12

Fig. 9

Remove ⁺2 three times.

$(^-3) \bullet (^+2) = {}^-6$

0   ⁻6

Fig. 10

Remove ⁻4 three times.

$(^-3) \bullet (^-4) = {}^+12$

0   ⁺12

Fig. 11   How many times must ⁺6 be added to get ⁺24?

$(^+24) \div (^+6) \quad {}^+4$

0   ⁺24

Fig. 12

How many times must ⁻6 be added to get ⁻24?

$(^-24) \div (^-6) = {}^+4$

0   ⁻24

times, then find the new charge on the jar. We cannot remove charges from an empty jar, however, so a change in representation is necessary. We must start with a zero-charge jar containing at least six (from 3 · 2) positive and six negative charges. See figure 9. For the problem (⁻3) · (⁻4), we must remove four negative charges three times from a jar having charge zero. Here we should start with a zero-charge jar having twelve (from 3 · 4) positive and twelve negative charges. See figure 10.

Division

Finally, we examine division. Consider first the case where the dividend and divisor have the same sign. To divide ⁺24 by ⁺6, *count* how many times ⁺6 must be added to a jar having charge zero to get ⁺24. We must *add* ⁺6 to the jar four times, so ⁺24 divided by ⁺6 is *positive* 4. See figure 11. To divide ⁻24 by ⁻6, count how many times ⁻6 must be added to an empty jar to get ⁻24. Since we must add ⁻6 to the jar four times, the quotient is ⁺4. See figure 12. In both cases, the quotient is positive because we must repeatedly add the divisor to the jar to get the dividend.

Now what about the case where the dividend and divisor have opposite

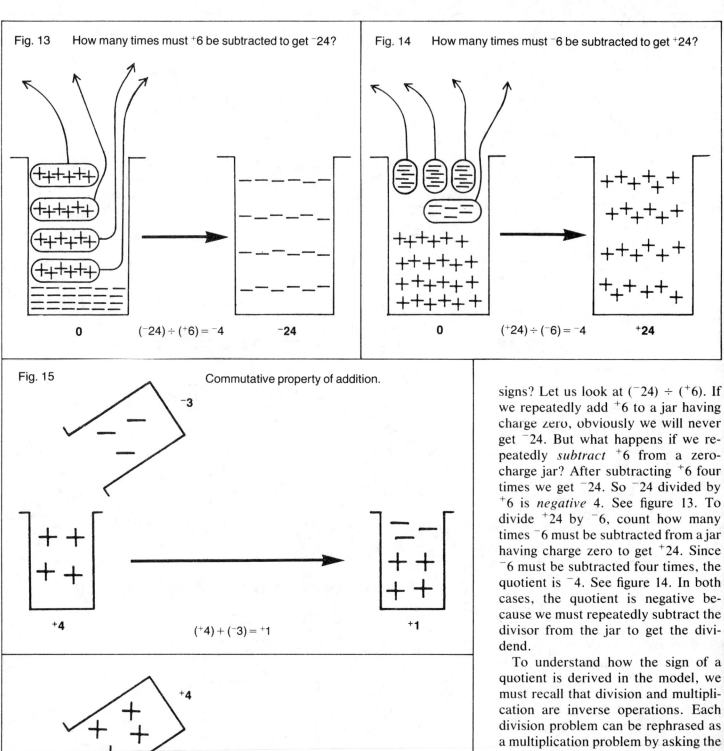

Fig. 13   How many times must ⁺6 be subtracted to get ⁻24?

0   (⁻24) ÷ (⁺6) = ⁻4   **⁻24**

Fig. 14   How many times must ⁻6 be subtracted to get ⁺24?

0   (⁺24) ÷ (⁻6) = ⁻4   **⁺24**

Fig. 15   Commutative property of addition.

⁻3

⁺4   (⁺4) + (⁻3) = ⁺1   **⁺1**

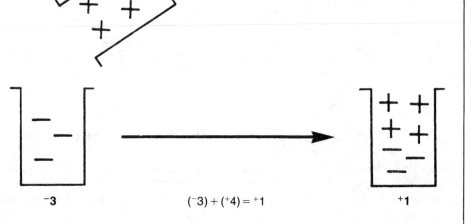

⁺4

⁻3   (⁻3) + (⁺4) = ⁺1   **⁺1**

signs? Let us look at (⁻24) ÷ (⁺6). If we repeatedly add ⁺6 to a jar having charge zero, obviously we will never get ⁻24. But what happens if we repeatedly *subtract* ⁺6 from a zero-charge jar? After subtracting ⁺6 four times we get ⁻24. So ⁻24 divided by ⁺6 is *negative* 4. See figure 13. To divide ⁺24 by ⁻6, count how many times ⁻6 must be subtracted from a jar having charge zero to get ⁺24. Since ⁻6 must be subtracted four times, the quotient is ⁻4. See figure 14. In both cases, the quotient is negative because we must repeatedly subtract the divisor from the jar to get the dividend.

To understand how the sign of a quotient is derived in the model, we must recall that division and multiplication are inverse operations. Each division problem can be rephrased as a multiplication problem by asking the question, What number must the divisor be multiplied by in order to get the dividend? For example, (⁺24) ÷ (⁺6) = X can be rephrased as $X \cdot$ (⁺6) = ⁺24. Thus, by posing each division problem as a multiplication problem, we see that the sign of the quotient is automatically determined by the way our model represents multiplication: If repeated addition is involved, the first factor (the quotient) is positive; if repeated subtraction is involved, the first factor (the quotient) is negative.

Conclusion

We have seen that all four basic operations on the set of integers can be represented with the positive-negative charge model. The model can also be used to illustrate important structural properties of the system of integers such as the commutative and associative properties, the existence of additive and multiplicative identities, and the existence of additive inverses. The commutative property of addition, for instance, can be illustrated as in figure 15. It is clearly seen in the figure that although $(^+4) + (^-3)$ and $(^-3) + (^+4)$ are different additions, the resulting sums are the same. A similar demonstration illustrates why there is *no* commutative property of subtraction.

Thus, the positive-negative charge model presents a useful aid for introducing students to operations on integers. The major advantages to using the model are twofold. First, the model is concrete. Many students receiving initial instruction on the integers need concrete representations of the concepts involved. The charge model's closest "competitor," the number line, is usually presented in a pictorial manner. Second, the model is complete; it can effectively represent all four basic operations on the set of integers. As each new operation is introduced, the same familiar model of the integers can be used. Students being introduced to the representations for multiplication and division can build on their knowledge of the representations for addition and subtraction, thus making the learning of the new operations more meaningful. So the completeness of the charge model serves to give students a more meaningful and coherent picture of the workings of the four basic operations on the set of integers.

References

Frand, Jason and Evelyn B. Granville. *Theory and Application of Mathematics for Teachers*, 2d ed. Belmont, Calif.: Wadsworth Publishing Company, 1978.

Grady, Merle B. "A Manipulative Aid for Adding and Subtracting Integers." *Arithmetic Teacher* 26 (November 1978):40. ◗

Geometry

2

String sculpture in the mathematics laboratory

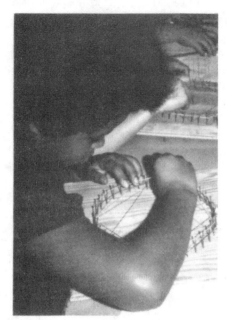

TERI PERL

Author of enrichment materials in mathematics, Teri Perl is mathematics consultant and resource teacher at Ventura Elementary School in Palo Alto, California. She is also presently doing graduate work in mathematics education at Stanford University.

Early last school year, during a parent's work night, a group of parents made a dozen 36- and 37-nail circular geoboards for our mathematics laboratory. This was the beginning of one of the most popular and successful activities in our mathematics laboratory that year—string sculpture.

First with colored rubber bands, then with string, students used the nail boards to discover the effects of various properties of numbers on designs. By hooking nails at intervals that are factors or relative primes of the number of nails on the boards, patterns were designed and combined in differing ways. Using these concepts, students were able to produce some extremely attractive "string sculpture" to take home.

To start, the students were told to hook a single rubber band on every twelfth nail of the 36-nail board. A triangle was formed. They were told to try another interval.

"Choose a rubber band of another color. Hook every ninth nail. What do you think the figure will look like? How many sides do you think it will have? Make a chart."

"Choose a rubber band of a third color. Hook every sixth nail. What do you think the figure will look like? How many sides do you think it will have? Notice that 6 × 6 = 36. Fill in the chart."

And so on, with the students using different colored rubber bands, hooking different intervals of nails, forming different figures, and filling in the chart after each figure was formed. The completed chart is shown in table 1. At this point the student

Table 1

Nail interval	Nails hooked	Shape of figure	Total number nails counted	Equation
12	3	triangle	36	12 × 3 = 36
9	4	square	36	9 × 4 = 36
6	6	hexagon	36	6 × 6 = 36
4	9	nonagon	36	4 × 9 = 36
3	12	dodecagon	36	3 × 12 = 36
2	18	18 sides	36	2 × 18 = 36

was led, we hoped, to realize that the intervals he had been stringing and the numbers of sides of the figures formed, were factors of 36.

On the next activity, a piece of colored string was tied on a nail of the 36-nail board. Students then were asked to hook every seventh nail on the board. It soon became apparent that the hooking did not terminate (get back to the first nail) once around the board. In fact, it did not terminate until every nail had been hooked. The design was very pretty. (Fig. 1)

Next the students were told to hook every eighth nail and they were asked what they thought was going to happen. (Fig. 2)

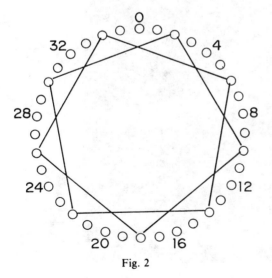

Fig. 1

Fig. 2

They tried other intervals. When every eleventh nail was hooked, the pattern went around and around. Every nail was hooked before the string got back to the starting nail. This was the same thing that had happened with 7 as an interval.

"Anything special about 7 and 11? Can you guess another interval that will behave this way? Try it and see if it works." We hoped that the students had noticed that something special was happening.

"Have you ever heard of a *prime* number? Does that give it away? Can you guess another interval that might behave this way? Try it and see if it works."

The last thing we did as part of the first experiment was try to hook *any* interval on the 37-nail geoboard. Here, no matter what number was tried, the string went around and around, hooking every nail before it returned to the start. Students were encouraged to try some of the intervals that had led to polygons on the 36-nail board. Nothing worked that way here. No interval formed polygons on the 37-nail board.

"Any ideas why? Anything special about 37?"

By contrasting the designs resulting from intervals that were factors of the number of nails on the board with intervals that were prime numbers, we were, we hoped, presenting a dramatic effect of "primeness." And all this in a very attractive setting.

We asked only one other question at this stage of our experiment. "Notice that a circle can be inscribed in each of the designs. Will the inscribed circle become larger or smaller as the number of nails hooked each time varies?"

For the next mathematics laboratory we planned a related activity that was very well received and provided a "take home" product—always a popular thing to do. Each student was given a square piece of poster board, 20 cm by 20 cm, and a template formed by 23 evenly spaced points on the circumference of a circle. The students placed the template on the poster board and punched through each point on the circle with the sharp end of a compass.

(This is more easily done if the first two points punched are at opposite ends of the board and the template is anchored on the board by putting paper fasteners through these first two holes.) When all the holes were punched, the template was removed and brass fasteners were put through each of the holes. The fasteners served as the nails had served in the previous activity. Strings of different colors were used for the various "nail" intervals to be hooked on the board.

"Why do you think we've chosen 23 nails as the number to form our circular figure? What other numbers of 'nails' might we have chosen to accomplish the same thing?" The answer, of course, is that 23 is a prime number. Any prime number would create the same result. On such a figure *any* interval (less than 23) that was strung would hit every nail before repeating.

We repeated the question, "How does the size of the circle that could be inscribed in the design vary with the size of the nail interval chosen?" The students tried various intervals and found that the larger the nail interval chosen, the smaller the inscribed circle, and vice versa. Students tried different colors and layers of circles; the

resulting "sculpture" couldn't miss being attractive.

This activity was done very successfully with students in grades three through five. Although we didn't plan to push any more of the mathematics than the students could handle, we felt it was important that the people supervising the activity understood what was happening. In this way they would be equipped to lead students to discover more of what was happening if the students were ready to do so.

The next time we use this activity, we plan to use a twenty-four point circle. Twenty-four is not a prime number and has several factors, 1, 2, 3, 4, 6, 8, 12, and 24. First, we will ask the students to hook intervals of 8 nails, then 6, then 4, and then 3. These intervals will generate regular polygons—triangle (by interval 8, since 8×3 is 24), square (by interval 6, since 6×4 is 24), hexagon (by interval 4, since 4×6 is 24) and octagon (by interval 3, since 3×8 is 24). (See fig. 3.) Then the students will be asked to choose an interval that they think will cause the string to hook every nail before it returns to the start. One of two things most likely will happen. We hope that everyone will know enough to choose

Table 2

		$24k + r = C$, where k = times around board r = remainder, or number of nail		
nth nail	C = total count (add 9 each time)	k	r	r = actual nail hooked
1	9	0	9	9th
2	18	0	18	18th
3	27	1	3	3rd
4	36	1	12	12th
5	45	1	21	21st
6	54	2	6	6th
7	63	2	15	15th
8	72	3	0 or 24	back to start

an interval that is not a factor of 24. Probably most students, if they remember what a prime number is, will choose a prime number less than 24, say 5, 7, 11, or 13. (Fig. 4) Suppose, however, that someone chooses to hook every ninth fastener. (See fig. 5.) The result is a star because 9 and 24 have *some* common factors. Let's examine what is happening here. As we hook every ninth nail we count 9, 18, 27, 36, and so on. However, since there are only 24 nails on the board, when we have counted 27, we are actually hooking the third nail since 3 is the remainder of 27 divided by 24. We have been around the board once, and are now hooking nail 3. The next nail hooked is 12, since 3 + 9 = 12, and so on. Table 2 shows

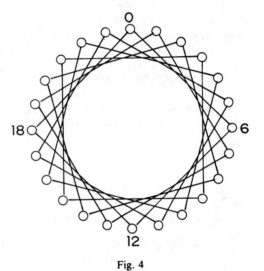

Fig. 4

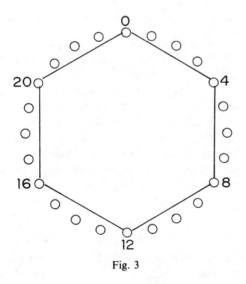

Fig. 3

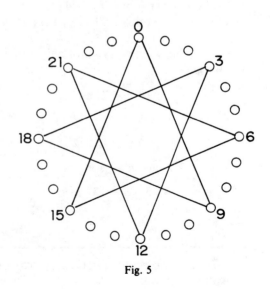

Fig. 5

Table 3

nth nail	C = total count (add 15 each time)	24 k + r = C where k = times round board r = remainder, or number of nail		r = actual nail hooked
		k	r	
1	15	0	15	15th
2	30	1	6	6th
3	45	1	21	21st
4	60	2	12	12th
5	75	3	3	3rd
6	90	3	18	18th
7	105	4	9	9th
8	120	5	0 or 24	back to start

the 8 nails that will have been hooked before the pattern repeats.

Suppose we had hooked every fifteenth nail. What would the figure look like? Can we predict what the figure will look like?

Let v = number of vertices of the figure, and
k = number of times around the board until the return to the start.

Then

$$15 \cdot v = k \cdot 24$$

$$3 \cdot 5 \cdot v = k \cdot 3 \cdot 8$$

$$v = 8 \text{ and } k = 5 \text{ is a solution.}$$

Thus, the figure will have 8 vertices and it will also be an 8-pointed star. Actually it is the same star as before (fig. 5) since 15 is the additive inverse of 9 mod 24 (15 + 9 = 24, and 24 ≡ 0 mod 24). The chart for 15 is shown in table 3.

Now try hooking every tenth nail. What will we get?

$$10 \cdot v = k \cdot 24$$

$$2 \cdot 5 \cdot v = k \cdot 3 \cdot 2^3$$

$$5 \cdot v = k \cdot 3 \cdot 2^2$$

$$v = 3 \cdot 2^2 \text{ and } k = 5 \text{ is a solution.}$$

$$v = 3 \cdot 2^2 = 12$$

This design will be a 12-pointed star that will be completed when we have cycled the board 5 times. (Fig. 6)

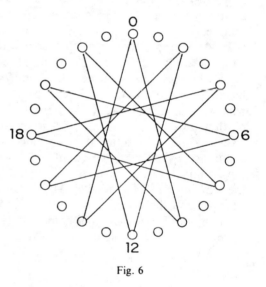

Fig. 6

To conclude, this is an excellent activity for the mathematics laboratory. It has several positive qualities. The products of the activity are extremely attractive and it can be done at many levels. It contains a lot of good mathematics—another way of thinking about factors, primes, relative primes, modular arithmetic. And perhaps, not the least important, students seem never to tire of making the designs.

Miscellaneous

MAKING TANGRAMS FOR THE CLASSROOM

What do you do when you want a supply of tangrams for use in a class? One solution is to prepare your own by using those clear, acetate folders in which college students often submit reports. Each, costing less than a quarter, provides excellent material from which to make two to twelve sets of tangrams, depending on the size desired. The sets are easy to cut, durable, inexpensive, functional, and come in many colors. A large set can be used readily with an overhead projector for demonstration purposes.

Experience has also shown that the same process works well with magic squares, too. The acetate squares hold marker fluid.

You may be able to think of other uses for this technique and material in your classroom. Why not give them a try?

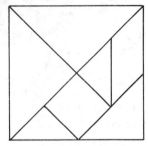

From the file of
AT-9-80   William D. Jamski, Indiana University Southeast, New Albany, Indiana.

Geometry

TESSELLATIONS—BY CRACKERS!

The teaching of tessellations can be made very clear—by crackers! This inexpensive, ready-made manipulative device for learning gives the pupils neat and accurate figures. Tessellations (in a plane) or tiling is the repeated use of geometric polygon shapes or other figures so that a surface is completely covered with no gaps or overlaps. All the shapes fit together like pieces of a puzzle.

(1) Distribute to each student a package containing an assortment of polygon-shape crackers. Crackers in various geometric shapes—squares, rectangles, equilateral triangles, circles—can be found in most supermarkets.

(2) Have students fit together each set of shapes. Which sets leave no gaps or overlaps?

Answers: As shown in the photographs, congruent equilateral triangles, regular hexagons, squares, and parallelograms (kites) will tessellate alone.

From the file of Gloria Sanok, Anthony Wayne Middle School, Wayne, New Jersey.

AT-9-79

Cardboard, Rubber Bands, and Polyhedron Models

By **Patricia F. Campbell**

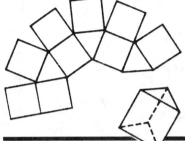

Young children's preschool years are filled with three-dimensional objects as the children come to understand spatial and topological ideas. These ideas, such as nearness, order, or enclosure, are based on the child's experiences and sensory impressions of shapes and solids. However, too often early school experiences with geometric concepts are limited to plane figures. This is because solids are difficult to represent on paper or the blackboard and young children have difficulty constructing models of three-dimensional figures with cardboard and paste. The "cut and paste" method of construction also produces permanent figures that are difficult to store.

The "cardboard–rubber band" method of constructing three-dimensional models (Stewart 1970) offers a successful alternative for the elementary school. Furthermore, this method allows construction of models that have tunnels, challenging the imagination of older students. Students in the intermediate grades have sufficient dexterity to cut the necessary panels from a pattern. In the younger grades, teachers can cut a set of panels that the children can then assemble into models. The models are easily taken apart and reassembled. One or two sets of panels can be used over and over to construct many different types

of solids, making this approach ideal for a learning-center activity. Storage is no problem; the panels from disassembled models and the rubber bands will fit into a manila envelope.

Preparing the Panels

To start with, triangular-shaped panels are sufficient. Later, you or your students may wish to experiment with panels in the shapes of squares, pentagons, or hexagons. The key is to make all sides of your panels, whatever the shape of the panels, the same length so you can combine them into a single solid.

The template

1. Place a piece of lightweight cardboard (either 2-ply bristol board or speech board) beneath the pattern shown in figure 1.

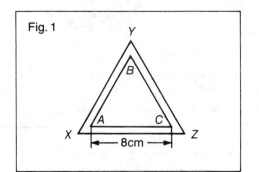

Fig. 1

2. Using a sharp-pointed instrument such as a geometry compass, make an impression at each of the six labeled corners (A, B, C and X, Y, Z).

3. Remove the cardboard. Using a ruler, draw lines connecting corners A, B, and C as well as corners X, Y, and Z.

4. Cut out the outer shape (along triangle XYZ).

5. Using either the point of a compass or a ballpoint pen, make small (diameter of a pencil point) marking holes at A, B, and C (corners of the inner shape).

This template is now used to construct the panels. Children in the intermediate grades may complete the following steps themselves, but teachers of primary-grade children will need to prepare panels.

The panels

1. Place the template on lightweight cardboard.

2. Trace the outside of the template.

3. Mark the inner corners through the marking holes with a pencil or ballpoint pen.

4. Remove the template. Cut out around the outer shape you traced.

5. Using a ruler and a pencil or ballpoint pen, connect the three inner corners. Press hard when you draw these lines, as you will fold along these lines later.

6. Using a hand paper punch (1/4-inch diameter for hole), punch three

Patricia Campbell teaches mathematics education courses at the University of Maryland, College Park, MD 20742. She is currently doing research on the learning of mathematics by elementary school children.

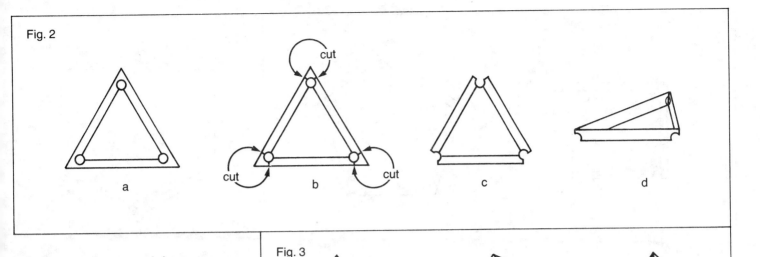

Fig. 2

a
b
c
d

holes centered over each inner corner (fig. 2a).

7. Using scissors, make two cuts toward the center of each hole. Each cut should be perpendicular to its nearest outer edge (fig. 2b).

8. Panel should now resemble figure 2c.

9. Fold up each tab along the lines connecting the holes. The panel should resemble figure 2d.

Repeat steps 1–9 until the required number of triangular panels for your models are completed. The ease of future model construction is related to the care taken in preparing the panels accurately.

Constructing a Model

A model is constructed by laying the panels side-by-side according to a pattern and by placing rubber bands over the tabs of all adjacent panels. Two-inch rubber bands work very well. As more rubber bands are added, the model takes on a three-dimensional shape. When all tabs are connected, the model is complete. Under this method of construction, the tabs are exposed. Students should be reminded that these projecting ridges are not part of the abstract forms the model represents.

Patterns for making eight different shapes of increasing complexity are given in figure 3. These models represent the eight deltahedra (plural for deltahedron). Each of these solids consists of panels or faces that are in the shape of equilateral triangles (like the Greek letter, delta) such that no two panels are in the same plane.

Fig. 3

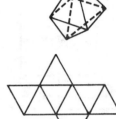

Tetrahedron

Triangular dipyramid

Octahedron

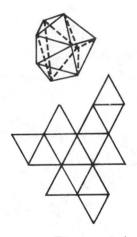

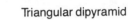

Pentagonal dipyramid

Siamese dodecahedron

Triaugmented triangular prism

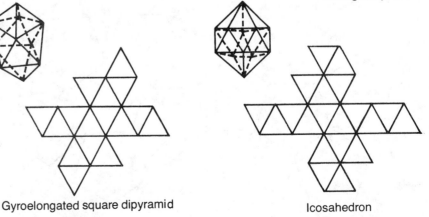

Gyroelongated square dipyramid

Icosahedron

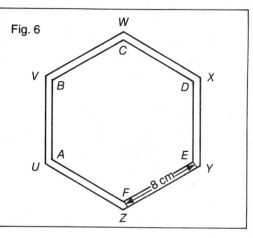

Fig. 4

Fig. 5

Fig. 6

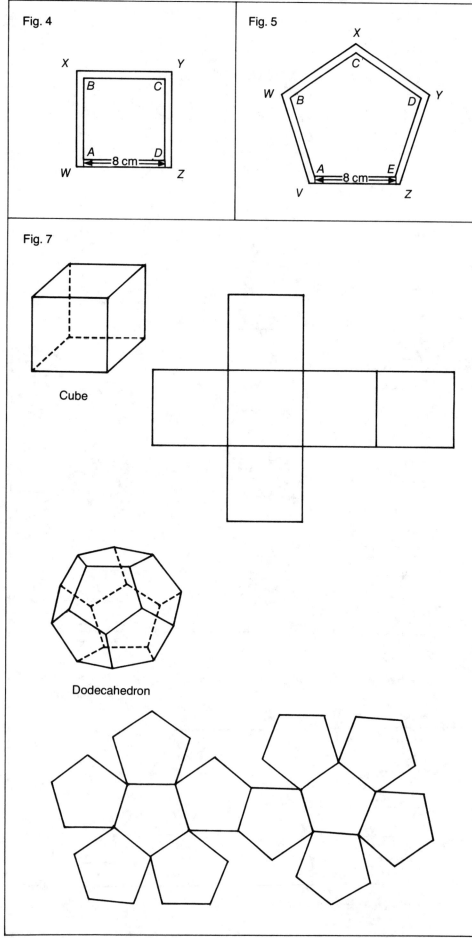

Fig. 7

Cube

Dodecahedron

More Patterns

Using the procedure just outlined, students can construct templates and panels in the shapes of squares, pentagons, and hexagons, using guides like those pictured in figures 4, 5, and 6.

The square- and pentagonal-shaped panels can be used to form a cube and a dodecahedron as patterned in figure 7. These shapes—along with the tetrahedron, octahedron, and icosahedron (patterns in fig. 3)—are called Platonic solids. The panels, or faces, of each of these solids consist of one type of a regular polygon (polygons with all sides the same length and all angles the same measure). These are the only five solids that fit this description.

Students enjoy constructing models involving panels of different shapes (fig. 8). If the corners of an octahedron are chopped off, the result is the truncated octahedron. Similarly, the cuboctahedron is a cube with all eight corners chopped off. Still other patterns can be found in Wenninger (1975) or Cundy and Rollett (1954).

For those students who like challenges, the patterns in figure 9 are offered. For these models, the students construct an outer "shell" and the inner "hole" as two separate figures. The "hole" is then covered by the "shell," joining all outside edges. These models represent a type of tunneled polyhedra known as toroids.

Ideas for Classroom Use

Three-dimensional models provide the basis for many interesting activi-

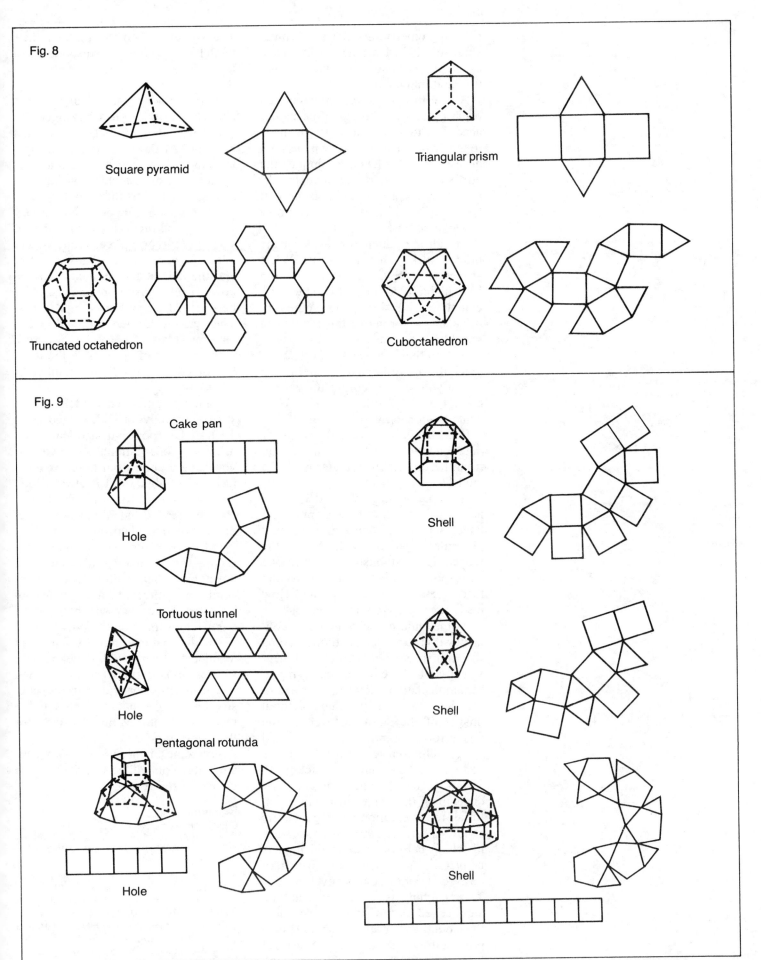

Fig. 8

Square pyramid

Triangular prism

Truncated octahedron

Cuboctahedron

Fig. 9

Cake pan

Hole

Tortuous tunnel

Hole

Pentagonal rotunda

Hole

Shell

Shell

Shell

ties in geometry. At the same time, students will be learning to view space as something they can understand, use, and manipulate.

At the primary level, students can begin by learning to place the panels according to a pattern. Patterns made to the actual measure of the panels are necessary at this level. Examining the attributes of constructed models may also lead to a valuable discussion. Questions such as the following may provoke comment:

Are all the panels (or faces) of the model alike or different? What shape(s) are the faces? (If the children have difficulty looking at one face of a complete solid, simply loosen the rubber bands and remove the panel. The panel now provides a two-dimensional pattern that can be traced on paper, yielding a more familiar shape.)

Can you tell one corner (or vertex) apart from any other corner? How could you check your answer?

Does the model look the same or different if you look at it from the side, from the top, or from underneath the model?

How many faces does the model have? (If orientation is a problem, have as many students as necessary place one hand on each face of the model. This establishes a one-to-one correspondence between students and faces, simplifying the counting.) How many corners? How many edges?

As the children become more proficient with the models, activities aiding the transition between two-dimensional and three-dimensional representations can be devised. For example, the patterns may include pictorial images of the solids as well as the layout for the panels (as in figs. 3 and 7). The children learn to refer to the picture to check their construction. In this way the students are gradually developing the ability to identify pictorial representations for geometric solids. Further activities, such as matching patterns with solid models or pictorial representations with patterns, can reinforce this development. This matching using patterns can then be checked as the students assemble the model. Yet another technique is to present drawings of three-dimensional figures from different points of view.

The students then try to hold their models in positions corresponding to the point of view represented in the drawing.

In the middle grades, surface area and volume take on a new meaning with three-dimensional models and patterns. At the same time, concepts such as a closed surface, region exterior or interior to a closed surface, or a closed surface as the boundary of an interior region can be explored. By counting and recording the number of vertices (corners), faces (panels), and edges of each of the Platonic solids and the deltahedra, students can discover a relationship among the numbers of edges, vertices, and faces. This relationship is expressed in Euler's formula $V - E + F = 2$, where V is the number of vertices, E the number of edges, and F the number of faces.

Hanging completed models from a string not only provides decoration for the classroom but also leads to a discussion of rotational symmetry. If you hang a cube from a vertex (or a face or an edge), will it always look just the same as you rotate it through 360 degrees? What about a tetrahedron or a dodecahedron?

In the elementary school mathematics program, geometry aids children in developing their ability to describe, compare, represent, and relate objects and shapes with which they have experience in their environment. Three-dimensional models can play an important part in this development. The cardboard–rubber band method of construction provides an inexpensive means of producing self-stabilizing solids, requiring no adhesives, for the classroom.

Try some of these ideas with your students. You will be surprised by the quality of the results.

References

Cundy, Henry M., and A. P. Rollett. *Mathematical Models*. London: Oxford University Press, 1954. (Available from Creative Publications.)

Stewart, B. M. *Adventures among the Toroids*. Published by the author, 1970. (Available from B. M. Stewart, 4494 Wausau Road, Okemas, MI 48864.)

Wenninger, Magnus J. *Polyhedron Models for the Classroom*, 2d ed. Reston, Va.: National Council of Teachers of Mathematics, 1975. ◆

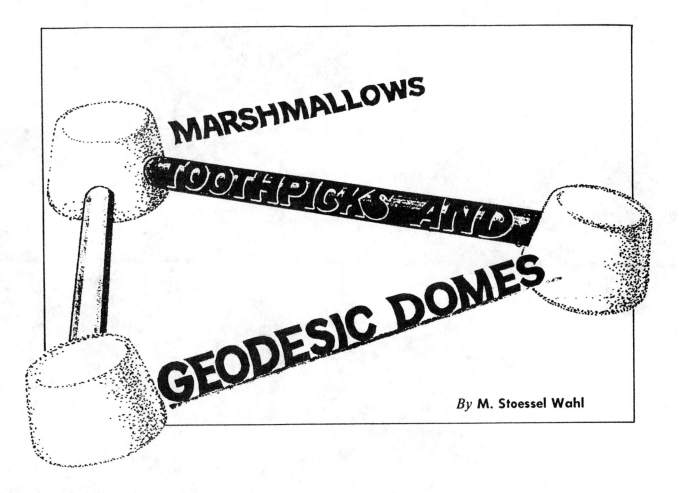

MARSHMALLOWS TOOTHPICKS AND GEODESIC DOMES

By **M. Stoessel Wahl**

Young children grow up in and adapt to a world of three-dimensional objects. Solids, however, are difficult to show on textbook pages and in chalkboard drawings, with the result that there is a tendency to limit early school geometric experiences to recognition of plane figures.

One successful learning approach to the three-dimensional world for young children can be made by having children construct geodesic domes with marshmallows and toothpicks. Since it involves physical activity, this approach also has been successful with young hyperkinetic children. The classroom construction of geodesic domes is an activity that is relevant to the world outside school, interesting for children, and fairly inexpensive to implement. Using miniature marshmallows and

round toothpicks along with a well-constructed pattern, first graders can make a small dome. Larger domes can be made by children in higher grades.

Patterns for Domes

Patterns for making two domes are shown in figures 1 and 2. The patterns

Fig. 1

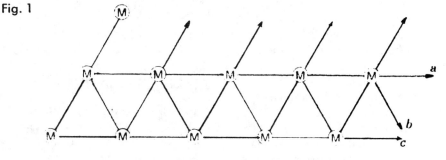
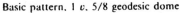

Basic pattern. 1 *v*. 5/8 geodesic dome

Fig. 2

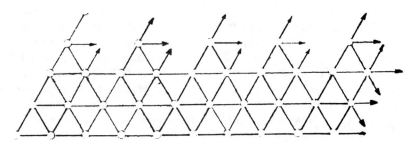

Basic pattern, 2 *v*, 5/8 geodesic dome

An associate professor of mathematics at Western Connecticut State College, Stacey Wahl has a special interest in the creative teaching of mathematics. Much of her material is first tried out in the classrooms of former students. She and her husband are the authors of I Can Count the Petals of a Flower, *a counting book for young children, published by the NCTM.*

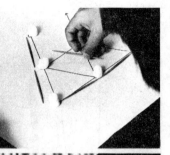

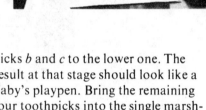

Using midget marshmallows and round toothpicks along with a well-constructed pattern, first graders can make a small dome.

are color coded to toothpick colors. (Colored cocktail toothpicks are available in supermarkets in four assorted colors—blue, green, yellow, and red.) When the larger domes are made cooperatively by several children, it is easier to assign sections to individual children by color. Even if plain toothpicks are used, it is helpful to have the pattern color coded. If the color coding is used consistently in all patterns, the various domes can be more easily compared and studied later.

Young children need patterns that are drawn to actual measures. To make such a pattern, first construct a dome. Then disconnect the dome from top to bottom and lay it flat on a piece of paper or cloth. Locate the positions of the marshmallows with black circles, and then draw in the colored connecting line segments so each pattern is in the desired one-to-one toothpick unit scale.

The storage of large permanent patterns often becomes a problem for a teacher. To minimize the storage problem, draw the patterns on light-colored cloth with dime-store crayons. After the pattern has been carefully checked

for accuracy, press it with a warm iron. The pressing melts the crayon marks into the cloth and the patterns can then be folded and put away—and even washed, if necessary.

Making Small Domes

Children in the primary grades can make the small domes (fig. 1). Give each child a teacher-made pattern (1:1 scale), eleven miniature marshallows, and twenty-five toothpicks. The child should spread out the pattern and then place the marshmallows, upright like a can, on each circle. The marshmallows are then connected with toothpicks, as indicated in the pattern. The toothpicks marked by arrows are not connected to marshmallows while the figure is in a flat position. Check that there is a bottom row of eight connected triangles and two partly opened ones. Then help the child tip this row on end and connect the open toothpick *a* to the upper marshmallow and tooth-

picks *b* and *c* to the lower one. The result at that stage should look like a baby's playpen. Bring the remaining four toothpicks into the single marshmallow at the top. The small geodesic dome is now completed.

Making Larger Domes

Children from the fourth grade up can successfully make the larger domes from patterns (fig. 2). The larger domes are more interesting and easy to make cooperatively. The miniature marshmallows should be dried, at least an hour on a dry day, before they are used to make a dome.

Before children attempt the largest dome (4 *v*), they should have experience in constructing smaller domes. Using several pairs of hands and a knowledgeable leader, the large dome is formed like the smaller ones; the lower row of triangles is connected first, and then, carefully, layer by layer, the upper triangles are put together. It is important to put the large dome over a volleyball or large inflated balloon to dry.

Since trouble often develops if the toothpicks are not well seated in the marshmallows, it is advisable to insert the toothpicks uniformly all the way

The larger domes are more interesting and easy to make cooperatively.

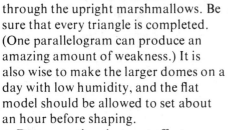

through the upright marshmallows. Be sure that every triangle is completed. (One parallelogram can produce an amazing amount of weakness.) It is also wise to make the larger domes on a day with low humidity, and the flat model should be allowed to set about an hour before shaping.

Damp weather does not affect gumdrops as readily as it does marshmallows, so some teachers might prefer to use gumdrops as connectors. The toothpicks, however, must be inserted at the correct mathematical angle in the gumdrops; the softness of the marshmallows lets the physical forces control the mathematical angle. If a more permanent, gumdrop model is desired, it would be wise to make a marshmallow model first; then make the gumdrop model one triangular layer at a time, carefully observing the angles of the toothpicks in each gumdrop.

Dome Sizes

The four sizes of domes are differentiated in *Dome Book II* by the designa-

tion of frequency: 1 v, 2 v, 3 v, 4 v, where v stands for frequency. The term *frequency* can be explained by reference to the construction of a simple icosahedron. If each side of each of the twenty equilateral triangles in the icosahedron is one toothpick in length, and if the lower five triangles of the icosahedron are removed, the resulting figure would be considered a 5/8, 1 v, geodesic dome. The dome is said to be of *one frequency* (1 v) because each of the basic equilateral triangles has sides one toothpick unit long. If each basic

equilateral triangle had sides two toothpick units long, it would be a *two frequency* (2 v) model. Similarly, a 3-v dome would have basic triangles three toothpick units on each side; and the 4 v dome, four toothpick units on each side. The 4-v dome is quite large and requires skill, patience, and cooperation in its construction.

Figure 3 represents a schematic picture of a basic, triangular unit for each of the four different sizes of the domes.

Observations

The construction of domes of the different sizes can lead to other mathematical ideas and activities. One fourth-grade class placed the four finished domes one inside the other. They

Fig. 3

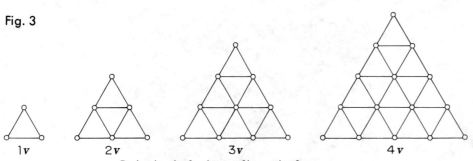

Basic triangles for domes of increasing frequency

were impressed by the changes in size and asked questions about area and volume changes. They had had previous experience with linear graphing and were quite surprised when their surface area graph produced a curved line. To graph the relative volumes they decided to line their domes with thin dry-cleaning bags and to fill them with big marshmallows. Thus their volume comparisons were made in big marshmallow units and they had a meaningful experience in making their first cubic graph.

Reference

Kahn, Lloyd. *Dome Book II*. Berkeley, Calif.: Pacific Domes, 1971. □

By **James V. Bruni** *and* **Helene Silverman,**
Herbert H. Lehman College, City University of New York

Using geostrips and "angle-fixers"

Geometry is an important, exciting part of elementary school mathematics. Children can be involved in relating mathematics to shapes in their environment. The activities described here suggest one way to help children develop some basic ideas about simple closed shapes, angles, and triangles. By constructing models of geometric shapes and physically transforming those models, children can examine the changes that occur with a transformation. This can help organize and synthesize thinking about basic geometric concepts. It can also serve as a foundation and a springboard for activities involving the use of a ruler, compass, or protractor.

The materials used in these activities are homemade geostrips, "angle-fixers," and brass fasteners, as shown in figure 1. (The angle-fixers are patterned after

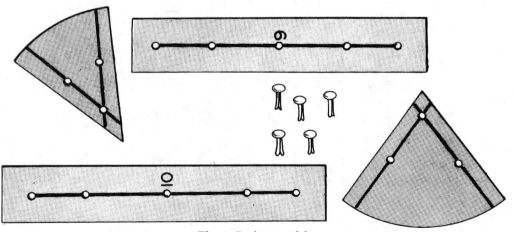

Fig. 1. Basic materials

Photograph by Clif Freedman

to develop ideas about shapes and angles

a material developed by Emma Castelnuovo, a teacher in Rome, Italy. The authors are indebted to Professor Castelnuovo for her pioneering efforts in the teaching of geometry through the transformation of models.) The geostrips and angle-fixers are made by using rubber cement to mount patterns like the ones in figures 2 and 3 onto oaktag and cutting along the black lines. The holes are made,

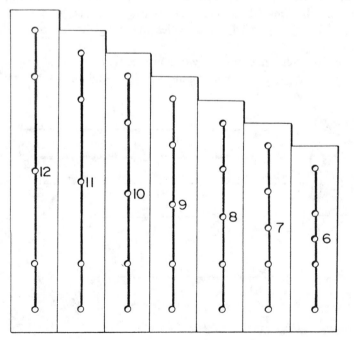

Fig. 2. Sample patterns for geostrips

as indicated, with a hole punch (preferably one that makes very small holes). It is convenient for the strips to be 2 centimeters wide and to have different lengths. The numbers indicated on the strips represent the distance in centimeters between the end-holes of the strips. In making models with the geostrips, this distance is the length. You will need strips ranging in length from 6 to 24 centimeters. Each strip has five holes: two holes that are 2 centimeters apart at each end of the strip and one hole at its midpoint.

To make the patterns for the angle-fixers, begin with a circle with a radius of 5 centimeters. Make "sectors" that vary in angle size. (Fig. 3.) The patterns for angle-fixers should include 30, 45, 60, 75, 90, 105, 135, 150, and 180 degree

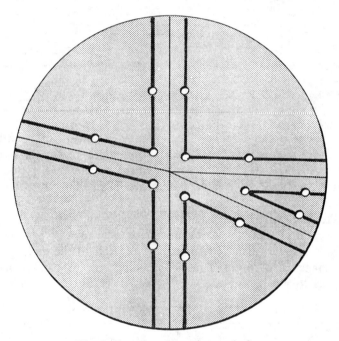

Fig. 3. Sample pattern for angle-fixer

angles, but initially they should not be labeled as such. You may wish to have the children label the angle-fixers in degrees later when you introduce the degree as a unit of angular measurement. On each sector draw a red line segment along each straight side ½ centimeter from the sides, as shown, and punch a hole where the segments intersect. Each of the holes along the "sides" of the angle-fixers should be 2 centimeters from this hole.

Simple closed shapes

Give children an opportunity to make different kinds of shapes using just the strips and brass fasteners. Encourage the children to talk about the shapes that are made: How are the shapes alike? How are they different? Once children have had ample opportunity to explore the materials, you might pose a challenge like the following.

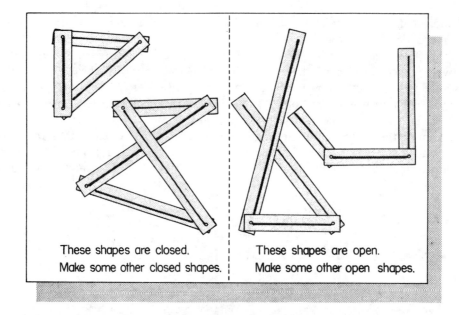

These shapes are closed.
Make some other closed shapes.

These shapes are open.
Make some other open shapes.

See if the children can discover the difference between an open shape and a closed shape from the examples. Let the children attempt to explain that difference in their own way. We are trying to make them realize that a closed curve has no "beginning" or "end." If a child moves his finger along the closed shape, he can keep going "around and around" along the shape. Once children can successfully make an open shape, ask them to make an open shape into a closed shape. When children can transform an open shape to a closed shape, and vice versa, you have a better assurance that they understand the concept. Notice that a shape can "cross itself" or not. That has nothing to do with being open or closed, which brings us to a second challenge. Again, when children can make a simple

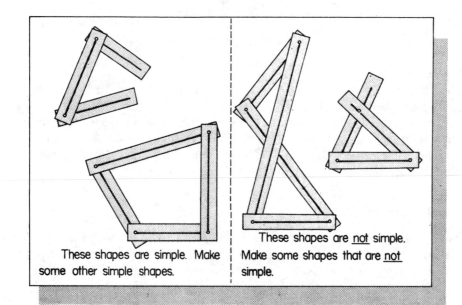

These shapes are simple. Make some other simple shapes.

These shapes are <u>not</u> simple. Make some shapes that are <u>not</u> simple.

shape, they should be asked to try to change the simple shape into one that is *not* simple, and vice versa.

Once children are familiar with the ideas of *simple* and *not simple* shapes, and *closed* and *open* shapes, they can try to make shapes that are both simple *and* closed at the same time. If each strip represents a line segment, these simple, closed shapes that are made up of line segments represent *polygons*.

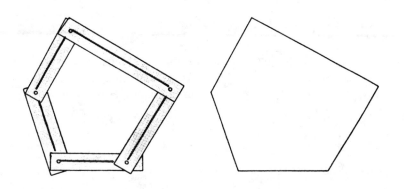

Shapes that are simple and open or not simple and closed, do *not* represent polygons. Children should be encouraged to transform these shapes that are not polygons into models of polygons.

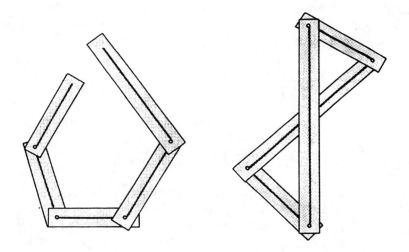

Angles

Before children are taught to measure the size of an angle with a protractor, they should have experience in making models of angles and in estimating the sizes of angles. Two strips joined by a brass fastener at their end holes can be thought of as a model of an angle. You can tell children to hold one strip still and rotate the other one about the brass fastener. Then ask, What is changing? Children should see that as one strip is turned the "amount of opening" between the strips changes. Ask the children, What is the largest opening you can make? What is the smallest opening you can make?

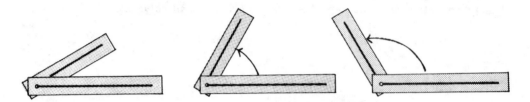

At this point the "angle-fixer" can be introduced. By using an angle-fixer you can keep the opening between two strips from changing; in other words, you can "fix" an angle. The children can use different angle-fixers and compare the resulting models.

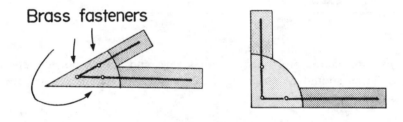

Brass fasteners

How can children show that one opening is larger than another? They can place one model on top of the other.

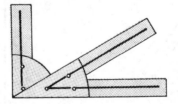

Children can also realize that the size of an opening does *not* depend on the length of the strips used. (How often do children confuse size of angle with length of "sides"?) As the children compare the sizes of openings, you might ask them to arrange the models in order from smallest to largest opening.

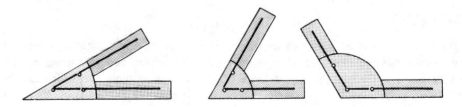

Once children realize how the angle-fixers influence the sizes of these models of angles, you can introduce activities such as the following to develop an understanding of specific kinds of angles.

Find an angle-fixer that makes an angle like the corner of a book.

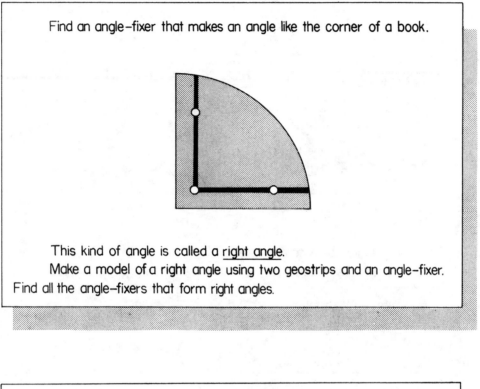

This kind of angle is called a right angle.
Make a model of a right angle using two geostrips and an angle-fixer.
Find all the angle-fixers that form right angles.

Find an angle-fixer that makes an angle like the edge of a book.

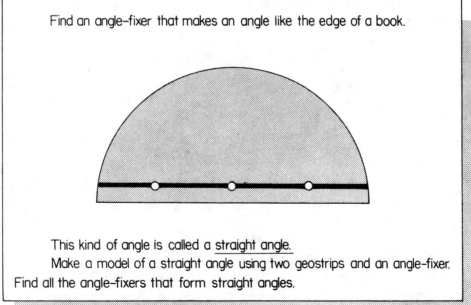

This kind of angle is called a straight angle.
Make a model of a straight angle using two geostrips and an angle-fixer.
Find all the angle-fixers that form straight angles.

When the right angle and the straight angle are understood, models of acute and obtuse angles can be made and identified.

Find all the angle-fixers that can form angles that are <u>smaller</u> than a right angle.

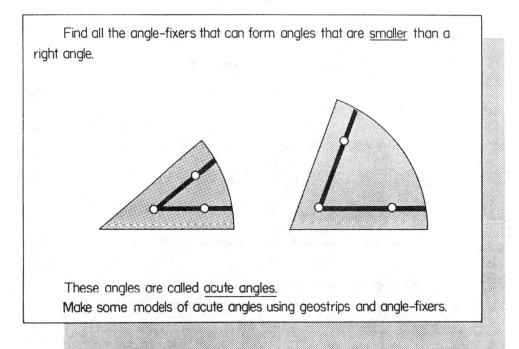

These angles are called <u>acute angles</u>.
Make some models of acute angles using geostrips and angle-fixers.

Find all the angle-fixers that can form angles that are <u>smaller</u> than a straight angle, but <u>larger</u> than a right angle.

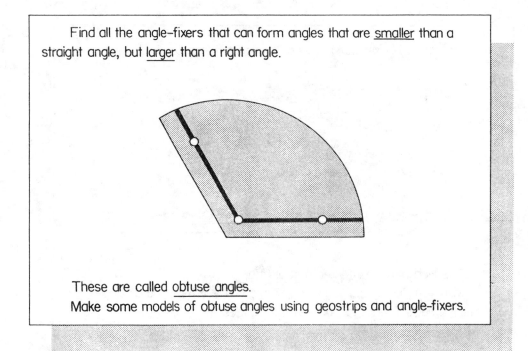

These are called <u>obtuse angles</u>.
Make some models of obtuse angles using geostrips and angle-fixers.

When you introduce the degree as a unit of angular measurement, the children can discover ways to find the measures of all the angle-fixers. Starting with an angle-fixer that can form the model of a right or 90° angle, children can find the number of degrees in the other angle-fixers. By placing smaller angle-fixers on top of the 90° angle-fixer, children can then figure out the number of degrees in the small angle-fixers.

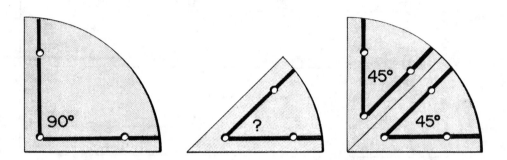

In a similar way the children can find the measure in degrees of all the angle-fixers without using a protractor. These kinds of experiences can give them a better understanding of angular measurement and increase their ability to estimate the size of an angle.

Triangles

In the previous activities the children found that a model of a simple closed shape made with the strips is a model of a polygon. They can discover that they need *at least* three strips to make a polygon. A three-sided polygon is called a triangle. Can children make a triangle with *any* three strips? An activity like the following can be interesting.

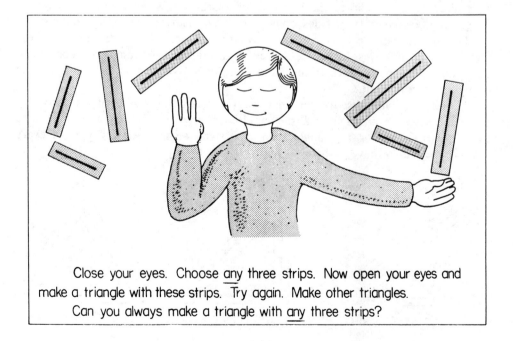

Close your eyes. Choose any three strips. Now open your eyes and make a triangle with these strips. Try again. Make other triangles.
Can you always make a triangle with any three strips?

The children should be encouraged to keep a record of when it is and when it is not possible to make a triangle with three strips. See what the children can discover about triangles from the chart.

Can You Make a Triangle?

Side 1	Side 2	Side 3	Yes or No
6	7	8	Yes
6	7	15	No
8	9	14	Yes
8	9	20	No
7	18	6	No
8	15	10	Yes
9	18	7	No

As the children make many different triangles you can ask them how they might sort the triangles into three piles, placing all those triangles that seem to belong together into the same pile. Children may sort or classify the triangles in different ways; discuss with the children how they chose to sort the triangles. This discussion can lead to the introduction of the terms *equilateral* (three sides congruent), *isosceles* (two sides congruent), and *scalene* (no sides congruent).

The children can use the angle-fixers to discover facts about the angles of these three kinds of triangles: All three angles of an equilateral triangle are congruent. Two angles of an isosceles triangle are congruent. No two angles of a scalene triangle are congruent.

Children may also discover another way of classifying the triangles according to their angles. You might ask the children if they can make a triangle with two obtuse angles, or a triangle with two right angles. And why does every triangle they make have to have *at least* two acute angles?

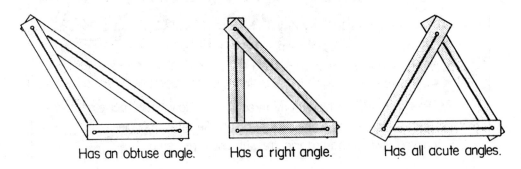

Has an obtuse angle.   Has a right angle.   Has all acute angles.

If the children can classify triangles in terms of sides and in terms of angles you can try an activity like the following.

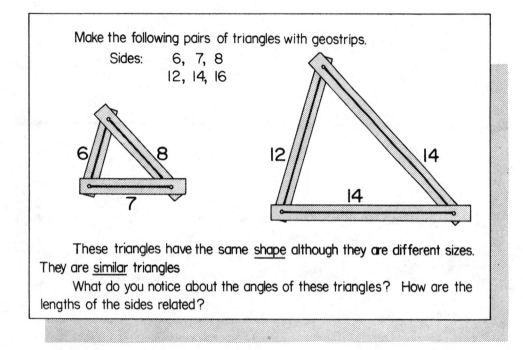

Make the following pairs of triangles with geostrips.

Sides: 6, 7, 8
         12, 14, 16

These triangles have the same <u>shape</u> although they are different sizes. They are <u>similar</u> triangles

What do you notice about the angles of these triangles? How are the lengths of the sides related?

Children can investigate the idea of similar triangles by making special pairs of triangles. Activities like the following can be used.

Each space below suggests a possible triangle, described according to its sides and according to its angles. For example, the triangle indicated is acute and scalene.

	Acute	Right	Obtuse	
Scalene	6 7 8 (triangle)		
Equilateral			No
Isosceles			

Can you make one that is right and scalene? Can you make one that is acute and equilateral? Which kinds of triangles are possible to make? Draw a picture of each one that you can make. Indicate which ones cannot be made.

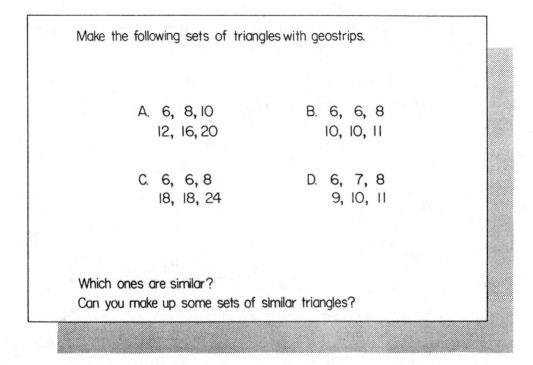

Make the following sets of triangles with geostrips.

A. 6, 8, 10   B. 6, 6, 8
   12, 16, 20   10, 10, 11

C. 6, 6, 8   D. 6, 7, 8
   18, 18, 24   9, 10, 11

Which ones are similar?
Can you make up some sets of similar triangles?

Investigating other shapes

You can encourage the investigation of many ideas about triangles or other polygons. For example, when the children make models of polygons with more than three sides, they find the models can be "pushed out of shape." (Fig. 4.) They cannot "push" a model of a triangle "out of shape," however; a triangle is a *rigid* figure. This makes the triangular shape very valuable for construction (as the shape of supporting structures).

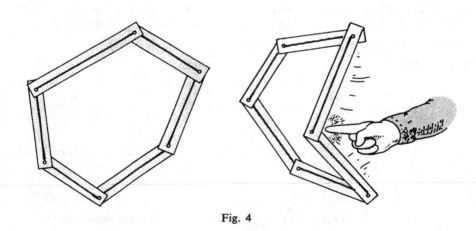

Fig. 4

The children can examine what happens when a polygon is "pushed out of shape." Notice that in this activity the perimeter remained the same as the area changed. Other questions can be raised: When is the area the greatest? How are the sizes of the angles changing?

Make a square with geostrips.

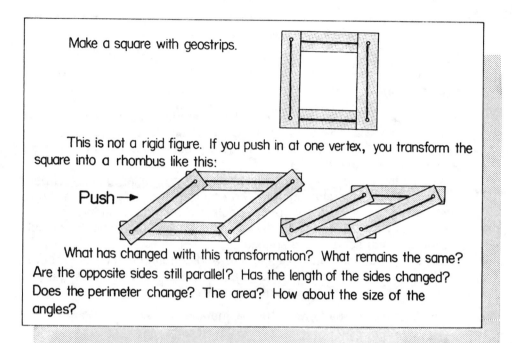

This is not a rigid figure. If you push in at one vertex, you transform the square into a rhombus like this:

Push →

What has changed with this transformation? What remains the same? Are the opposite sides still parallel? Has the length of the sides changed? Does the perimeter change? The area? How about the size of the angles?

By using geostrips and angle-fixers to actually make models of geometric shapes and by transforming those models, children can gain a great deal of insight and understanding about basic geometric ideas.

Photograph by Clif Freedman

Geometry

USING CERAMIC TILES

Ceramic tiles are good manipulative materials to use when you are teaching area. Not only are they more sturdy than cardboard squares, but they are also very inexpensive. (A square foot yields 144 one-inch tiles and costs about one dollar.)

I begin my unit by drawing geometric shapes on a large piece of paper and then having the students use the one-inch tiles to determine the approximate area of each shape. This activity helps the students to understand what we mean by area; it also leads them to discovering the formulas for the areas of some of the shapes.

Students also learn that placing tiles and counting them will not always work, as in trying to find the area of a circle. But work with tiles is a good forerunner to discussing the formula for the area of a circular region.

From the file of Linda Lewis, Muncie, Indiana

AT-5-81

Miscellaneous

MORE ON CERAMIC TILES

Ceramic tiles are very useful manipulative materials. They are durable and inexpensive. Some tile companies will donate tiles that are left over from a job or that have been used for color samples, so ask before you buy. You can get 1-inch and 2-inch square tiles, and hexagonal and rectangular tiles.

You can spray paint tiles if you want many of one color. Tiles can be used to make patterns. They can also be used to show areas. In drawing geometric shapes for which the children are to determine the area, make some in which certain tiles will fit neatly and others in which tiles of one size will fit, but not tiles of another size.

Magnetic tape can also be glued to the back of tiles for use on a magnetic board or on the side of a file cabinet. Write numerals, operation signs, order signs, and equal signs on tiles; then place them randomly on your file cabinet. Watch how children make number-fact sentences or generate a counting sequence. All undirected!

From the file of
Elaine Bologna, Summit School, Reynolda Estates, Winston-Salem, North Carolina.

AT-4-82

Measurement

METRICS
WITH MARCEL AND MARCETTE

By **Bernard R. Yvon**

> **Editor's note:** During my teacher workshops the participants came up with some very good ideas. One teacher made the snakes out of alternating segments with each segment ten centimeters, or one decimeter, long. The finished snake had ten segments of alternating colors to show the relationship of decimeters to meters. Another suggestion is to use laundry markers and make the centimeters on the snake's tummy. Children really enjoy using this aid. In kindergarten they started counting the centimeter markings without being told what they were for. For the traditionalists, these snakes can also be adapted to the English system of measurement. Make the snakes one yard long and name them Yancy and Yolanda Yard!

As a novel addition to the tools of metric measurement, try metrics with Marcel and Marcette. More than just stuffed snakes, Marcel and Marcette are metersticks with personalities, and they will charm students in the lower elementary grades. As the children work and play, they will painlessly absorb the meaning of the meter and even the centimeter. If children like stuffed toys, they'll enjoy Marcel and Marcette.

Marcel and his feminine counterpart, Marcette, are quickly and easily made. The total cost per snake is approximately $2.50, depending on the fabric. For each snake, you'll need a piece of fabric 20 cm by 110 cm. Plain material is preferable if you intend to mark the centimeters on the belly.

Fold the fabric in half lengthwise. With a pen or pencil, sketch the curve of the snake's body directly onto the material. (See fig. 1.) The widest point of the head should occur 5 cm in from the tip of Marcel's nose. At this point, the head should be about 7 cm wide (be sure to allow about 1.5 cm leeway between nose and edge of fabric), then taper down to 4.5 cm wide at the tail.

Stitch on the sketched outline, but don't stitch up the tail end. Trim the seam, clip the curves, and turn the snake inside out. Stuff the snake firmly with cotton batting. You can use a pencil to work the cotton down from the tail to the nose.

Next, beginning with the nose, mark off centimeters, from 1 to 100, with a laundry marker and a metric ruler. Allow the 1.5 cm leeway at the 100-cm mark, and clip off the rest of the fabric. Turn the raw edges to the inside, and close up the tail by hand. (See fig. 2.)

Sew on the eyes, which can be purchased at a fabric store in packages of eight. The mustache consists of two small strips of black felt either glued or sewn on.

For the beret, take a circle of felt 10 cm in diameter. (See fig. 3.) Keep folding opposite ends in towards the center (steps *b* and *c*). When there are eight folds (step *d*), press them so that they all lie the same way. Tack down each fold with needle and thread (step *e*). Cut a tiny strip (5 mm by 10 mm), and make a tiny matching slit (about 5 mm wide) in the center of the beret. Insert the strip into the slit and sew the underside end to the beret. Sew beret onto the head at a jaunty angle, et voici Marcel. With the addition of yarn hair and removal of mustache, voila Marcette.

Activities that have been used successfully in the classroom include letting pairs of children first estimate, then measure, the dimensions of the room with Marcel. They can compare estimates with actual measurements.

Children quickly become good at guessing objects in the room that are the same length as Marcel, but try asking them what objects are two times, or three times, the snake's length.

If you have marked the centimeters on the snake's belly, children will enjoy measuring each other. Although they can estimate heights to the nearest half snake, this is really not accurate enough. Using centimeters, they can make graphs comparing the heights of classmates. They will especially like to get the teacher's height on the graph—the difference between your height and theirs tends to be dramatic.

There are may more activities that you can devise using these toys. Any idea that involves using a meterstick may be adapted for Marcel and Marcette. Both are also flexible enough to measure girths.

You will find that Marcell and Marcette quickly assume a prominent and popular place in your classroom. And once they have become a part of your classroom, the concepts of meter and centimeter will become familiar ones to the children in your class. □

An associate professor of education and child development at the University of Maine in Orono, Bernard Yvon teaches preservice and in-service mathematics education courses at the graduate and undergraduate levels. He was a visiting lecturer at Keswick Hall College of Education in Norwich, England, during 1976 and 1977.

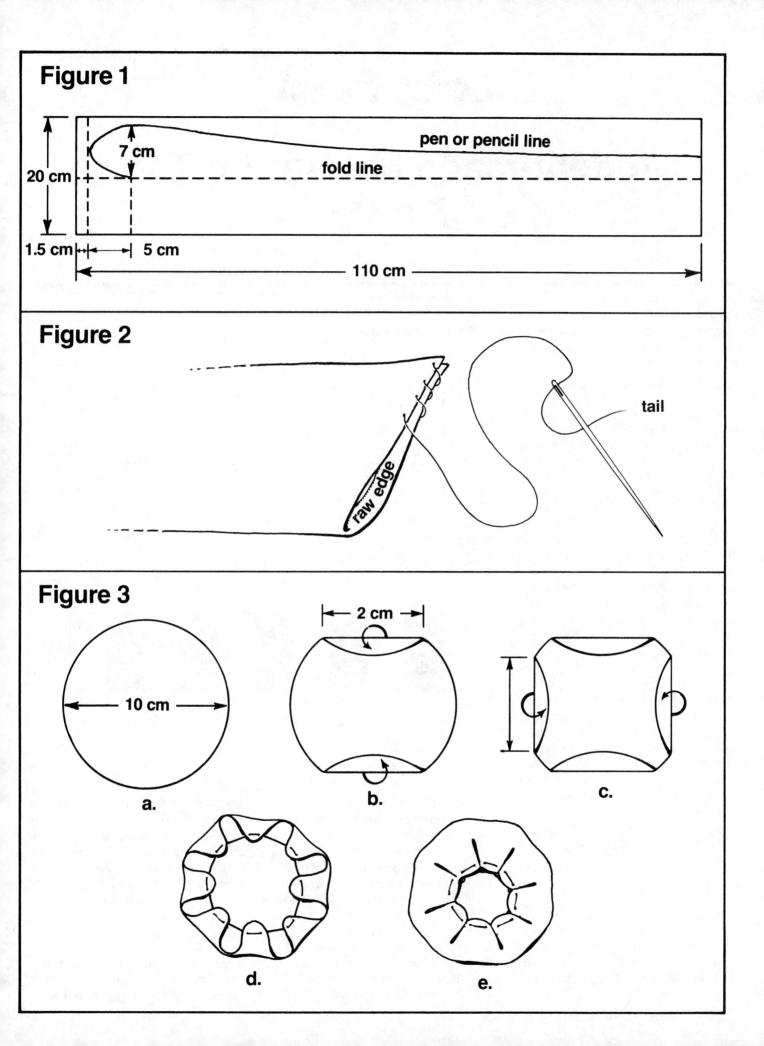

Figure 1

pen or pencil line

7 cm

fold line

20 cm

1.5 cm

5 cm

110 cm

Figure 2

raw edge

tail

Figure 3

10 cm

a.

2 cm

b.

c.

d.

e.

Let's Do It

Student-made Measuring Tools

By **Jean M. Shaw**
University of Mississippi, University, MS 38677

Let's Do It—activity approaches to teaching and learning mathematics in the primary grades, with extensions through grade six.

Mr. Kevin, a fifth-grade mathematics teacher, strongly believes that measurement should be taught using hands-on activities, but he has only two metersticks, three tape measures, and one balance scale in his room. Ms. Williams, a second-grade teacher, wants her pupils to measure objects to the nearest centimeter. She finds, however, that the rulers the children buy, calibrated in millimeters, confuse many of the children. If these teachers worked with their students to make their own measuring devices, they would find partial answers to their dilemmas.

When students make their own measuring devices, they produce valuable tools to use in measuring experiences. They learn much about the units of measurement as well as take pride in the measuring tools they have made themselves. Students can use their materials to share some of the skills they are mastering with their families.

Measuring Tools and Activities

Decimeter strips

Reproduce a decimeter strip (fig. 1) for each student. Have the students cut them out carefully, leaving the corners as straight and even as possible. Have the students label the strip *1 decimeter* and *1 dm*.

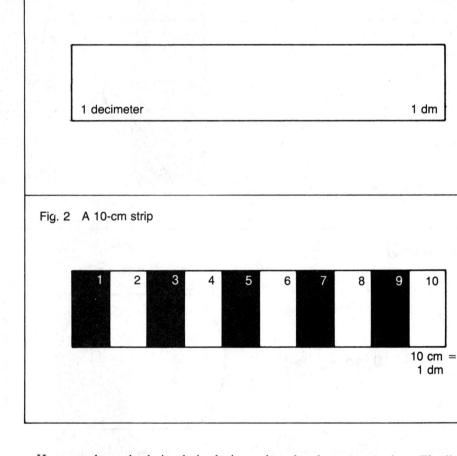

Fig. 1   A decimeter strip

1 decimeter   1 dm

Fig. 2   A 10-cm strip

| 1 | 2 | 3 | 4 | 5 | 6 | 7 | 8 | 9 | 10 |

10 cm = 1 dm

Have students look in their desks and pockets and around the classroom for objects close to 1 dm in size. Have students hold thier 1-dm strips next to objects to compare their sizes. Let students show each other objects that have one dimension of 1 dm or close to 1 dm. Now have students fill in a chart on the chalkboard listing objects that have measurements less than 1 dm, approximately 1 dm, and greater than 1 dm. Ask students to find and discuss some body parts that have a length close to 1 dm. Finally, as homework, ask students to use their decimeter strips at home to find objects close to 1 dm in one dimension. They can share their results in a class discussion, or they can bring objects to school to show to their classmates.

Centimeter strips

Reproduce a 10-cm strip for each student. Have students color every other section of their strips (fig. 2) and num-

ber each section. Lead students to compare their decimeter strips to their 10-cm strips. Develop the idea that 10 cm = 1 dm and have students label their strips *10 cm = 1 dm*. Ask students to work in groups to collect several small objects, estimate the length of each object in centimeters, and then use their strips to measure each object in centimeters.

Meter tapes

Have each student make a meter-long measuring tape from ten 1-decimeter sections. Reproduce the pattern shown in figure 3. Have students color five of the decimeter sections and leave the other five blank. Students should carefully cut out each section and overlap and tape them together end to end, alternating colored and blank sections. Have students number each decimeter section and carefully reinforce the joints with more tape.

When the tapes are completed, review the idea that 10 dm = 1 m; each student has just made a concrete representation of this idea. Have students compare the lengths of their tapes with a machine-produced meterstick. Talk about the reasons for slight variations in lengths.

Discuss some instances where measuring with a tape is easier than measuring with a flat ruler. Students might mention body parts and objects with curved edges. Let your students sug-

Fig. 3   A meter tape

Use this section for overlap.

Use this section for overlap.

The finished tape will look like this.

gest a list of things they could measure with their tapes. Ask students to work in pairs and choose ten items from the list to estimate and measure. Students might use their meter tapes to get approximate measures of their waists, ankles, heads, or shoulders. They might measure classroom objects such as books, furniture, the perimeter of the television screen, or the circumference of large containers. Let students discuss any objects they found that were longer than 1 m, shorter than 2 dm, or about 1/2 m. Assign homework involving use of the meter tapes to measure people or objects.

Calibrated measures of volume

Show students how to use a standard of volume to calibrate a transparent or translucent plastic container. To illustrate the idea, cut the top off a plastic bottle with heavy scissors, as shown in figure 4. Tape a piece of masking tape to the bottle. Use a standard measuring cup calibrated in 25 mL intervals. Fill the standard measure with water. For your demonstration you might add a few drops of food coloring to the water to make the water level easy to see. Carefully pour 25 mL of water into the bottle. Mark the 25 mL water level on the masking tape. Pour another 25 mL of water into the bottle and mark the 50 mL level on the tape. Continue the process until the bottle is calibrated as far as possible. If the bottle's sides are curved, the calibrations will not be equally spaced. If the bottle has straight sides, the calibration marks should occur at even intervals.

Have students help you to calibrate a larger container, such as a large milk jug, of translucent plastic. For a large container, use a larger unit for calibration; 500 mL units would be appropriate for a large jug. You could calibrate a gallon milk jug from 500 mL to 3000 mL, or 3 L. Use scissors to trim the milk jug (fig. 4) to make a large convenient opening. Use a ball-point pen or permanent markers to mark the units on tape attached to the side of the milk jug.

Ask students to bring in a plastic container suitable for calibration. Let

Fig. 4 Calibrated containers

Fig. 5

HOUSEHOLD VOLUMES

pairs of students work to calibrate their containers, using either measuring cups or calibrated laboratory measures as standard measures.

When all the students have finished a calibrated measure of volume, set up a laboratory session during which students can use their measures. Ask students to estimate and measure the volumes of various containers of water, sand, rice, and styrofoam bits. Have students take their measures

home to find the volumes of containers such as cans, soup bowls, mixing bowls, or even the kitchen sink! As a sharing experience, ask students to write the volumes of several household objects on paper. Let students take turns placing their papers on a bulletin board such as the one shown in figure 5. Measures of volume will become meaningful as students learn to associate them with familiar objects.

A balance scale

You can make a fairly sensitive balance scale with these materials: a half-gallon milk carton, an inexpensive ruler, two spring clothespins, a piece of metal coat hanger, two styrofoam cups or small aluminum pans, some sand, some yarn, and two paper clips. The ruler should have three to five holes already drilled in it. Many inexpensive rulers sold in variety or school-supply stores have holes for easy insertion into a notebook. These rulers are ideal for making the balance scale.

Have students work together in groups of four to make the balance scale. Help students cut a straight section of a wire coat hanger 15–20 cm long. Show them how to assemble the balance scale (fig. 6) by clipping a clothespin to the top of the milk carton, inserting the piece of wire through the hole in the clothespin's spring, putting the ruler on the wire through the middle hole, and finally, clipping on the second clothespin to hold the wire in place. Next, have the students insert a partially opened paper clip in each end hole of the ruler to hold the cups onto the balance scale. Have the students check the scale and see if the ruler hangs in a horizontal position. If the ruler hangs too low on one side, the students can balance it by adding a tiny piece of tape to the higher end.

Students can construct the cups for the balance scale by carefully punching three equally spaced holes in the tops of two styrofoam cups or small aluminum pie pans. They should insert yarn through the holes and carefully tie the yarn together at the top to support each cup (fig. 7). Students should hang the empty cups on the paper-clip hangers. Once again, students should check to see that the ruler hangs in a horizontal position and make necessary adjustments if it does not.

Students can use standard masses to establish the masses of some readily available materials that would be appropriate for balancing objects on the scale. If you do not have plastic or brass masses marked in units of 1 g, 2 g, 5 g, 10 g, and 25 g, a teacher in your

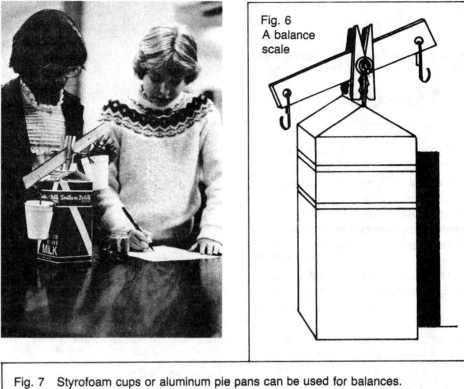

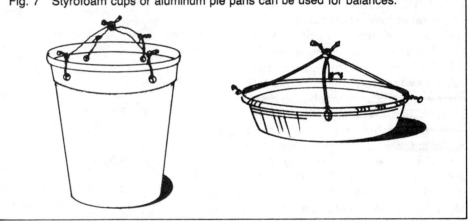

Fig. 7   Styrofoam cups or aluminum pie pans can be used for balances.

district's junior or senior high school science department may be able to loan you some. Students will see that objects such as small paper clips or one raisin have a mass of approximately 1 gram and that a nickel has a mass of about 5 grams. These objects can be used as standards for subsequent measuring activities.

Have students work in groups and gather small objects to weigh on the homemade balance scale. Each group of four students should select at least ten objects. They should record or estimate the mass of each object, then place it in one cup of the balanced scale. Next they should carefully add to the other cup the small objects they have gathered to use as standard masses. When the cups balance, the

students can count the standard masses and determine the approximate mass of their small objects. For most students, much practice in estimating masses is necessary before well-developed mental images of masses are established. You will want to have groups of students use their balance scales for many other experiences dealing with mass.

Conclusion

Student-made measuring tools are not substitutes for finely calibrated, precisely made manufactured tools, but their economy and the lessons learned in constructing them makes them valuable aids in the elementary school mathematics classroom. ◆

Geometry for the Intermediate Grades

By **James V. Bruni**

If you examine current, upper-grade, mathematics textbooks, you will find that they usually include a good deal of geometry. But in actual practice geometry does not constitute a significant part of the mathematics programs in elementary schools. Geometry activities usually are considered a "frill," a topic that is covered, if time permits. "Sure, geometry activities are great. But who has time? There's too much 'basic' arithmetic to do," was the comment of one fifth-grade teacher.

This attitude toward geometry is unfortunate. Children are naturally interested in shapes, and they have ideas about shape before they become acquainted with number concepts. As the study of shapes in space, geometry can offer children wonderful opportunities to explore the properties of shapes in their world and to be involved in highly motivating problem-solving situations.

Even when there is a commitment to including geometry in the elementary school programs, geometry is too often limited to memorizing definitions of geometric terms, identifying geometric shapes, or involvement in activities that seem to have little to do with "mathematics" from the children's, parents', or teachers' perspectives. Geometry activities in the elementary school should give children a chance to create different two-dimensional and three-dimensional shapes and to investigate properties of those shapes in a concrete, purposeful way. The following are examples of such activities.

In this series of activities, children are involved in making a variety of pa-

As a professor and chairman of the Department of Early Childhood and Elementary Education at Herbert H. Lehman College, City University of New York, Jim Bruni teaches mathematics methods courses for preservice and inservice elementary school teachers. Through speaking and writing, he has been an active proponent of more geometry in elementary school programs.

per boxes as they gain an understanding of the concept of volume, the development of three-dimensional shapes from two-dimensional patterns, and the use of two-dimensional diagrams to represent three-dimensional shapes.

First Activity

Materials needed

Wooden cubes, 1 by 1 by 1

Four paper or oaktag boxes. The dimensions of the boxes might be as follows:

E	3 by 2 by 2
F	3 by 5 by 1
G	2 by 8 by 1
H	2 by 4 by 2

Problem (see fig. 1)

Fig. 1

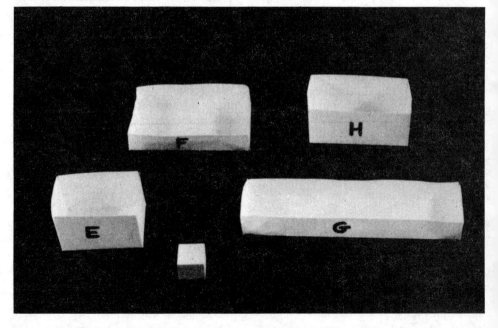

Which box is the biggest?

Which box is the smallest?

How many wooden cubes would fit in each box?

Discussion

The questions are deliberately ambiguous. What is meant by *biggest*? Is the longest box the biggest one? Is the tallest box the biggest? After talking about what *biggest* can mean, you can develop the idea of the biggest box as being the one that holds the most cubes and thus relate *biggest* to volume. Note: Boxes G and H are *both* the biggest. It is interesting to watch how the children formulate their guesses. Do they use the wooden cube as a reference? They can check their answers by actually filling the boxes with cubes.

Editor's note: A very simple aid for working with volume is sugar cubes. These can be used if a large supply of wooden or plastic blocks isn't available. "Cocktail" sugar cubes, when available, are a good substitute for centimeter cubes. The cocktail cubes are just slightly larger than a cubic centimeter. The difference isn't even noticed if a ruler is not near.

Second Activity

Materials needed

Wooden cubes
Four paper boxes, (similar to those used in the first activity but with faces that are marked off in squares congruent to the faces of the wooden cubes).

Problem (see fig. 2)

Which box is the biggest?
Which box is the smallest?
How many wooden cubes would fit into each box?

Discussion

This time the faces of the boxes are marked off in squares. Do the children find these squares helpful in arriving at their estimates of the number of cubes needed to fill each box? Do they merely count the squares (confusing surface area and volume)? Again, they can check their estimates by actually filling the boxes with cubes.

Third Activity

Materials needed

Wooden cubes
Scissors
Graph paper, with squares congruent to faces of wooden cubes used
Patterns for boxes (see fig. 3).

Problem (see fig. 3)

Look at these patterns for boxes.
Guess how many wooden cubes would fit into each box.

Discussion

Can the children visualize what the boxes will look like? How do they formulate their estimates? Do they merely count all the squares in the pattern? After children have made their guesses, they can cut out the patterns, form the boxes, and check their estimates.

Fourth Activity

Materials needed

Wooden cubes
Scissors
Graph paper, with squares congruent to faces of the cubes
Cellophane tape

Fig. 2

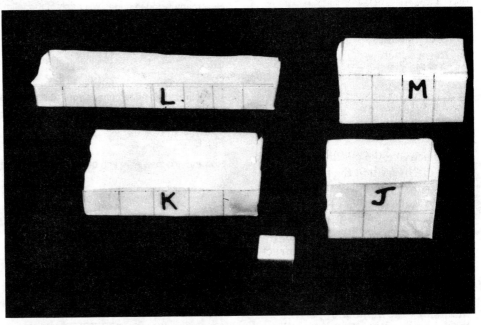

Fig. 3

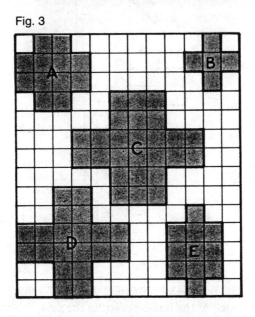

Fig. 4

Problem (see fig. 4)

Can you make a box, using graph paper, that holds exactly 6 cubes? How many *different* boxes can you make that hold exactly 6 cubes?

Can you make a box that holds 8 cubes? 12 cubes? 18? 24?

Make a collection of all the boxes you can make that hold the same number of cubes. How are they different? How are they the same?

Discussion

In solving this problem, children are investigating the factors of a given number. For example, boxes that hold 12 cubes have dimensions of 12, 1, 1; 6, 2, 1; 4, 3, 1; 2, 6, 1; 3, 4, 1; and so on. But the box that is 6 by 2 by 1 is really the same size and shape as the box that is 2 by 6 by 1. The same is true for the boxes that are 4 by 3 by 1 and 3 by 4 by 1, respectively.

An interesting extension of this activity is to give individual children one sheet of graph paper and to challenge them to make the largest possible box with that sheet (i.e., the box that holds the most cubes). Another challenge might be to have the children find out which of the boxes that hold a given number of cubes has the smallest number of squares on its faces (i.e., minimum surface area).

Fifth Activity

Materials needed

- Wooden cubes
- Graph paper
- Scissors
- Cellophane tape

Problem (see fig. 5)

Discussion

In this activity, the children are guided to the discovery that the product of the numbers for length, width, and height of a box is the number of cubes needed to fill the box—the basic formula for the volume of a rectangular solid. Some children may need to construct the box each time. Others may need to find out only how many cubes cover the base of the box and multiply that number by the number of "layers." Have children talk about how the resulting boxes will look.

Sixth Activity

Materials needed

- Scissors
- Graph paper
- Wooden cubes

Problem (see fig. 6)

Discussion

This time, larger numbers are used. After the children have responded to the given questions, ask them questions like, How did you get your answers? What will each box look like? How many cubes will cover the bottom of each box? How many "layers" of cubes will each box have?

Groups of children can work together on making a model of any one of these boxes. Do they recognize that the product of these three numbers (length, width, and height) represents the number of cubes that fit into each box?

Seventh Activity

Materials needed

- Diagrams of boxes, with congruent squares outlined on the faces (fig. 5).

Problem (see fig. 7)

Fig. 5

How many wooden cubes will each of the following boxes hold?

	length	width	height	guess	answer
Box A	2	2	3	_____	_____
Box B	4	2	3	_____	_____
Box C	9	2	1	_____	_____
Box D	5	2	2	_____	_____

Using the graph paper, check your guess by making the box and filling it with cubes.

What is an easy way to figure out how many cubes a box holds without having to fill it with cubes?

Fig. 6

How many cubes will each of the following boxes hold?

	length	width	height	guess
Box H	5	12	3	_____
Box I	6	3	4	_____
Box J	7	3	5	_____
Box K	12	10	3	_____
Box L	15	107	10	_____
Box M	52	10	5	_____

Fig. 7

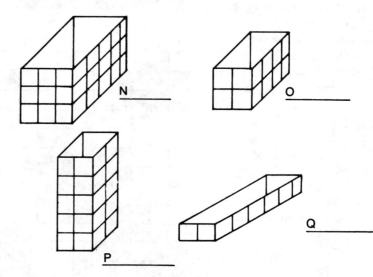

How many cubes will you need to fill each of the boxes shown in the diagram?

Discussion

This activity can help teachers to see if the children have developed an understanding of volume. How do the children arrive at their answers? Do they still confuse volume with surface area, counting the squares on each face of the box? Do they merely count the squares along the base of each box? Or can they use previous experiences in making and filling boxes to visualize filling these boxes with cubes?

At this point you might wish to pose more challenging questions like the following:

How many cubes would it take to fill a box with dimensions

4 by 3 by 1½?   6 by 2 by ½?   2 by 4 by ¼?

Have the children discuss the ways they try to solve these problems.

Summary

Through activities like these, upper-grade children can gain the kinds of firsthand experiences with ideas about two-dimensional and three-dimensional shapes and volume that textbook exercises rarely provide. Geometry is not an isolated subject; it clearly becomes an integral part of mathematics as the children deal with concepts of shape, number, and measurement in a meaningful way.□

Money on the number line

VERENA SHARKEY

*Having previously taught elementary and middle school,
Verena Sharkey presently divides her time between the Newark
(Delaware) School District, where she is a mathematics specialist,
and the University of Delaware, where she is a mathematics methods instructor.
She is active in NCTM and has been a speaker at state and regional
meetings. In addition, she has organized laboratory workshops
throughout the state of Delaware.*

Everyone wants money! Everyone needs money! Everyone uses money! Since these are all true statements teachers often relate other mathematical concepts to money as a means to foster the understanding of number value.

Teaching place value in base ten using money as the manipulative is an example of such a relationship. Pupils are encouraged to use place value charts showing pennies for ones place, dimes for tens place, and dollars for hundreds place. Grouping begins with pennies, exchanging ten of them for one dime and exchanging ten dimes for one dollar. While some teachers report a measure of success using this method for place value, other teachers of children in the primary grades find pupils lack the ability to equate coin value to number value. Many pupils are unable to give the correct coins for a stated money value.

If a teacher intends to teach by relating one concept to another, then he should not assume that children understand money value simply because they are accustomed to spending and saving money. It seems more credible to relate number value to money first and then use the money concept in relation to other concepts. The question is, how does one begin?

The number line is a manipulative and visual aid most primary teachers use for presenting the concepts of *greater than* and *less than, order,* and *number value.* Children familiar with this device can quite

easily relate number values from the number line to the number value of coins.

The introduction to this concept can be started as early as first grade by using pennies, a nickel, and a number line to five. (See fig. 1.) The child can learn to read the number value on the coins (one cent on the penny and five cents on the nickel). The

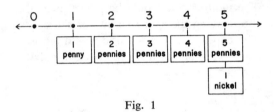

Fig. 1

next step would be to introduce the pennies one at a time with the numbers on the number line. When five pennies are equated with the five on the number line then the nickel can be introduced as another way to express five cents. Development of the concept continues from five on the number line to ten, number by number. Ten is then equated with ten pennies, two nickels, five pennies and a nickel, and finally a dime. (See fig. 2.) The same type of development would continue until all coins have been introduced with a value on the number line. A complete number line for coins would end with 50 for the half-dollar. (See fig. 3.)

The teacher should construct a number line of predetermined length prior to class. Small cards with 5 pennies, 1 nickel, 1 dime, and so on, (fig. 1) should also be

---

Editor's note: Another useful idea would be to make pieces of paper with pictures of coins on them to hang from the number line. A set of coin stamps can greatly facilitate this activity.

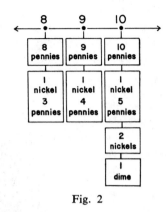

Fig. 2

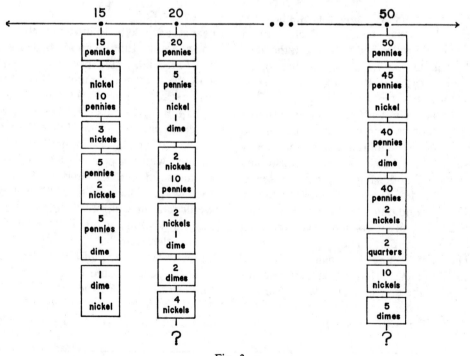

Fig. 3

prepared in advance and when the children have concluded that a particular point on the number line would include that name, the teacher, or a child can fasten the card under that point. Additional cards can be made as children discover other ways of representing a number with coins. Wide paper, similar to shelf paper, could be used. The number line would be placed near the top, leaving the space below for the cards. The completed number line would be used for a reference or a quick check in solving problems.

Of course, the most logical culmination of this activity would be "playing store." Articles could be real or pictures of articles, each with a price tag attached. The children would be expected to pay the exact amount for the articles and later count the exact change. This method of instruction can continue through third grade if necessary. It could be supplemented with games involving the use of money; practice in naming coins and giving their value; adding and subtracting using coins of various values; and exercises to give a specified amount of money using the least number of coins.

For example, teachers could construct a game in which the goal is to present the least amount of coins for a given number. It could be either a team game or one involving two or three individuals. Numbers could be drawn from a "pot" and the first pupil to show or answer with the least amount of coins for that number would score a point. A student monitor could use the number line to check any questionable answer. Such a game would be suited to grades one through four.

A Single-Handed Approach to Telling Time

By **Charles S. Thompson**, *University of Louisville, Louisville, Kentucky*
and **John Van de Walle**, *Virginia Commonwealth University, Richmond, Virginia*

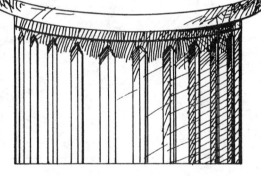

Many school children have difficulty learning to tell time via traditional teaching methods because some clock times are read "after the hour" whereas others are read "before the hour." Some children also have trouble telling time because minute numbers are not written on their clocks. Still other children learn to tell time, but do not have good concepts of the duration of time. They keep wanting to know, for example, when five minutes will elapse before they go to recess.

The teaching strategy described in this article attempts to avoid the difficulties described above. It emphasizes initial use of only one hand—the hour hand—and, consequently, names all times in relation to that one hand as "after the hour." Additionally, it uses clocks that have the minute numbers written on them so that the child can easily determine the number of minutes that have elapsed. Finally, in conjunction with reading clocks, activities are suggested that help children acquire the concepts of minutes and hours. Learning the time concepts along with reading clocks enables children to attach meaning to times they report, such as "forty minutes after two."

A Sundial

A simple sundial is a good introduction to telling time and using clocks. The sundial gives children a good picture of the passage of time because of the changing position of the sun's shadow. The sundial also looks somewhat like a clock face, especially when numerals are written in to correspond to shadows at various times of the day.

A first activity is to make a simple sundial as shown in figure 1. The sundial is then placed in a south-facing window (or outside). The sundial need not be permanent or stationary but its position should be carefully marked so that it can be placed in the same location the next day. The shadows are drawn in to correspond to various classroom activities during the day. Choose activities that occur at the same time every day—school begins, lunch time, recess, music, school ends. Label the shadow lines by writing the name of the activity beside the shadow line to which it corresponds (fig. 2). Then, on subsequent days when a regular activity begins, have children look at the sundial to see if the current shadow line corresponds with the one drawn previously. For several days the correspondence will be very close.

Next, use the same sundial and have children draw the shadows when the clock shows exact hour times. Good choices are 9, 10, 11, 12, 1, 2, and 3 o'clock (fig. 3). Draw and label these shadows with a different color marker than was used previously. Discuss with children that, as the shadow moves, the corresponding numbers increase in value. Then question children regarding the times that daily activities occur. For example, "What time is it when we begin story time?" Stress terminology such as "*about* eleven," "*a little after* one," "*about halfway between* nine and ten," and "*a little before* three."

A possible follow-up exercise is to give each child a drawing of a sundial that has only the exact hour shadows and the corresponding numerals drawn. Have children draw shadow lines from memory to correspond to activities which you, the teacher, specify. Use familiar events such as lunch time, art time, and mathematics time. This exercise helps children mentally connect the daily activities with the sundial times and it also helps them to put their daily activities into sequential order.

One-Handed Clocks

Though sundials are a good introduction to telling time, they have inherent difficulties as well. Ask children why they would not want to depend on sundials for telling time. Some answers that children frequently give are, "What would you do when it's cloudy or raining?" "They are no good at night," and "Sometimes they are not exact enough." This discussion provides a good lead-in to the use of clocks, a time-telling device that's accurate and works even when the sun is not shining.

We suggest that the first clock to use with children is one that has only one hand—the hour hand. There are several options for obtaining these one-handed clocks. The best is to buy a wind-up alarm clock or an inexpensive electric clock from a garage sale and then cut off the minute hand. Another good option is to obtain any clock and paint the minute hand a different color from the hour hand and then have children focus on the hour hand only. It is important that the one-handed clock be in working order.

Initial activities with this clock should be similar to the later activities with the sundial. The hour hand re-

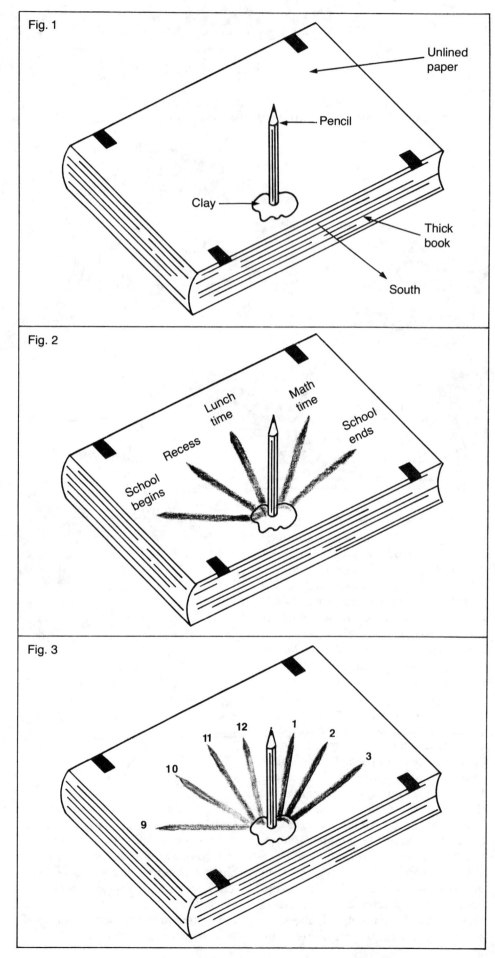

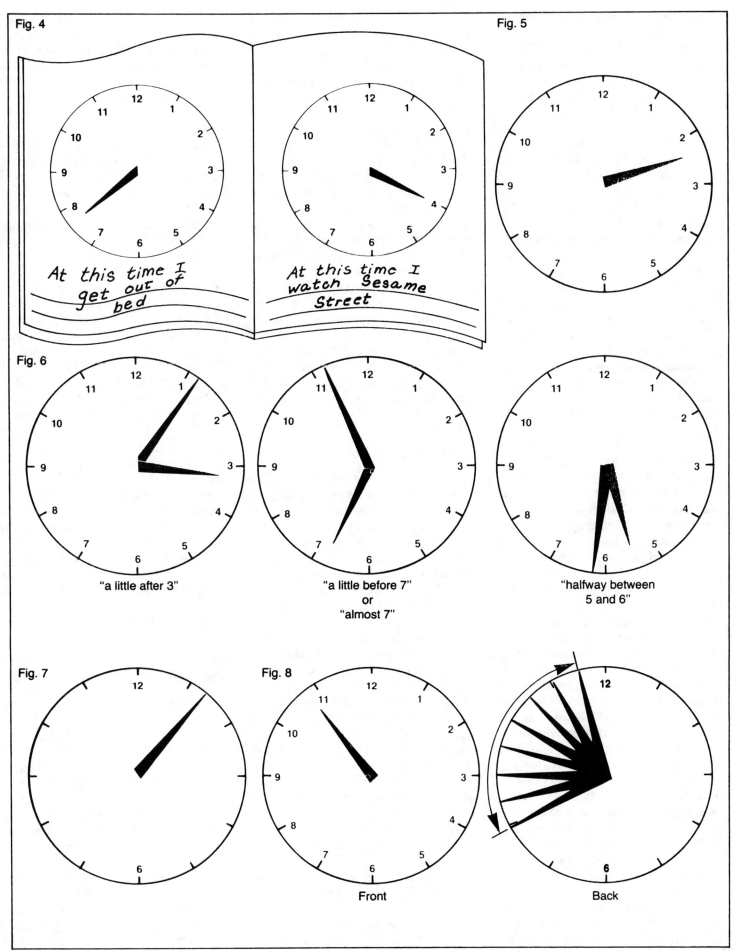

Fig. 4

At this time I get out of bed

At this time I watch Sesame Street

Fig. 5

Fig. 6

"a little after 3"

"a little before 7"
or
"almost 7"

"halfway between 5 and 6"

Fig. 7

Fig. 8

Front

Back

places the shadow. Instead of the sun causing the shadow to move, the mechanism makes the hour hand move. Have children read times and relate them to their daily events. Use the same terminology as was suggested with the sundial. For example, "Lunch time is *a little after eleven*," and "We go to the library *in the middle between* one and two." A motivating and worthwhile activity is to have children make personal time books like those shown in figure 4. In the book the children name activities that they do regularly and mark the corresponding times on clocks drawn in the booklet, using the hour hand only. The booklet is simply made by duplicating clock faces on both the front and the back of unlined paper and stapling the pages together. The books can be placed in a reading area for other children to enjoy.

Concurrent with these clock-reading activities, teachers should use activities that develop children's concepts of time and the passage of time. Use a one-handed clock and talk about the length of one hour. Discuss what can be done in an hour. Ask children what television shows last an hour. Discuss the number of hours in a school day and the number of hours they sleep. Discussions like these can cause children to develop concepts about the duration of time and the length of an hour.

Teachers will also want to have children practice setting one-handed clocks to specified times and to have children read specified times set by the teacher. Paper-plate clocks are fine for students to use but a larger, more durable one is suggested for teacher use. One that is easy to construct is shown in figure 5. The clock face and the separate hour hand are first drawn on posterboard and then laminated or covered with clear adhesive. Heavy cardboard may also be used as backing if desired. Note that the hour hand is made to be the same color as the hour numerals. The hour hand is attached to the clock face with a brass fastener so that it can rotate freely. On the underside of the hour hand, at the end near the point, place a small loop of tape with the adhesive side facing outward. This tape will enable the teacher to place the hand in any position on the

clock and have it stay fixed. It can then be easily moved to any other position as well.

A very important activity in helping children learn to tell time is one that is done in the children's homes. Simply write a note to moms and dads and explain to them that their child is learning to tell time and as a first step the child is learning to tell time by using only the hour hand. Point out that times can be read fairly accurately by using only the hour hand. Initially, the minute hand is ignored. Then ask the parents to occasionally question their child about the correct time using the approximate language we have been suggesting. Give the parents some sample clocks and indicate how they would be read (fig. 6). Also suggest some questions or tasks for the parents to pose. For example, "Johnny, is it six o'clock yet?" or "Sally, will you tell me when it's halfway between six and seven," or simply, "Tonya, about what time is it?"

The Minute Hand

The introduction of the minute hand should serve to relate its motion to the motion of the hour hand (instead of noting where it is on the hour or half past the hour as is traditional). This relationship is best made by using a geared clock—either a real clock which may be manipulated manually or a commercially produced teaching clock which is geared to coordinate the motions of the hour hand and the minute hand. As you manipulate the clock, ask the children about the positions of the hands. "Where is the long hand (minute hand) when the hour hand points directly at an hour number?" (It's straight up, or it points to the 12.) "Let's watch what the long hand does as the hour hand goes from two o'clock to three o'clock. How far does it go?" (It goes all the way around, back to the twelve.)

It is also important to stress the *direction* the hands move. Continue asking questions which elicit responses relating the movements of the two hands. For example, ask the children how far the long hand moves as the hour hand moves from three o'clock to midway between three and four. Of course, the

goal is to have children know—though they won't be able to state the concept in this manner—that, as the hour hand moves a fractional part of the distance from one hour number to the next, the long hand moves the same fractional portion of the distance around the clockface.

To reinforce this concept try the following activity. Provide children with paper-plate clocks that have only a long (minute) hand as in figure 7. Note that the numerals are omitted except for the 12 and 6. These are included only to provide a top and bottom orientation to the clock face.

Initially, ask the children to show on their clocks the position of the long hand as you display the hour hand on the large one-handed demonstration clock shown in figure 3. Set times such as, (a) 7 o'clock, (b) a little after 10 o'clock, (c) almost 5 o'clock, and (d) halfway between 1 o'clock and 2 o'clock. As you set the hour hand, use the appropriate language to report the time. Later present times using only the verbal format. For example, "Show me where the long hand would be if the time is almost three o'clock."

Other practice activities could make use of flash cards like the one shown in figure 8. On the front of the card is an hour clock with the hour hand drawn in. The child must determine the approximate position of the long hand using a paper-plate clock as shown in figure 5. Then he or she turns over the card to determine if the answer is acceptable.

Digital Time

Of course the major reason for using a minute hand is to measure and report time more accurately. This is accomplished by dividing one revolution of the long hand (one hour) into 60 equal parts (called minutes). The clock reader simply determines how many of the 60 minutes have been passed by the minute hand. The time is then reported as that number of minutes after the hour. When times are reported this way, we shall refer to it as "telling time digitally."

When beginning to teach children how to read clocks illustrating minutes after the hour, provide them with a

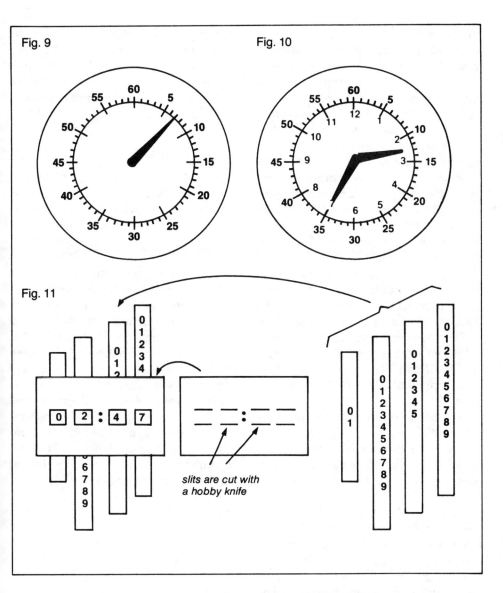

Fig. 9

Fig. 10

Fig. 11

slits are cut with
a hobby knife

about 5 minutes or about 10 minutes.
Examples are the time it takes for a
spelling test, to call roll, to walk
around the playground, to write the al-
phabet neatly, or for the entire class to
line up and each sharpen one pencil.
These and similar activities help give
children a feeling for the duration of
specific time intervals. Concepts regarding the passage of time are difficult and slowly acquired, but they are
very important. Reading a clock without a conception of the passage of time
is comparatively easy.

The next activities for telling time
digitally use clocks that have both the
hour numbers and the minute numbers
written on them. The clocks should be
in two colors, with the color of the
minute numerals and markings corresponding to the color of the minute
hand, and the color of the hour numerals corresponding to the color of the
hour hand (fig. 10). For a demonstration clock it is probably best to make a
new clock showing minutes and hours
in different colors. Cover the clock
with plastic laminate as before and attach pieces of tape to the two hands so
that they can be positioned on the
clock face where desired.

The procedure for telling time with
this clock is simple and is identical to
the method described at the beginning
of this section. The student first looks
at the hour hand and determines which
hour number it has just passed, for example two. This number represents the
hour time. Then the student looks at
the minute hand and determines the
minute number that the minute hand
has just passed, say for example thirty-
five. The student then reports the time
as "thirty-five minutes after two
o'clock."

Activities to reinforce telling time
digitally should again be related to
children's daily events. Ask children to
set a clock to show the exact time that
lunch begins, for example. Then have
them report that time digitally. Another activity is to pass out a sheet of
clocks and to have children draw in the
times, to the minute, that various
school routines begin. One activity that
has proved particularly enjoyable to
children is to have them use clocks to
show "funny times." Times which children classify as "funny" are ones such

minute-hand clock showing 60 minutes, as in figure 9. Be certain that the
minute hand and the minute numerals
are the same color. Have children
count the intervals between numbers to
help them locate "minute times" such
as "23 minutes after" and "48 minutes
after."

Early activities with this clock
should again relate the movement of its
minute hand to the movement of an
hour hand. Set your geared, two-
handed clock in any position, verbally
describe the time—"a little past six
o'clock," for example, and have children predict the location of the minute
hand by using their minute clocks (fig.
7). Ask them to report the minute
hand's position by saying the number
of minutes after the hour, such as
"seven minutes after six." Repeat this
activity with many other times until
children have a visual image of the

general locations of the minute numbers of the clocks. They learn quickly
that 30 minutes corresponds to half a
revolution of the minute hand and that
60 minutes represents a complete revolution. Associations with the other
numbers proceed more slowly.

As the idea of minutes after the hour
is being developed, short activities,
which develop a feeling for the length
of 1 minute, 5 minutes, and 10 minutes, should be conducted. Have children determine how many times they
can tie and untie a shoe in 1 minute,
how many times they can write their
names, and how many times they can
bounce a basketball. Have them close
their eyes and raise their hands when
they feel 1 minute has elapsed. Similar
activities should also be done for 5
minutes and 10 minutes. For these intervals you might consider having children find things to do that require

as 1 minute after 1, 2 minutes after 2, and so forth. These times are good times to practice with for they cause children to focus specifically on the different sets of numbers on the clock.

Another device that is good for time-telling practice (see fig. 11) is made to show written times digitally. This digital clock is made simply by sliding number strips through a small sheet of posterboard that has four pairs of slits in it. Note that the hour numbers and minute numbers are color coded to correspond with the clock shown in figure 10. Use this digital clock in conjunction with the two-handed clock. For example, display the digital clock (say 02:47) and have children set or draw in the hands on a two-handed clock to correspond with this time. "Funny times" look funny on a digital clock, too. For example, 6 minutes after 6 is written 06:06.

Regular Clocks

The changes from clocks with minute numbers to clocks without them becomes easy for children during the late primary years. They know how to count by fives and they also learn to multiply the hour numbers on a regular clock by five to determine the minute numbers that aren't present.

The standard curriculum will probably continue to include the terms *half past*, *quarter after*, and *quarter 'til* even though the move toward digital time reading is quite prevalent in our society. Certainly this terminology must be taught and understood by children. We have found, however, that when the traditional sequence of clock reading instruction is followed ("___o'clock," followed by "half past," followed by "quarter after" or "quarter 'til," followed by "minutes after" and "minutes before") each new level requires new concepts to be learned. Children who learn "quarter after" and "half past" have little to help them with "minutes after" or "minutes before."

We have found that by teaching time initially as minutes after the hour provides a conceptual framework into which all of the other usual clock terminology can be fit. To teach clock reading as suggested does admittedly require some modification in the usual sequence. We suggest that the terminology of *half past*, *quarter 'til*, and so on, be taught *after* the child can read a standard clock digitally.

Conclusion

This method of teaching children to tell time has been used effectively by many teachers with children ranging from age five through age twenty. Many older children are able to use this method to learn to tell time because all times are treated as "after the hour." Furthermore, the presence of the minute numbers on the clock eliminates extra mental calculating that must be completed with regular clocks.

It should be emphasized, however, that telling time (clock reading) and acquiring time concepts are not necessarily related. Many children can read clocks but don't possess good concepts about the passage of time. A good educational program, however, teaches children about the passage of time as they learn to read clocks. ●

Editor's note: A useful manipulative for learning to tell time on the digital clock can be made from a roll of adding machine tape. A strip of tape twenty-four feet long can be stretched across the room with the twenty-four hours marked on it, beginning with midnight. Have the children mark on it the times they get up, get on the bus, have lunch, go to bed, and so on. This type of aid will help teach both duration and sequencing. This model is very similar to that of having a week of seven days on a linear model. The children can be told that when the day ends, they merely go back to the left end and start all over for the next day. The digital clock is especially useful for the special education student who has particular difficulty with telling time. Special education teachers have commented that if it weren't for the digital clock, many of their students would never learn to tell time. However, it is important to provide a concrete model such as this digital number line.

Let's Do It

Teaching Time with Slit Clocks

By **Virginia M. Horak** *and* **Willis J. Horak**
College of Education, University of Arizona, Tucson, Arizona

The teaching of time in the primary grades should consist of activities of two distinct types. The first focuses on developing an understanding of the *concept* of time. This deals with the passage of time, the chronological sequencing of events, and the duration of time periods. The second type focuses on *telling* time. This includes reading a clock, recording time, and predicting times after determined intervals.

Concept-of-Time Activities

Children in the primary grades quite often are able to associate the positions of the hands of a clock with the occurrence of an event, such as eating dinner when the long hand is on 12

and the short hand is on 6. They may also be able to read the numerals representing an "exact" time from a digital clock. These abilities, however, do not insure that the children meaningfully grasp the idea of the passage of time. Activities of the following type are designed to develop this ability.

Activity one

This activity is designed to give children experiences in ordering and sequencing the events in their day. The teacher may begin with a class discussion on important things the children do on a typical day. A list containing such things as eating meals, catching the school bus, practicing soccer, starting school, doing mathematics,

and going to bed may be generated. The children then draw or collect pictures representing four or five of these events. The children next practice putting their pictures and those of other classmates in order. Later, the pictures can be assembled into a booklet entitled "Events in My Day" which the child can take home.

Activity two

Activity one deals with the passing of time in a day; children also need to sequence events over longer periods of time. Sprouting and growing of plants can be an effective means of doing this. Over a two week period, children draw pictures of planting and growing their individual bean plant. Later, from a scrambled set, they assemble these into the correct order. The teacher may then discuss with the children other events that happened during the same period of time—such things as a national holiday, a child's birthday, or a school assembly. In this way, the children begin to gain a "feeling" for longer periods of time.

Activity three

It is also useful to have children compare durations of time. This helps them begin to think about "how long" it takes to do certain things. A list may be made of the various activities done during the school day. It could include such things as recess, cleaning up the classroom, music class, reading class, and eating lunch. The children then vote on which activity they believe takes the least amount of time and which the most time. They may also be asked to compare various pairs of other activities, for example eating breakfast—eating dinner, riding to school—walking to school, and brushing teeth—taking a bath. The accuracy of their predictions can later be checked by actually timing the occurrences.

Activity four

Once children have worked with putting daily activities in chronological order, they are ready to begin estimating short durations of time. This is best done by beginning with one-minute intervals. Initially, the teacher must give children opportunities to experience one-minute periods. This can be done in a variety of ways, such as reading a book to the class for one minute, or having a child run in place for a minute.

The next step is to have the children estimate one-minute intervals. To do this they first put their heads down with their eyes closed. After the teacher says, "Begin," the children are to raise their heads when they think one minute has elapsed. Since some children may count to 60 during this activity, they may then be asked to estimate the time while doing something. This could include such events as singing a song or reading aloud. These activities help develop an intu-

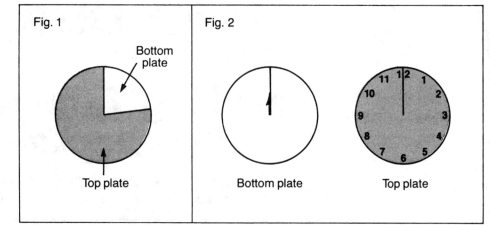

Fig. 1   Bottom plate   Top plate

Fig. 2   Bottom plate   Top plate

itive feeling for a common, basic unit of time. They also point out to the children that what they are doing affects their perception of the passing of time.

Activity five

After estimating intervals of one minute, children may be asked to consider longer periods of time. For example, the children can estimate the length of time it takes to play some songs on a record. This experience can then be extended to discussions about even longer time intervals such as lunch time, recess time, time until dismissal, and reading time. Children often underestimate the time they spend on "fun" activities and overestimate the time they spend doing tedious chores. Therefore, this activity can lead to a meaningful discussion about factors that affect our ability to estimate the duration of time.

Telling-Time Activities

Once the children are ready to begin "telling time," they will need a variety of activities with clock-type faces. Although digital clocks are commonplace, we suggest that most telling-time activities be done with circular model clocks. Digital clocks allow children to read time quickly and accurately, but they do not let children see what times come before or after a certain time. For example, it is difficult to "see" that 1:57 is almost 2:00 on a digital clock. Likewise, it is difficult to work with time concepts such as determining 30 minutes from 9:40.

Circular clock models (slit clocks) are made from inexpensive 9-inch pa-

per plates. They are an alternative to the commonly used numbered face with moveable hands. These slit clocks are advantageous because they allow the children to focus their attention on each aspect of telling time separately.

All slit clock faces are constructed similarly. The fronts of two paper plates are painted in contrasting colors. The two plates are stacked and a cut is made in both of them from the edge to the geometric center. Hold the two plates so the slit is vertical at the top of the plate. Open the slit, raising the left side of both plates. The bottom plate is then rotated clockwise as it comes from behind and covers the front plate. An example of the resulting interlocking plates is shown in figure 1.

Hour-face clocks

Initially, the children will be working with only the short (hour) hand and its associated numerals. It is helpful if every pair of children has a set of "clock faces" with which to work. The top plate is divided into 12 parts and numbered like a standard clock face. To make it easier for the students to do this, the teacher can cut notches in another paper plate at the location of the numbers. The students can then use this notched plate to mark their own clocks into twelfths. A thick, black arrow is marked on the left edge of the slit in the bottom plate. This arrow indicates the hour hand, and thus should extend only part of the way to the edge of the plate. Then the plates are again stacked together. Figure 2 illustrates this set of plates.

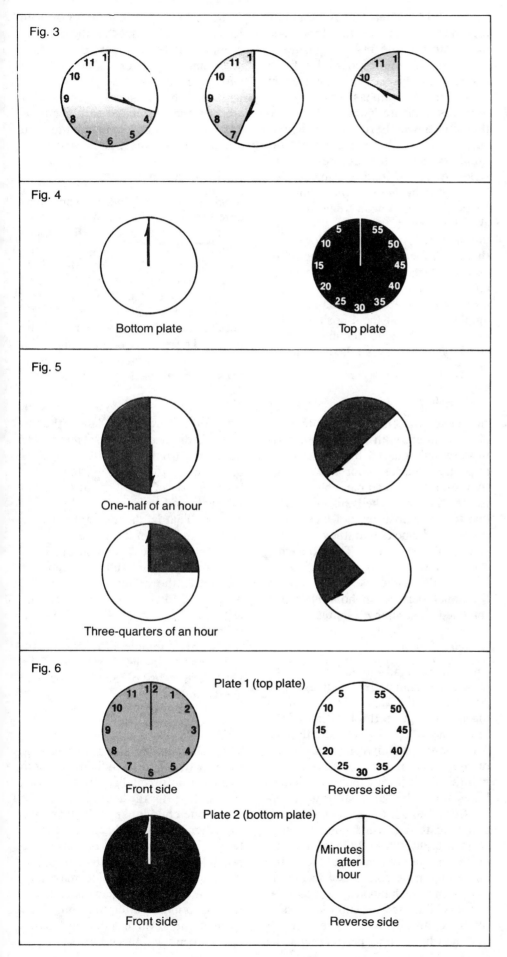

Fig. 3

Fig. 4

Bottom plate

Top plate

Fig. 5

One-half of an hour

Three-quarters of an hour

Fig. 6

Plate 1 (top plate)

Front side

Reverse side

Plate 2 (bottom plate)

Front side

Minutes after hour

Reverse side

Activity one

To begin working with these hour-face clocks, the teacher and children first rotate the bottom plate so that the short hand points to various numerals on the face. Explain that these show ''on-the-hour'' times, such as 2 o'clock, and 7 o'clock. Once the children recognize these positions, they are ready for approximate before-the-hour and after-the-hour times. Children need much practice on this activity so that later they will look first at the hour hand when they are reading clocks like those in figure 3. For example, the children should recognize the faces in figure 3 as representing ''a little after 3 o'clock,'' ''a little before 7 o'clock,'' and ''almost 10 o'clock.''

Activity two

The hour-face clocks can now be used to display approximate times of important happenings. The children can be asked to locate the position of the short hand at lunch time, recess, mathematics class, dinner time, and bedtime—to name a few events. This activity again reinforces the importance of the position of the short hand.

Activity three

Another activity that uses these hour-face clocks emphasizes the change in the position of the short hand during specific time intervals. One half of the class can be asked to set their short hands to indicate a specific hour. The other half of the class must then set their hand to indicate the time two hours later. Lastly, this same approach can be used when the hands start out a little before or a little after the hour.

Minute-face clocks

Before children work with telling time using the minute hand, they need experiences designed to acquaint them with common fractional parts of the hour. This can be done effectively with unnumbered clock faces. Another pair of plates is used, the top one is marked with 12 lines at the five minute intervals and the bottom one is marked with the long (minute) hand on the left side of the slit. This un-numbered minute-face clock is used in activity one. For activities two through four, the teacher and the children will need to make sets of numbered minute-face clocks, which are made in the following manner. One plate is divided into 12 equal segments, which are numbered by fives from 0 to 55 inclusive. On the other plate, a thick, black arrow is marked to represent the long (minute) hand. These are illustrated in figure 4. The plates are then stacked with the numbered plate on top and the bottom plate rotated in the usual manner. We suggest that this pair of plates be a different combination of colors than those previously constructed. In this way, the children themselves can easily select the clock faces appropriate for the various activities.

Activity one

To start out this activity, the teacher takes the unnumbered minute-face clocks and rotates the bottom plate clockwise one full turn. Children are able to watch the minute hand move and to see and learn that this indicates the passing of one full hour. The teacher may wish to begin with the slit in other locations, such as at the 3 or 6 positions, before making the full turn.

After seeing that a full, one-hour turn can begin anywhere, the children are ready to start investigating half-hour and quarter-hour turns. By manipulating the faces, the children are able to recognize one-half the clock face in various positions. Similarly, they need to become familiar with one-quarter and three-quarters of the clock face in various positions. Throughout this activity, the teacher must focus the children's attention on the colored fractional parts of the circles, not on the location of the clock hand. (See fig. 5.)

Activity two

Being able to count by fives is an important prerequisite to an understanding of telling time using the minute hand. Once the children can count by fives it is then necessary, for telling time, to associate each of these numbers with a position on the clock face.

To do this, the teacher and children together can rotate the long-hand plate, stop at the marked positions, and simultaneously count by fives. Along with this activity the teacher may want to emphasize that these numbers indicate minutes after on-the-hour times. Furthermore, it may be pointed out that these are not the numbers used for before-the-hour times. After the children can count by fives with the help of the numbered clock face, they can reinforce this skill by testing themselves with the unnumbered minute-face clock. On this clock face the children should be able to start at any marked position and count the number of minutes to another designated position. For example, starting at the 4-position, children should be able to count by fives to thirty as they move the hand to the 10-position.

Activity three

In this activity children learn to associate numbers with the geometrically represented quarter-hour, half-hour and three-quarters-hour turns of activity four. For example, children can rotate the unmarked plates into a quarter-hour position and then rotate the marked clocks until they show the same colored region. Thus the children can *see* that one quarter of an hour is the same as 15 minutes; a fractional part of an hour is simply renamed as so many minutes.

Activity four

The minute-hand clocks can also be used to develop understandings of the passing of time. This is done by showing the change in the location of the long hand after certain time intervals. The first interval investigated should, of course, be 30 minutes since it uses half the clock face. Children, originally, establish the half hour as the interval from 0 to 30; the idea can then be extended to a consideration of other 30-minute intervals. By looking at the entire, numbered minute face, the children can be challenged to find as many other such intervals as possible. Some children will subtract, while others count by fives. They should find half-hour time periods such as

from 5 to 35, from 20 to 50, or from 10 to 40. It is important that the children realize that the numbers on the face still stand for minutes after-the-hour, while the intervals they are working with tell the passing of time. This work is then extended to other periods of time such as 15 minutes, 20 minutes, 40 minutes, and 45 minutes.

Self-checking clocks

Since regular clock faces are not numbered from 5 to 55, it is necessary for children to be able to associate these quantities with their locations on the clock face. That is, they should be able to state that when the long hand points to four, it is 20 minutes after the hour. To help children do this another set of the slit clocks can be made. These are self-checking with the number of minutes after the hour shown on the back side of the clock face.

Once again, two colored plates with slits in them are used. Plate 1 (the top plate) is divided into 12 segments and numbered from 1 to 12. The multiples of 5, from 5 to 55, are written on the reverse side of this plate at the usual intervals and in counterclockwise direction. That is, the numeral 5 will be directly in back of the 1, the 10 directly in back of the 2, and so on. Both sides of plate 1 are shown in figure 6.

Plate 2 (the bottom plate) has the usual long arrow marked along the left-hand edge of the slit on the front side. On the reverse side of this plate, the words "minute after hour" are written along the left-hand edge of the slit. Both sides of plate 2 are also shown in figure 6.

Activity one

The self-checking slit clocks can be used by the children individually or in pairs to reinforce telling time in terms of minutes after the hour. To do this in pairs, one child looks at the front and the other child at the back of the clock faces. The hand may be turned to point to a numeral on the front. The child looking at this side may then say, "When the long hand is on the 9, it is 45 minutes after the hour." By reading the reverse side, the child's partner can tell if this is correct. Alter-

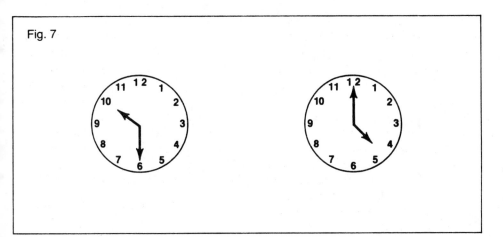

Fig. 7

nately, the clocks could be turned and the child looking at the reverse could state, "When it is 25 minutes after the hour, the long hand is on 5." By reading the front side of the clocks, the partner can tell if this is correct.

Activity two

An extension of activity one is to make a set of slit clocks that tells before-the-hour times. These clocks are similar to those in figure 6, except that the reverse side of plate 1 is numbered from 5 to 55 in a *clockwise* direction. Also, the reverse side of plate 2 should read "minutes before the hour." Since in our everyday communications we rarely go beyond 25 minutes before the hour, the teacher may wish to stop numbering at 25. As in the preceding activity, these clocks are used in a self-checking manner.

Two-hand clock face

After working with the slit clocks that show the long and short hands independently, the children are ready for activities with two-hand clocks. Initial activities should be done with old clocks whose hands are still geared to move together. For other activities it will be necessary for the children to make a two-hand clock from one numbered paper plate, two cardboard hands, and a brass fastener.

Activity one

After children are proficient at using the hour-face clock (with its associated short hand) and the minute-face clock (with its associated long hand),

they are ready to incorporate the two concepts into a single clock. To do this, the standard clock face with both hands is used. By moving the hands of such a clock, the children can actually *see* that the long, minute hand makes one complete turn (revolution) while the short, hour hand moves from one numeral to the next.

Children should now be ready to practice positioning both hands of a clock for given times. This can be done by first having the children make their own clock faces with moveable hands. In all of the previous activities, children were working with one-hand clock faces only and consequently did not write down times in the common hour:minute notation. The teacher may want to introduce this notation and provide practice with it. This could involve the teacher saying, "The time is 15 minutes after two o'clock" or "It is seven thirty-five," while the children write 2:15 and 7:35 respectively. After this, the children can position the hands of their clock to show the given times. Much of the early work should center around the exact hour and half-hour times, since the children can position the hour hand accurately for these times. For other times, children only need to understand a little less than half way and a little more than half way between the numerals for the hour hand.

Activity two

Another worthwhile activity is for children to recognize and demonstrate impossible combinations of hand positions on their clocks. This is necessary since the hands can be put in any

position on the student-made clock. Some of the impossible combinations are shown in figure 7.

Children may not realize the related positions of the hands, with the current emphasis on digital clocks. On a digital clock, they see the hour numerals remain the same for the entire one-hour period, and then move in one jump as the minute numerals change from 59. They expect the hour hand on the clock to move in a comparable way.

Activity three

Finally, children may use their two-hand clocks to show the passage of time. Children need to be aware of the fact that a clock measures the passage of time no matter where the hands begin. For example, beginning with the minute hand on 6 and the hour hand between 10 and 11, the children should be able to predict where both hands will be after 30 minutes. Everyday situations can be used to reinforce this concept. If spelling class starts at 10:45 and lasts for 20 minutes, the children should be able to state that the class is over when the long, minute hand is on one and the short, hour hand is just after 11. Similarly, if they are to clean-up 10 minutes before lunch, they should know when to begin.

Summary

A set of self-made, slit clocks provides a concrete approach to developing the concept of time. The progression of clock faces, each a little more detailed than the preceding one, allows children to focus on each part of the clock independently. The activities also allow children to work with spoken as well as written time. This is useful since the children's first exposure to time is their families' verbal reference to it in everyday situations. Although the activities dealing with the passage of time were discussed in this article prior to those focusing on the telling of time, it is better if both concepts can be developed together. Concepts of time develop slowly and the paper-plate models need to be available throughout the year. ◗

4

Graphs and Charts

Let's Do It

Collecting and Displaying the Data Around Us

By **Virginia M. Horak** and **Willis J. Horak**, *College of Education, University of Arizona, Tucson, Arizona*

Fig. 1

Young children are interested in answering questions about themselves and their surroundings—What colors of eyes do the children in our class have? How many in the class are left-handed? How many of our class were born in the spring, summer, fall and winter? Questions like these can be answered by constructing charts and graphs to present the information.

Graphing is a means of organizing and representing information in order to make it meaningful and useful. Graphs can range from the very concrete kind that uses actual objects to more complex forms such as circle and line graphs. The activities in this article deal with representing student-collected information by means of reusable pictorial graphs, tally charts, bar graphs, and circle graphs.

Reusable Teaching Aids

Directions for making three teaching aids are included here. These reusable aids are large enough to be used for classroom discussion. Their use may be supplemented with smaller, individual copies for use by students.

Pictorial graph board

The reusable teaching aid for pictorial graphs is made by covering a 60-cm-by-100-cm rectangular piece of cardboard or light-weight soft wood with flannel material. This board can be used with the longer dimension either horizonal or vertical. Actual objects or cut-out figures are thumb tacked to the board in rows or columns to represent collected data. Figure 1 is a picture of such a board with student-collected data displayed.

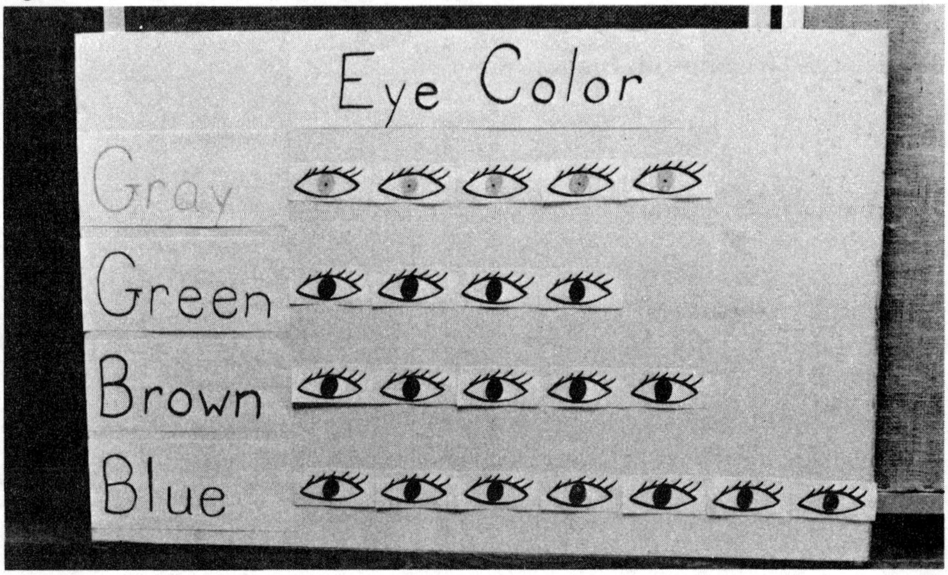

Tally chart

The second teaching aid is a reusable tally chart. Commercially produced pocket charts are available, but you can construct one of your own. For the self-constructed type, a finished chart that is 60 cm by 100 cm is sufficient. To construct a chart this size, you will need a piece of cardboard 60 cm by 100 cm and a piece of construction paper 120 cm by 100 cm. Measuring along the long side of construction paper, lines for folding are drawn at the following intervals:

2 cm, 12 cm, 7 cm, 19 cm, 7 cm, 19 cm, 7 cm, 19 cm, 7 cm, 19 cm, and 2 cm

The folds 2 cm from the top and bottom will fold around the cardboard backing. The construction paper is folded back and forth along the other lines to produce the four pockets as illustrated in figure 2. The folded con-

struction paper is then stapled securely to the cardboard backing.

Ribbon bar graph

A third type of graph usable at the primary level is the bar graph. A reusable, ribbon bar graph can be made from a sheet of white tagboard about 56 cm by 65 cm and two rolls of ribbon, one white and one red, that are about 4 cm wide. The longer sides of the tagboard will be the top and bottom of the bar graph. About 15 cm from the left edge of the board, cut 5 vertical slits. These slits should be 4.5 cm long and 6 cm apart, beginning about 5 cm from the top. A second set of slits is made directly opposite the first set and 5 cm from the right edge. The slits should be cut out to make them about 0.5 cm wide. This extra width in the slit allows the ribbon to move smoothly through the slit. This is especially necessary for the places

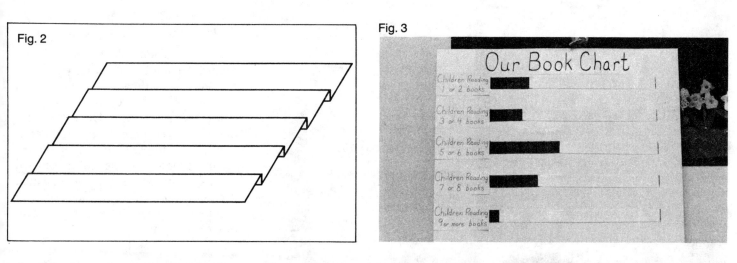

Fig. 2

Fig. 3

where the two colors are sewn together.

Two strips of ribbon are cut, one white and one colored, and each about 56 cm long (the distance between the slits on the board.) The two pieces of ribbon are joined (sewed) together at one end. The two-color, long ribbon is then strung through a pair of slits and the remaining ends are connected to form a loop. This is repeated for the five pairs of slits. When the ribbons are in place, the colored ribbons are each marked off at intervals of 2 cm. Figure 3 shows a completed bar graph representing data about the number of books read by children in a second-grade class during a two-week period.

When you begin to use the ribbon graph, the white ribbon is showing on the front of the graph. As the ribbon is pulled through the slits, the contrasting ribbon color represents the quantity for a given category. The markings on the colored ribbon show you how far to pull the colored ribbon.

To facilitate changing the categories on the chart from one graph to another, the space along the sides of the left slits can be covered with clear Contact paper. It is then easy to write categories with a grease pencil and to erase them. Contact paper can also be used on the tally chart in the same manner.

Graphing Activities

The data collected in the activities that follow can be displayed on more than one of the charts described. Young children must begin with concrete activities that make use of actual

objects. The pictorial graph board and tally chart are useful in this regard. The bar graph can be used most successfully after children have had experiences with concrete, hands-on materials.

Personal data activities

Effective introductory activities may involve collecting data relating to the physical characteristics of the students. This type of data is easy to collect directly in the classroom.

Activity one

The tally chart is the easiest to use for these activities. All that is needed is for each student to have a card with her or his name on it. For example, to construct a chart displaying data relating to hair color, the children and teacher must first identify the categories—blond, brown, and so on. These are listed on the tally chart. Each child then places her or his name card alongside the appropriate category.

This same approach can be used to display data collected about eye color, sex, month of birth, height, right- and left-handedness, number of siblings living in the home, and so on. For physical characteristics such as heights, which require measurement, the teacher may have to identify the relevant categories. Broad categories such as "less than four feet tall" and "four feet tall or over" could be used. Finer divisions can be used to give more categories.

A pictorial graph can also be used to display physical data. This might be especially useful for young children or for those experiencing their first work

with graphing. To make this type of graph with eye-color data, cut out felt or construction paper eyes of various colors. Children then choose the color of eye appropriate for themselves and attach it to the chart. The visual display is very concrete and can precede the tally-chart activities if necessary.

In displaying data about a class, it is not necessary to identify individual children. For example, one child may be asked to stand in front of the class, call out the category names, count the number of children who stand as each category is called, and record this data on the tally chart. The data is recorded with impersonal tally markers, such as strips of paper or popsicle sticks, rather than with name cards. This extends the data-displaying scheme to a slightly more abstract form.

Activity two

Children may also collect data relating to larger groups of students. This usually involves gathering information on personal preferences. With your help, children can develop a questionnaire relating to some of their likes and dislikes. Frequently used preference polls include topics such as favorite ice cream flavor, color, television program, outdoor activity, and so on. Initially you may want to select topics with only two choices, such as chocolate milk and white milk. For other topics, it may be necessary to list only the most common categories for a topic and to group various single choices under the heading, "other." The preference questionnaire can also be used to collect data on children in

Fig. 4

Activity one

Children can be asked to count and record the number of doors, windows, and mirrors in their homes. This data can then be represented on tally charts or histograms. Once the children try to represent large numbers of doors or windows, they will soon see the need for letting one picture or card represent more than one object. Thus, it may be convenient for one pictorial window to represent ten counted windows.

Activity two

A second type of home data collected relates to measurable quantities. These may include such things as distance from school, the amount of water or electricity used in a month, or the length of the longest wall in the house. The amount of water or electricity used can be read directly from the monthly bill.

Once again, the data can be represented in the two ways discussed in the preceding activity three. The method you select depends on the types of questions you want answered. If you want to focus on data collected by individual children, then a chart listing their names would be appropriate. If you want to focus on group data and overall trends, then charts identifying broad categories of the measured quantity would be appropriate. The following questions are some suggestions: What is the most common number of windows in the homes? Who lives the farthest from school? Who has the longest room in her or his house? How many houses have the least number of doors? What is the most amount of water used in a home?

School grounds data activities

The school grounds offer many opportunities for children to collect meaningful data. The grounds also allow children to collect and present different types of data about the same items.

Activity one

Playground equipment is a source of much data. Initially, the children can

other designated classrooms, such as all the third grade classes.

An alternative activity can involve children in one class collecting preference data and then making inferences about the preferences of children in other classrooms. Figure 4 represents preference data from a third grade class related to children's favorite team sport. The following questions can be discussed based on this graph. What team sport do you think will be the favorite in the other two third grade classes? There are 58 pupils in the other two classes, how many of them do you think will like baseball/softball? What do you think will be the least favorite sport among the other third graders? Can you determine boys' and girls' preferences from the chart? Do you think first graders will like the same sports third graders do? These inferences can then be checked by giving the questionnaire to children in the other classes. Through an activity like this, children can become aware of the possible errors in conclusions drawn from sampling procedures.

Activity three

A third type of data that can be collected from individual students pertains to their personal accomplishments. These may involve physical activities such as ball throwing, jump-ing rope, doing sit-ups, distance jumps, and timed running. Student accomplishments may also include academic achievements such as spelling scores, number of mathematics facts mastered, books read, and papers completed without errors.

The collected data can be displayed in either of two ways. You can list an activity and some of the children's names on the bar graph. The selected children then in turn record their results by moving the appropriate colored ribbon on the chart. To do this each segment of the colored ribbon must represent a convenient unit. Other children may later display their data for different events.

The second way of representing the data involves using the tally chart or pictorial graph. Select the activity and identify the outcome levels for that activity. For jumping rope, for example, the categories might include 5 or less, 6 to 10, 11 to 15, 16 to 20, and 21 or over. For the tally chart, the children place their own name cards in the correct place. For the pictorial graph, children attach a picture or cut-out shape of an appropriate figure to represent themselves.

Home data activities

The children's homes also offer many opportunities for collecting data.

determine how many there are of each type of equipment. For example, they can count the number of swings, sand-boxes, monkey bars, slides, balance beams, and so on. This data can then be displayed on a pictorial graph, a talley chart, or a bar graph. The categories for the graphs are the various types of equipment.

Activity two

After the types of equipment have been identified, the children can collect data concerning the number of students who use each of the types of equipment. This can be done most easily by designating a before-school time as "counting time." At the appropriate time, each pair of children is responsible for counting the number of children on a particular piece of playground equipment. This information is brought to the classroom and once again displayed on an appropriate chart or graph.

Activity three

Another type of data about the playground equipment that can be collected and displayed on a graph involves the children or the teacher finding out the cost of each piece of playground equipment. Usually this requires that the teacher look up the information in a catalog in the main offices. This data can then be displayed on a bar graph.

Making use of graphs

The data collected in the preceding three activities can be used simultaneously to draw conclusions and make inferences. Since the data cannot all be displayed at once on the charts you have made, it will be necessary for the students to reproduce the graphs on paper for their own use. You may conduct classroom discussions about the data and the relationships between them. Some questions cannot be answered directly from the graphs, as the following questions illustrate: What is the most popular playground equipment? What is the least popular playground equipment? The school has the least of which type of equipment? Which equipment is used mostly by boys? by girls? Is the

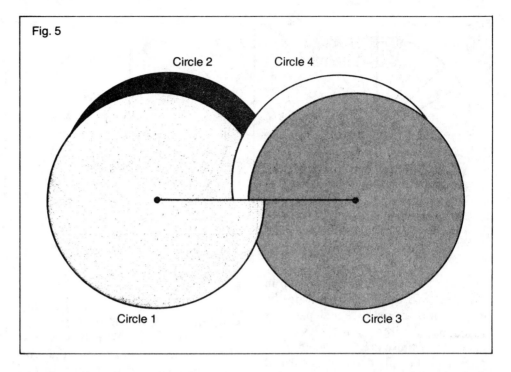

Fig. 5

Circle 2
Circle 4
Circle 1
Circle 3

cheapest equipment used by the least number of children? If the school could buy one more type of equipment, what should it buy? Why? By discussing questions such as these, children begin to realize the importance of graphs and charts in problem solving and everyday decision-making.

Along with the previous activities it is important that children be made aware of data that is reported in magazines and newspapers. You may wish to construct a data bulletin board that contains clippings the children have brought to school. Some of the data available in newspapers and magazines may pertain to scientific topics; public opinion polls; advertisement-related data, such as price comparisons; and historical information. For younger children such an activity is important since it points out the widespread use by adults of data, graphs, and charts. In the upper elementary grades, this data can be used to create numerous other graphs and charts that lead to further discussions.

Circle Graphs

Along with pictorial graphs, tally charts, and bar graphs, it is important that children gain an understanding of circle graphs. The circle graph is most useful after children have grasped the basic ideas of representing data. Circle graphs are important because they display a fractional comparison of quantities. This topic is frequently postponed until the intermediate grades, however, when the children have had a formal introduction to angle measurement. Teachers in the lower elementary grades can help children gain intuitive feelings for the relationships displayed by circle graphs by using the following types of activities.

Reusable circle graph

A reusable circle graph can be made from three or four circular shapes cut from heavy paper. The circular shapes should be of different colors and approximately 45 cm in diameter. One cut is made in each, from the center of the circle, along a radius, to the outside edge. The circular shapes are then entwined as shown in figure 5. By rotating the various shapes, children can represent approximate fractional comparisons of collected data.

Using a circle graph

Activity one

Personal data collected in the classroom can be displayed on a circle graph providing you prepare the circle

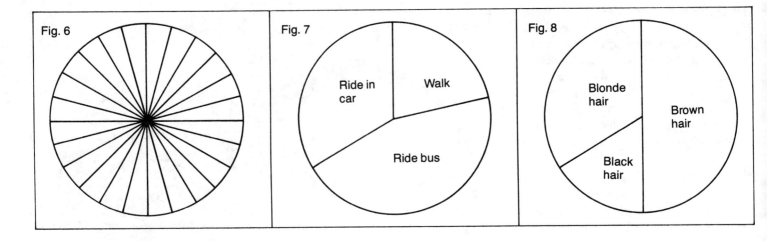

Fig. 6

Fig. 7

Ride in car

Walk

Ride bus

Fig. 8

Blonde hair

Brown hair

Black hair

graph to fit the number of children in the class. To do this, first divide the circles into as many equal parts as there are children in the class. For example, if there are 24 students, the circles must be divided into 24 parts of equal size. This is done by dividing 360° by 24, giving 15°. Using a protractor, the teacher begins at the slit and measures successive angles of 15°. Figure 6 shows a circular shape separated into 24 parts. Since the children will be dealing with general observations, it is not necessary to worry about "exact" fractional parts of a degree. The main objective is to get the circles divided into parts of approximately equal size.

Collecting data for these circle graphs can be very similar to the activities for collecting personal data. For example, children can be asked if they walked, rode the bus, or rode in a car to get to school. One circle of the interlocking circle graph then represents the number of children who walked, a second circle represents those who rode to school in a car. The results are displayed on the circle graph by moving the interlocking circles the appropriate number of segments. Figure 7 shows a circle graph constructed for a class of 24 students in which 5 walked to school, 11 rode the bus and 8 rode to school in a car.

Other similar graphs can be constructed using data collected about such things as type of shoe worn, type of lunch eaten, national origin, and sex. In addition to these, many of the other previously discussed personal characteristics can be displayed on the circle graphs.

Activity two

Simpler circle graphs can be constructed if you wish to work with fractional parts such as halves, thirds, and fourths. This will require that you use somewhat contrived situations to get the fractions you want. For example, a group of twelve children can be used to collect personal data for these graphs. Children will readily see that a subgroup of six students is 1/2 of the total group and thus must be represented on the circle graph by 1/2 of a circle. Similarly, a subgroup of three students must be represented by 1/4 of one of the circles. With a little foresight, it is easy to choose a group of twelve children such that six have brown hair, four have blond hair, and two have black hair. This would result in the circle graph showing 1/2, 1/3, and 1/6 in figure 8.

Circle graphs are especially helpful when children want to consider the data collected as a whole. From the graph in figure 8, it is easy to see that the number of brown-haired children is equal to the number of black-haired children combined with the number of blond-haired children. It is also easy to see that if this graph represents the hair color for a group of ten children, then five of them will have brown hair. Thus, relative comparisons are easier to make with circle graphs than with tally charts or bar graphs.

Summary

The preceding activities were meant to supplement the drill and practice activities necessary in the primary grades. The activities introduce children to one of the ways mathematics is used every day. They also make children apply the number data they collect to solve problems. Graphs can be important for children of all ability levels. The graphs can vary from highly concrete representations where children put actual objects on the displays to abstract forms where one symbol or unit represents a large quantity. Making mathematics meaningful can be as simple as counting heads. ▰

Graphing for Any Grade

By **William Nibbelink**

This article reports an instructional sequence for teaching graphing that has been extensively field tested in each of grades kindergarten through six. What is outlined in this article need not be used as a "graphing unit" in the usual sense. Graphing is better treated as an ongoing activity. Too often it is treated in a "crash course" manner just before standardized test time. The field testing of the sequences described here showed that even sixth graders who had studied several of the traditional "crash course" graphing units demonstrated a remarkable lack of basic concept learning. The instructional sequence advocated here is atypical in the following ways:

1. It begins with point graphs and later introduces bar graphs and pictographs as merely ornamental forms.

2. It employs a "slider" or "movable y-axis" to begin with minimal clutter and low perceptual demands on children.

3. Graphs are constructed before reading graphs is required.

Any chalkboard or bulletin board will do. If the board to be used has a track, the slider may be designed as shown by figure 1. If not, the chalk tray may be used to carry the slider as shown in figure 2. The latter is second best, since the slider may tend to obscure the x-scale a bit—a minor problem, however.

The slider should be constructed so

William Nibbelink is a member of the division of elementary and early childhood education at the University of Iowa, Iowa City. His more recent work focuses primarily on grades K–2.

that y-scales are easily removed and replaced. Scales used in the various field testings included a 0-to-10 scale, as shown by figure 1; a 0-to-100 scale; a clinical thermometer scale; and two outdoor thermometer scales. The grade level of the children places limits on the complexity of the scales. For example, the kindergarten classes used only a 0-to-10 scale and a 0-to-20 scale for situations calling for numbered scales. The grade level also determines what pace is reasonable and to which step in the following sequence the instruction should be carried.

Step one

Use discrete x-data such as days of the week, months of the year, children's names. For each x-coordinate, move the slider to that position and draw a point to match the corresponding y-coordinate. *No horizontal or vertical lines* appear on the graph at this time, only points. To read the graph, move the slider (y-axis) to the x-coordinate of interest and then read the y-coordinate matching the point. *Only after children participate in making several graphs* should they be required to read graphs already made.

At least two different y-scales should be used during step 1. Examples of x, y pairs that can be used are day, number of children ill; month, number of birthdays; day, high temperature; name, shoe size; day, number of spills in the lunchroom—whatever it takes to capture the children's interest, within the limits of decency, of course. As a general rule, the data should be determined easily by chil-

dren as a graph is constructed, or should be presented in table form before construction of a graph begins.

Step two

Suggest that the graphs of step one appear a bit plain to some folks, or suggest that to some the little points (dots) may be difficult to see. The solution: heavy lines to connect each x-entry to its little dot. Stress that the graphs are still the same, only a bit fancier to some folks' way of thinking. Figure 2 shows figure 1 modified to the bar-graph form. The same advice holds for step two as for step one: only after children participate in making several bar graphs should they be required to read bar graphs already made. In making bar graphs, (1) move the slider into position, (2) draw the dot as with step one, (3) pause, and (4) draw the bar (line) using the slider as the straightedge.

Step three

Suggest that for an even more pleasing effect, some folks prefer "fancy bars," bars made of little pictures of the things being talked about. Beyond being very fancy, the pictograph allows the clever person to read the graph without actually moving the slider.

To introduce the idea of one picture representing a fixed number of referents, use the 0-to-100 y-scale and "complain" that too much drawing and ridiculously small pictures would result from drawing a picture for each unit. The instructional sequence for step three is identical to that for step two.

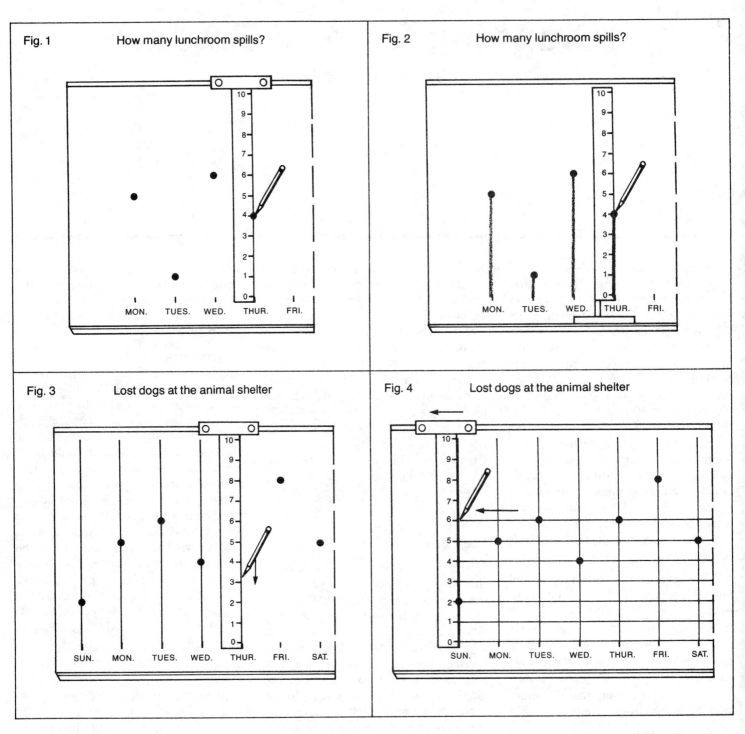

Fig. 1   How many lunchroom spills?

Fig. 2   How many lunchroom spills?

Fig. 3   Lost dogs at the animal shelter

Fig. 4   Lost dogs at the animal shelter

Step four

With an easy-to-read *point graph posted*, make up a story: over the coming weekend a witch (or a grinch or whoever is in season) will nail or glue the slider to the left of the graph. The challenge: to somehow fix the graph so that it will be readable after this evil befalls the slider over the weekend.

The first concern is that it may be difficult for some to see which point is "straight above" which x-entry. By a short forced-discovery discussion, get agreement to the idea of drawing a light vertical line for each x-entry. *Use the slider as a straightedge for each such line, as shown by figure 3.*

The second concern is that it may be difficult to tell just which number on the slider matches a point when the slider is nailed or glued to the left. Again, by a little discussion, get agreement to the idea of drawing a horizontal line for each y-entry. Draw each horizontal line as follows: *hold a marker at the number and move the*

slider all the way from right to left, as shown in figure 4.

After thus completing the usual vertical and horizontal lines, pretend that the slider is fixed in place to the left. To read an entry, (1) point to the x-entry, (2) move the finger up the line to the point, (3) pause, (4) move the finger along the line to the left, and (5) read the number from the slider/ (*Note:* Especially with younger children, this one-finger procedure is critical to success.)

Step four should be repeated for

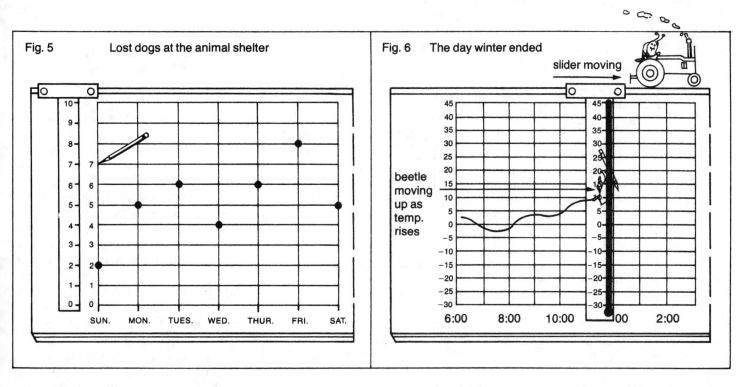

Fig. 5   Lost dogs at the animal shelter

Fig. 6   The day winter ended

slider moving

beetle moving up as temp. rises

both bar graphs and pictographs. Call attention to the fact that with these graph forms the vertical lines are not needed and are usually not included.

Step five

With an easy-to-read *point graph posted*, announce that over the coming weekend the slider will actually be stolen ("borrowed" would do also). Draw the vertical and horizontal lines as with step four, mainly as review. Then, by a short discussion, get agreement to simply copying the numbers from the slider to the left of the graph, as shown by figure 5. If considered necessary, repeat this for a bar graph and for a pictograph.

Step six

Using graph paper, have children construct and read a variety of point graphs, bar graphs, and pictographs. With younger children, use widely spaced vertical and horizontal lines to make the graphs perceptually easy and to allow the children to use a finger to read them. Give children plenty of practice. This step should be considered to be a time for "overlearning" to insure retention.

Step seven

Introduce horizontal bar graphs and pictographs. To read an entry, point

to the item of interest on the left, move to the right to the end of the bar, and drop down to read the *x*-entry. Explain simply that some folks, at times, think horizontal bars are more pleasing to look at than vertical bars.

Step eight

Repeat step six, but with a mix of vertical and horizontal graphs. This is another practice period to insure retention.

Step nine

Create a pair of creatures, like Bert and Bertha Beetle, who specialize in the art of making graphs. Attach a small tractor to the slider, as shown in figure 6. The tractor is to be driven by one of the beetles. (It's Bertha's turn today.) Use a temperature scale on the slider. Give the second beetle (that will be Bert) a pencil and allow him to run up and down the slider with the pencil. Use time of day for the *x*-scale, as shown in figure 6.

Now explain how these remarkable beetles construct "continuous graphs." Bertha will drive the tractor very steadily so that the slider will reach "10:00" at exactly ten o'clock, "12:00" at exactly twelve o'clock, and so on. Bert will keep the pencil exactly at the correct temperature at all times, climbing up the slider as the

temperature rises and backing down as the temperature falls. Then, slowly move the slider from left to right with one hand while moving Bert with his pencil up or down. Allow members of the class to make up weather conditions as time flies by. Figure 7 shows a possible result. To read the graph after it is constructed, remove the beetles and the slider and use the one-finger procedure described by step four.

Several such continuous graphs should be constructed and then read. A variety of *y*-scales may be used to cover such information as the time of day, wind speed; time of day, classroom noise level; and so on. (Bert and Bertha should take turns driving the tractor in order to avoid sex stereotyping.)

Step ten

Study a wide variety of graphs from books, newspapers, magazines—wherever. Many variations not covered by steps one through nine will show up, such as multiple graphs, bar graphs using a single picture for each bar, graphs showing area under a curve, and so forth. By this time, however, all the basic concepts of graphing should be established. The study is that of exploring the number of options available to the creative mind.

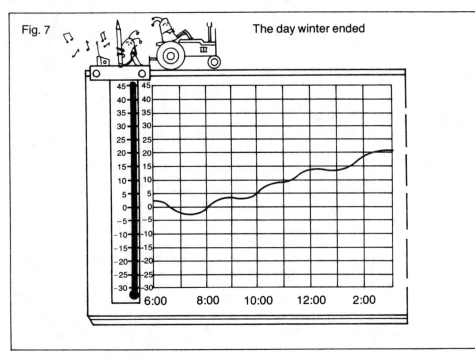

Fig. 7

The day winter ended

Other Considerations

Introducing children to the usual vocabulary that goes with graphing may be done either during the instructional sequence or after its completion. In general, it is better to delay the introduction of a term (word) until after the corresponding concept is established.

The usual business—locating points given ordered pairs of numbers, and writing ordered pairs of numbers given points—is not an integral part of the instructional sequence presented here. It may be either delayed until after completion of the instructional sequence or inserted at any point after step four. While knowledgeable adults know that graphs are sets of order pairs, many elementary school children fail to see the plotting and reading of points in the plane as even related to graphing. When (if) this topic should be included may be determined primarily by the level of mathematical maturity of the children.

How far to carry the instructional sequence (through which step) also should be determined by the level of mathematical maturity of the children. Two of the kindergarten classes who field-tested the sequence easily completed step six, sometimes using pictures to represent *x*-coordinates. All of the kindergarten classes easily completed step four.

Notes on Design

Many graphing units and textbook treatments of the topic begin with horizontal graphs. The vertical was treated first by this sequence for the following reasons:

1. To the degree that children will be required to or encouraged to associate graphing with measurement concepts, comparisons of heights relative to a common base are easier. This is especially true for younger children who may still suffer left-right reversal tendencies.

2. The construction of a slider featuring a horizontal axis presents more of an engineering problem than most teachers would accept.

Perhaps even more important for younger children, this two-step, physical manipulation—both to construct and to read a graph—relieves the child of any requirement to consider two variables simultaneously. Steps one through five and the reading parts of steps six through eight are appropriate to the intuitive, preoperational stage a la Piaget. Moving the slider into place, the necessary first step, is done by focusing only on one variable. Making a point or reading a point's location, the second step also is done by focusing only on one variable. The "one-finger procedure" stressed by step 4 insures that the child will persist in

dealing with the two variables in order rather than simultaneously, even after the slider becomes fixed to the left and, then, is removed. Briefly, it insures that thought will be dominated by memories of actions involving objects.

As to whether graphing is (should be) introduced as a counting or as a measurement activity, the suggested instructional sequence allows for either and demands neither. Only recognizing proximity is required of the child. For example, pictures of a bird, a squirrel, and a puppy could serve as *x*-entries with pictures of a nest, a hole in a tree, and a dog house serving as *y*-entries. The procedure for assigning animals to homes would be the same as for dealing with pairs involving measurement or counting. Rather than requiring either measurement or counting, the graphing method described offers a vehicle for encountering such topics. Anyone's point of view on which of these topics should be stressed and in what order may be honored by the appropriate selection of scales and situations. In fact, both may be stressed at once by the use of a *y*-scale that represents height by toothpicks glued end to end.

To keep the maximum number of interpretations open to the child regarding counting and measurement, equal distances between entries on scales are appropriate. Furthermore, equal distances between entries look better to the writer's (and probably to most readers') traditional sense of comeliness.

Granted, constructing a slider and scales may mean a trip to the lumber yard or hardware store and an evening's work. It is time well spent. ♥

Probability and Statistics

Let's Do It

Looking at Facts

By **David R. O'Neil** *and* **Rosalie Jensen,** *Georgia State University, Atlanta, Georgia*

The teaching of concepts of statistics and probability in the elementary school offers many opportunities to use "real" data, as well as to provide practice in fundamental operations with numbers. It is important that children begin early in their study of mathematics to develop the techniques of collecting, organizing, and analyzing data. These skills should lead naturally to the making of predictions and, thus, to the study of probability.

We believe the study of probability and statistics should be of an exploratory nature in the elementary school. Emphasis should be on an informal approach encompassing experimentation and exploration. The experiences suggested in this article will provide students with opportunities to learn the desired concepts through informal, exploratory activities.

Statistics

The first statistics concepts children are exposed to in the elementary mathematics classroom usually are those of interpreting and organizing data. This is accomplished most meaningfully if data collected or supplied by the students themselves are used. Activity one suggests data you might ask students to gather, plus several ways of "graphing" that data.

Activity one

With the children, survey your class to determine students' favorite ice cream flavor. Make a table similar to the one in figure 1 to record the results. Transfer the data from the table to a bar graph or a pictograph like the uncompleted one in figure 2.

Before constructing the suggested table or graph, students might use any of the following techniques to record the data they collect.

(1) Make card labels for each brand of ice cream chosen and stack blocks by each one to represent the votes each brand received (fig. 3). Students would thus form a three-dimensional graph of their data.

(2) Use an abacus or a counting frame and beads to represent the data by category. A narrow piece of wood with dowel sticks stuck in it works well for this activity (fig. 4).

(3) Use gummed labels upon which students write their favorite ice cream. Stick the labels on a piece of poster board or construction paper (fig. 5).

Ask questions about the completed graph:

• What kind of ice cream is liked by the most students?
• Did any kinds of ice cream receive the same number of votes?
• Which kind of ice cream received the fewest votes?

After students have had several experiences gathering and graphing data of their own, ask them to interpret already prepared simple graphs like the bar graph in figure 6. For younger students you may wish to include horizontal lines representing the values on the vertical scale, which will make the graph easier to read. You might also have them convert the bar graph to a pictograph or three-dimensional "block" graph like the one in figure 3.

Activity two

Give students a graph showing the number of hours five different children spent watching television on a particular day (fig. 6). Ask questions about the graph:

• Who watched the most TV?
• Who watched the least TV?
• Of the five children questioned, did any *not* watch TV?
• What else can you conclude from the graph?

Activity three

Many times in "real life" it is necessary to sift through data to determine what is necessary or relevant in order to solve a particular problem. We believe students should be given numerous situations in which both relevant and irrelevant data are presented, thus requiring the students to decide what is needed.

This activity is such a problem of this type. Discuss with your students what data they would need if they were to—

• make a graph or table showing the day of the week each student was born on;
• make a graph or table showing the size shoe each student wears;
• make a graph or table showing how each student got to school.

To help children recognize extraneous information, ask questions about what information is needed. For example, in gathering data for the first graph, ask questions such as, Would you need to know the age of each student? Would you need to know the time of day each student was born?

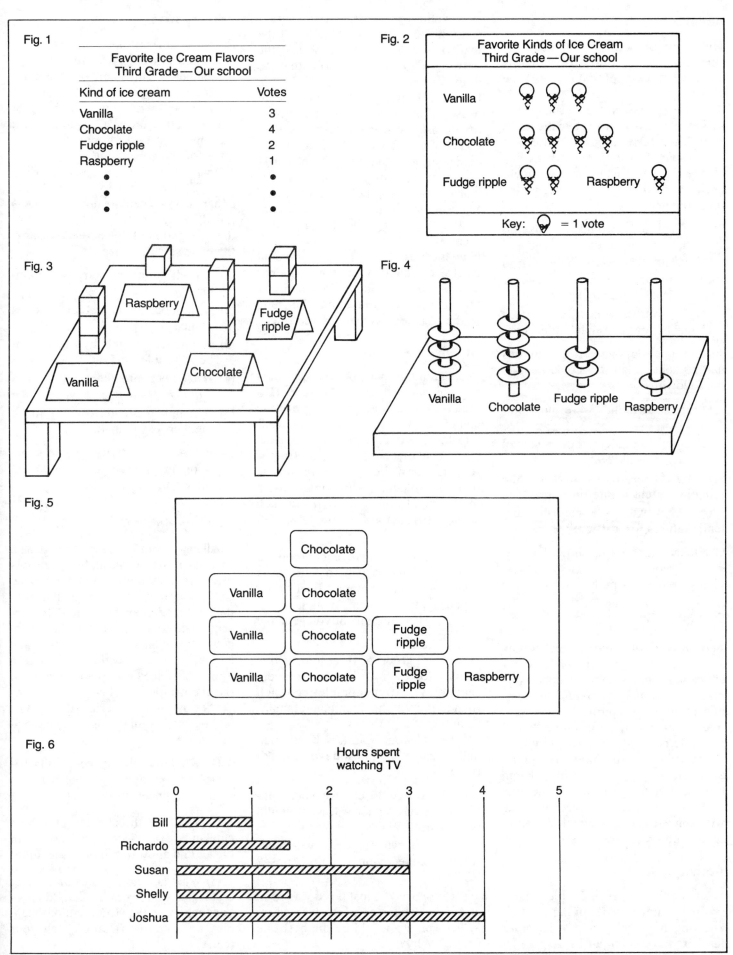

Fig. 1

Favorite Ice Cream Flavors
Third Grade — Our school

Kind of ice cream	Votes
Vanilla	3
Chocolate	4
Fudge ripple	2
Raspberry	1
•	•
•	•
•	•

Fig. 2

Favorite Kinds of Ice Cream
Third Grade — Our school

Vanilla

Chocolate

Fudge ripple   Raspberry

Key: = 1 vote

Fig. 3

Raspberry

Fudge ripple

Vanilla

Chocolate

Fig. 4

Vanilla   Chocolate   Fudge ripple   Raspberry

Fig. 5

Chocolate

Vanilla   Chocolate

Vanilla   Chocolate   Fudge ripple

Vanilla   Chocolate   Fudge ripple   Raspberry

Fig. 6

Hours spent
watching TV

Bill
Richardo
Susan
Shelly
Joshua

Activity four

This type of activity will help the students decide, prior to gathering data, what type of data should be obtained.

Figure 7 shows the results of a survey of teachers who gave the make of car they currently owned, the year it was manufactured, and when they planned to buy a new car. You might use such a table to ask questions like the following:

(1) What data would you use to show how old each teacher's car is?

(2) What data would you use to show how many years each teacher plans to wait before buying a new car?

(3) Can you show how many years each teacher has driven her or his car?

Additional data-gathering activities that students might try could include the following:

(1) In what month were most students born?

(2) How do students get to school (bus, car, or walk)?

(3) What kinds of cars drive past the school in a ten-minute time span?

(4) What were the median daily temperatures for last week?

Challenge students to show their results in more than one way (tables, pictographs, bar graphs, and so on).

Probability

The probability activities that follow are suggested for students in the early elementary grades. No emphasis is placed on formal terminology or symbolization. The approach is merely one of developing an intuitive "feel" for basic concepts of probability.

For students who have little or no experience with probability, begin with a situation similar to the one suggested in activity five. Students with some understanding of probability may go on to activity six.

Activity five

Place 6 red markers and 2 blue markers in a container without the children knowing how many and what color markers have been put in. Ask a stu-dent volunteer to draw one marker from the box. Record the color of the marker, replace it, and repeat the drawing allowing the volunteer to draw one marker for each student in the class. Better yet, let each student draw a marker. After numerous draws, ask the students to guess what colors of markers they think are in the container. Are the numbers of markers of each color the same? If not, which color has the most markers? Show them the contents of the container. Were they able to guess that there were more red markers than blue ones? Ask them how they would change the contents of the container so that their "chance" of drawing a blue maker would be about the same as the chance of drawing a red one.

Activity six

Make multiple sets of four spinners like the ones shown in figure 8. (Directions for making spinners are at the end of this article.) Separate the class into three groups of about the same size. Assign a color to each group—red, blue, or white. Then form subsets of three students, with one student from each of the color groups in each subset. Instruct the students as follows:

> I am going to give each group a spinner. I want you to take turns spinning the spinner. Each time your color is spun, you get one point. Play until one of you gets five points.

Have each group of three repeat this activity for each of the four spinners separately. After completing each round, record the results in tabular form (fig. 9).

When all four spinners have been used, ask students questions like these:

(1) If you could choose your winning color on spinner #3, what would you choose? Why?

(2) If your winning color was blue, which spinner would you choose? Why?

(3) Suppose you lost if red was spun and won if blue or white was spun. Which spinner would be the best one to use? Why?

Activity seven

Each student will need a die or cube numbered 1 through 6 for this activity. A numbered cube can be made by placing masking tape on each face of the cube and writing the numerals on the respective faces. (A spinner with six congruent sectors may be substituted for the cube or die).

Ask students to guess which of the following would have a better chance of happening when the number cube is rolled. Why do they think so? Let them experiment by actually rolling the cube several times.

(1) An odd number or an even number

(2) A number greater than 3 or a number less than 3

(3) A number divisible by 2 or a number divisible by 5

(4) A number greater than 6 or a number less than 3

(5) A number greater than 0 or a number less than 10

Note that this activity involves the ideas of an impossible event and a certain event.

Activity eight

Challenge your students to design their own simple probability experiment. Instruct them to run repeated trials and record their results. Students should then be invited to present their findings to the class. Encourage students in the class to make a guess as to whether there is a "good" chance or a "poor" chance of the event happening before they know the results of an experiment. The following are some possible experiments:

(1) What are the chances of a blindfolded person touching his or her nose with a forefinger on the first try?

(2) What are the chances of a dixie cup landing on its side if it is tossed in the air and allowed to fall to the floor?

(3) What are the chances of walking on the sidewalk from the front door of your school to the street without stepping on a crack? (Don't watch your feet.)

Fig. 7

Teacher	Make of Car	Year Made	Next New Car
Ms. Kraus	Chevrolet	1973	1985
Mr. McCoy	Plymouth	1972	1982
Ms. Pitts	Chevrolet	1974	1984
Ms. Sikes	Datsun	1978	1985
Ms. Woi	Toyota	1980	1984
Mr. Davis	Cadillac	1977	1982

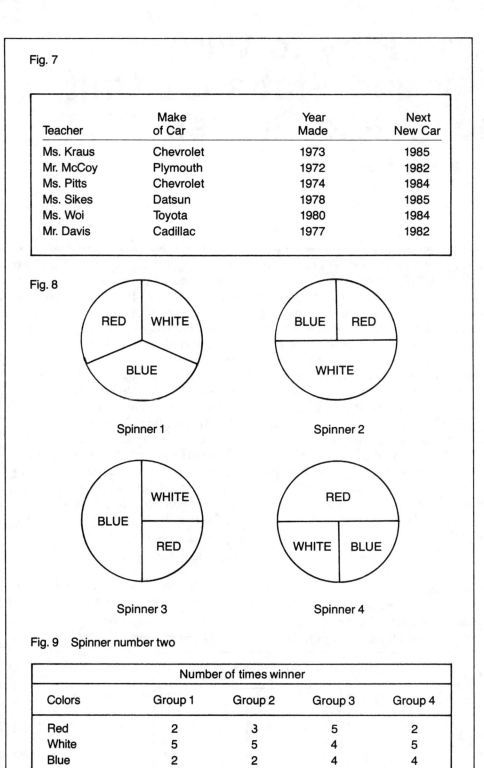

Fig. 8

Spinner 1

Spinner 2

Spinner 3

Spinner 4

Fig. 9   Spinner number two

	Number of times winner			
Colors	Group 1	Group 2	Group 3	Group 4
Red	2	3	5	2
White	5	5	4	5
Blue	2	2	4	4

clip, button, and a plastic arrow cut from any plastic lid. (1) Bend the paper clip as shown below and place the straightened end through the center of the circular numbered wheel from the bottom side so it acts as a spindle. (2) Place a button over the spindle. (3) Put the plastic arrow on top of the button.

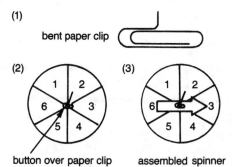

(1)

bent paper clip

(2)

button over paper clip

(3)

assembled spinner

If the arrow does not spin smoothly, use scissors to trim it so it balances. (Caution: If the width of the arrow is too great, a hard spin will turn it into a vertical propeller.) ☛

Summary

The activities suggested here are of an introductory nature. They can easily be extended for more able or advanced students by including such concepts as mean, median, mode, and range. The concepts of sample space and theoretical probability are natural outgrowths of the introductory probability activities suggested.

Whatever the abilities of your students, remember to begin each topic with a "hands-on" activity in which students use "real" data and have an opportunity to "see" their results.

Note to the teacher

An inexpensive highly effective spinner can be created by using a paper

Ya Gotta Play to Win:
A Probability and Statistics Unit for the Middle Grades

By **Francis (Skip) Fennell**

Probability and statistics are part of our daily lives in an ever increasing number of ways. State lotteries, casino gambling, and sports at all levels continue to fascinate millions of people.

With the number of people who invest time, energy, and—more importantly—money in activities involving probability, it is time that we use this social phenomenon to relate probability, statistics, and particularly gaming to the curriculum in grades 5–8. This article discusses such a unit.

Unit preplanning

Before beginning the study of probability, ask the pupils to bring in some of their favorite games of chance. Explain that a game of chance contains dice, a wheel, a spinner, cards, or other devices to decide moves, chances, and so on. Some examples of the more popular games are Monopoly, Chutes and Ladders, old maid, Yahtzee, Kismet, Cootie, Pay Day, and Gambler.

Purchase several pairs of dice, decks of cards, spinners, polyhedra dice, and other probability materials for unit instruction and follow-up activities. If applicable, display state lottery materials and information.

Inform parents of the probability and statistics activities. Although so-

cial applications involving probability and statistics are to be encouraged, care must be taken in presenting a unit on gaming. A letter or an evening session describing the intent of instruction involving gaming, along with an opportunity to discuss the activities, should be given to all parents. Although gambling is presented here as a social and practical application of probability and statistics, students are cautioned about the actual odds against their likelihood of winning. In fact, by understanding how probability and statistics can be applied to gaming, students are likely to see the statistical hazards involved in any gambling activity.

Day one

Construct an overhead Plexiglas transparency spinner similar to that shown in figure 1. Use two 25 cm × 25 cm pieces of Plexiglas. A hole can be

drilled through the middle of the two pieces and a spinner attached with a screw and nut. Interchangeable colored transparency circles divided into thirds, fourths, sixths, and so on, can be inserted between the Plexiglas pieces.

Using the Plexiglas and the transparency circles divided into thirds, discuss the outcomes of the spinner. Ask the students how many possible outcomes there are on the spinning wheel. The probability of an event can be described as the numerical way to express what the chance is that an event will occur. The probability of an event is most frequently written as a proper fraction. For example,

probability of an event

$$= \frac{\text{the number of ways the event can occur (successes)}}{\text{total number of events (outcomes)}}$$

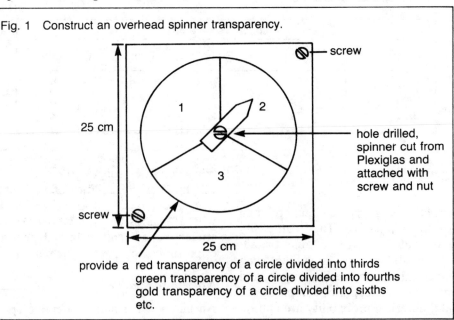

Fig. 1   Construct an overhead spinner transparency.

25 cm

25 cm

screw

screw

1

2

3

hole drilled, spinner cut from Plexiglas and attached with screw and nut

provide a red transparency of a circle divided into thirds
green transparency of a circle divided into fourths
gold transparency of a circle divided into sixths
etc.

Skip Fennell teaches mathematics methods for preservice and in-service elementary teachers and directs a mathematics clinic at Western Maryland College, Westminster, MD 21157. He is interested in the diagnosis, remediation, and applications of mathematics.

So the probability that the spinner will land on 2 is 1/3. The transparency divided into fourths can now be used with the Plexiglas overhead spinner to reinforce the definition of the probability of an event. In addition, use a coin to provide an additional example of using chance. What is the probability of flipping a head? A tail? (1/2)

The next step in reinforcing the concept is to provide an example of tallying or recording. Try flicking the spinner sixty times and having the class record the results. A similar tally can be made with fifty tosses of a coin. Some charts for recording the results are shown in figure 2.

The tallying experiment will approximate closely the equally likely outcomes of these events if a large number of tallies is recorded. An optional activity is to use a spinner transparency divided into four unequal sections (see fig. 3). Ask the students to predict results and discuss the fairness of this wheel.

Days two and three

Provide a regular die for each small group of pupils. Have the pupils determine the probability of rolling each number. Use the die to assist in defining odds. The odds against an event may be defined as the ratio of the number of unfavorable events to the

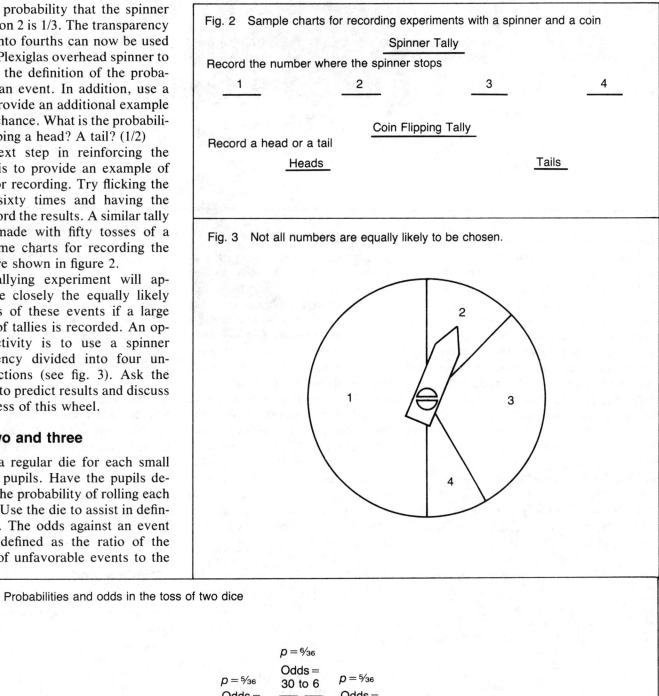

Fig. 2   Sample charts for recording experiments with a spinner and a coin

Spinner Tally

Record the number where the spinner stops

| 1 | 2 | 3 | 4 |

Coin Flipping Tally

Record a head or a tail

Heads   Tails

Fig. 3   Not all numbers are equally likely to be chosen.

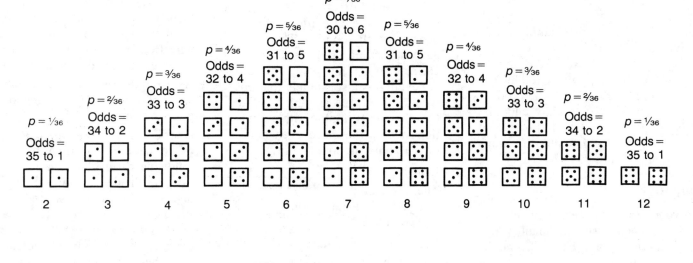

Fig. 4   Probabilities and odds in the toss of two dice

number of favorable events.

For example, when a die is rolled, the odds are 5 to 1, or 5:1, against someone rolling a 1 because only one of the die's six sides is a 1 and the other five sides are not:

odds against an event occurring

$$= \left(\begin{array}{c} \text{number of} \\ \text{unfavorable events} \end{array}\right)$$
$$\left(\begin{array}{c} \text{number of} \\ \text{favorable events} \end{array}\right)$$

Next, make sure that each student has a pair of dice. Encourage the students to roll the dice and define the probability and odds of all events involving two dice. Students should then construct a chart similar to that in figure 4, illustrating the probable occurrences of each roll. The outcomes in figures 5 and 6 present the sums and products using two dice.

The probabilities of sums and products provide an opportunity to analyze basic addition and multiplication fact combinations. Which sum(s) or product(s) is/are most likely to occur? Least likely? How can we use the probability of rolling sums and products to help us in learning facts or in winning games? Have the pupils roll and record sums according to the chart in figure 7. Using a tally or frequency count aids pupils in determining the total sum of all fifty rolls and the average, or mean, roll of the fifty rolls. Pupils can also find the most frequent sum and can arrange the dice sums in bar or line-graph format similar to the sample graph provided in figure 7.

Pupils may find it interesting to repeat the dice activity by rolling and recording fifty products. The product distribution, the average, and the most frequent product will provide an interesting comparison to the sums recorded in figure 7.

Day four

Provide standard decks of playing cards for each of several small groups in your classroom. Have the pupils determine the probability and odds of the following:

Fig. 5 All possible sums in the toss of two dice

+	1	2	3	4	5	6
1	2	3	4	5	6	7
2	3	4	5	6	7	8
3	4	5	6	7	8	9
4	5	6	7	8	9	10
5	6	7	8	9	10	11
6	7	8	9	10	11	12

1. Drawing a face card

   The probability is 12 of 52, since 12 of the 52 cards are face cards. This fraction can be restated in its lowest terms as 3/13, consistent with the fact that there are 3 face cards for each suit of 13 cards. The odds against drawing a face card are 40 to 12, expressed in its simplest form as 10 to 3. Thus, in each suit of 13 cards, 10 will not be and 3 will be face cards. Teachers interested in having probabilities and odds expressed in lowest terms, have to assume a knowledge of fractions or provide instruction.

2. Drawing a red card

   The probability is 26/52, or 1/2, since 26 of the 52 cards are either hearts or diamonds. The odds against drawing a red card are 26 to 26, or 1 to 1. Therefore, the odds are even; it is just as likely that one would draw a red as a black card. Can the pupils think of other situations where there are even odds? (What about flipping a coin?)

3. Drawing a 3

   The probability is 4/52, or 1/13. The odds against drawing a 3 are 48 to 4, or 12 to 1.

4. Drawing a 4 of spades

   The probability is 1/52; the odds against this are 51 to 1.

5. Drawing a diamond

   The probability is 13/52, or 1/4. The odds against drawing a diamond are 39 to 13. The same results would hold even if the question dealt with clubs, hearts, or spades.

Provide additional examples using the cards. These activities would be an excellent extension of previously learned fraction concepts.

Days five and six

Following the introductory activities of the first four days, the two-day sequence described below presents probability in a gaming format.

1. Construct a carnival wheel similar to that shown in figure 8. The wheel can be constructed of triple thickness cardboard or plywood.

2. Ask your pupils what the probability is of the wheel stopping on a given number?

3. Distribute five $1 bills in play money to each pupil; then play the following carnival simulation. The "carny" leader can dress accordingly in a straw hat, striped shirt, sunglasses, and arm garters. Each pupil is to wager $1 on a number for each of five spins of the carnival wheel. Students may change their wagers for each spin of the

Fig. 6 All possible products in the toss of two dice

X	1	2	3	4	5	6
1	1	2	3	4	5	6
2	2	4	6	8	10	12
3	3	6	9	12	15	18
4	4	8	12	16	20	24
5	5	10	15	20	25	30
6	6	12	18	24	30	36

Fig. 7 Sums of two dice in 50 tosses

Sum	Tally or frequency	Total (sum times tally)
2					6
3	⊮	15
4					12
5	⊮	25
6	⊮		36
(7)	⊮ |||	56
8	⊮		48
9	⊮	45
10						40
11					33
12				24
	TOTAL SUM	340

1. Average or mean sum $= \dfrac{\text{total sum}}{50 \text{ rolls}} = \dfrac{340}{50} = 6.8$

2. Circle the most frequent sum

(Sample) line and bar graph presenting results of 50 dice sums

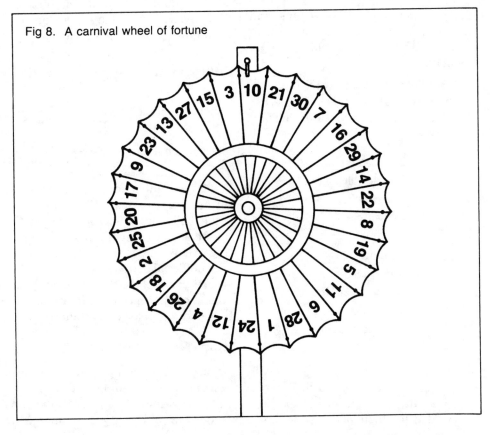

Frequency vs Sums 2 3 4 5 6 7 8 9 10 11 12

wheel. Winners of each round receive their $1 wager back plus $1 more, for a total of $2.

4. Keep a running account for each spin of the wheel. Run the introductory game for five spins of the wheel. An example of an introductory game for a class of thirty students is shown in table 1.

Find out how many pupils actually won money at the end of the five spins. Discuss the excitement of gaming. Describe the social problems of people hooked on gambling. Introduce materials related to horse racing and casino gambling as applications of probability. Would the results change if $10 bets were permitted?

5. Use the overhead transparency spinner shown in figure 1 and replicate part of this lesson. Have the pupils identify probability and odds and keep track of individual winnings and the carnival's totals.

Day seven

Pass out decks of cards to small groups of pupils. Introduce the game of blackjack, or twenty-one. Number cards are worth their designated number in this common game. Face cards are worth ten points and aces are worth either 1 or 11 points, at the

Table 1
An Introductory Game for 30 Students

Spin	Winning no.	Winners	Losers	Carnival collected	Carnival paid
1	27	2	28	$28	$2
2	13	2	28	$28	$2
3	12	1	29	$29	$1
4	11	1	29	$29	$1
5	4	1	29	$29	$1
				$143	$7

Fig 8. A carnival wheel of fortune

player's discretion. Each player receives his or her first card face down from the dealer. The second card is dealt face up. The object of the game is to get as close to 21 points as possible without exceeding 21. To get additional cards, a player requests a "hit," an additional card placed face up. A sum over 21 immediately disqualifies the player. Encourage pupils to keep track of their winning rounds and to use probability and odds as they compare the other cards to their own. Encourage pupils to be aware of probability and odd's when playing games out of class as well.

Day eight

Sporting events provide many opportunities for a variety of applications oriented toward probability and statistics. The following baseball card game is an activity that incorporates both probability and statistics. This game could be demonstrated first to the whole class, but it is more appropriately played in small groups.

1. Have pupils bring in their favorite baseball cards. Organize two teams of major-league players according to pupil interests.

2. Have pupils on the visiting and home teams position their cards in a simulated playing field and begin play.

3. The fielding player rolls one die, and the batting player rolls the other. The following sums indicate moves:

> 2 = home run
> 3 = double play
> 4 = double
> 5 = single
> 6 = out
> 7 = out
> 8 = single
> 9 = wild pitch
> 10 = stolen base
> 11 = sacrifice fly
> 12 = triple

4. Pupils may use individual baseball player statistics on baseball cards to aid them in figuring out the sum needed for their play. If the base-

ball player on a card has a batting average of .280 or above for the season, the die is rolled two times and the player plays the better of the two rolls. The designated hitter rule would apply for this activity, since the batting average for pitchers is not recorded on baseball cards. You can revise the strategy by allowing players hitting above .280 to take a chance on a second or even a third roll of the dice, but then they *must* play their "chance" roll. Pupils should refer back to the probability of each outcome of the dice so that they can plan a game strategy.

5. As a continuation of this baseball activity, pupils may calculate the following baseball statistics:

$$\text{batting average} = \frac{\text{hits}}{\text{times at bat}}$$

$$\text{fielding average} = \frac{\text{errors}}{\text{fielding chances}}$$

$$\text{earned-run average} = \frac{\text{earned runs}}{\text{games pitched}}$$

Player comparisons and discussions of the previous season's averages for each ball player as reported on the baseball cards can provide an interesting extension of this activity.

Additional activities involving other sports can include the probability and statistical aspects of golf, horse racing, football, basketball, and track.

Day nine (optional)

If applicable, bring in and discuss information regarding statewide lottery programs. Ask pupils questions about the probability of winning, the

odds, and go on. Examine lottery literature and schedule a visit by a lottery representative.

Day ten

This unit contains many applications for reinforcing probability concepts and involves the games that the pupils brought in at the beginning of the unit as a culminating unit activity. Games should be reviewed according to the format shown in table 2. Remember, ya gotta play to win!

Conclusion

Teaching probability and statistics is important because of the popularity of the various applications of these subjects in our daily lives. The activities suggested in this article are only several among many that could be chosen. Many interesting and thought-provoking problems could be used. These subjects are a rich source on which we can draw in our efforts to implement *An Agenda for Action* (1980).

Bibliography

Dubisch, Roy. *Basic Concepts of Mathematics for Elementary Teachers*, pp. 381–97. Reading, Mass: Addison-Wesley Publishing Co., 1977.

Heddens, James W. *Today's Mathematics*, pp. 536–51. 93d ed. Chicago: Science Research Associates, 1974.

National Council of Teachers of Mathematics. *An Agenda for Action: Recommendations for School Mathematics for the 1980s.* Reston, Va.: The Council, 1980.

Wykes, Alan. *The Complete Illustrated Guide to Gambling.* New York: Doubleday & Co., 1964. ♥

Table 2

| | | Game Review | |
Title	Element of Chance	Use of Statistics	Probability, Odds used
Yahtzee	dice	recording scores	Combinations of 4 dice used. The probability of getting Yahtzee is $\frac{1}{1296}$. Other sums and combinations occur more frequently.

From the File

Measurement

PLANTING, PREDICTING, AND PROBABILITY

Spring is an excellent time in which to integrate mathematics and science in one lesson and show elementary children how important mathematics is to a scientist. An exciting and interesting exercise for young children is to plant seeds such as wax beans, corn, or white and red radishes. Have the children make observations about the seeds and draw inferences about the growth of the plants: In what ways are the different seeds alike in appearance and size? In what ways are they different? Which plants do you think will grow the fastest? Will the plants all look alike? Red and white radish seeds, for example, look almost exactly the same, but are different as plants.

Children enjoy making and recording observations and predicting the results. They can make various charts to show the information they have—frequency charts (tallies in cells) to show seeds by color, length, and so on; bar graphs to show the number of seeds in each category that grow; and line graphs to show the rate of plant growth.

Mathematics is easily and obviously incorporated in measuring and recording seed size and in recording plant growth in centimeters. Probability can also be involved by counting the exact number of seeds planted and then observing the number that germinate, thereby determining the probability of germination of certain seeds. This exercise is even more interesting if old seeds (not packed for the current year) can be used and students can discuss the reasons why they may not all germinate.

From the file of
Brian Lockard, Elementary Supervisor, Carroll County Schools, Westminster, Maryland.

AT-9-81

Problem Solving

6

Functioning with a Sticky Model

By **Robert E. Reys**

Searching for patterns is an integral part of mathematics, and arithmetic provides excellent opportunities for students to look for patterns, make conjectures to continue a pattern, and then to check these predictions. The early study of functions is a natural place to reinforce basic computational skills as well as develop some pattern-finding techniques. "Guess my rule" or "Find my number" are effective activities that are frequently used. For example, consider the following exchange between a child and a teacher:

T: I am going to pretend to be a machine. Give me a number and then I will give you a number back.
C: Two.
T: Five.
C: Four.
T: Seven.
C: Ten.
T: Thirteen.
C: I think I know how the machine works.
T: Okay, let's see if you do. You pretend you are the machine and that I give you a number, say eight.
C: Eleven—I think.
T: Right! How about twenty?
C: Twenty-three! You just add three.
T: That's it! You guessed my rule.

This game takes many forms but the underlying principle uses some rule to assign one number to another. Basal elementary school texts provide similar activities. Children are asked to complete tables of numbers or to identify the rules used in the tables (fig. 1).

Robert E. Reys is professor of mathematics education at the University of Missouri at Columbia.

Fig. 1 Function Activities from Several Elementary Mathematics Textbook Series
Input-output table

Add 3	
Input	*Output*
1	4
3	6
	7
8	

Holt School Mathematics. New York: Holt, Rinehart and Winston, Inc. 1974.

Finding rules

Maxine's machine shorted a circuit. It started using its own rules and printing only a few answers. What rule did the machine use for this table?

What are the missing numbers?

3	9
4	10
2	8
0	
5	
7	
8	

Mathematics Around Us. Glenview, Ill.: Scott, Foresman and Company, 1975.

Complete the Number Pattern

x	1	2	3	4	5	6	7	8	9
2	2	4	6	8	?	?	?	?	?

Modern School Mathematics: Structure and Use. Boston: Houghton-Mifflin Company, 1972.

These are valuable activities for children for the following reasons in particular:

1. They epitomize the problem-solving process. Furthermore, the difficulty can be easily adjusted to accommodate children's ability and maturity.

2. They provide raw data, which must be organized, analyzed, and synthesized for patterns. These conjectures and predictions of the next number(s) are not only encouraged but become vital to the successful completion of the activity.

3. They provide much practice with basic facts, including mental computation.

Function tables such as those in figure 1 represent a type of mathematical puzzle that is challenging and inherently motivating, provided children have had the necessary prerequisite activities.

The most obvious limitation of these function tables is that they are completely symbolic. Before working with such tables, children should have some similar concrete experiences. For example, table 1 shows a typical function encountered in primary grades. It takes on new meaning in the context of a real problem. Suppose that the square, representing the number of cars, is replaced by a picture of a car and the triangle, representing the number of wheels, is replaced by a picture of a wheel, as in table 2. Completing table 2 has a meaning that completing table 1 alone does not provide. In this context a rebus is highly effective, in terms of both clarity and motivation. Use of pictures rather than abstract symbols reduces the level of complexity initially required. It may be clearer that

is a function (both linguistically and mathematically) of

Although care must be taken to insure that the bridge from the concrete to the abstract is recognized and crossed by children, the most important consideration is that early experiences be meaningful.

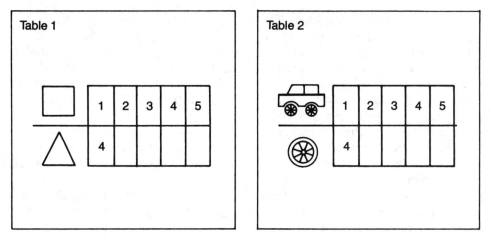

Table 1					
□	1	2	3	4	5
△	4				

Table 2					
car	1	2	3	4	5
wheel	4				

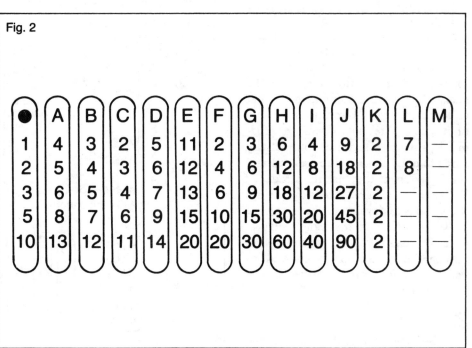

Fig. 2

●	A	B	C	D	E	F	G	H	I	J	K	L	M
1	4	3	2	5	11	2	3	6	4	9	2	7	—
2	5	4	3	6	12	4	6	12	8	18	2	8	—
3	6	5	4	7	13	6	9	18	12	27	2	—	—
5	8	7	6	9	15	10	15	30	20	45	2	—	—
10	13	12	11	14	20	20	30	60	40	90	2	—	—

Various models can be effectively used to develop the notion of function and provide varied practice. In addition to some typical textbook developments shown in figure 1, the approach by the Comprehensive School Mathematics Project and the development of functions with hand calculators are both interesting and effective (Frederique 1968 and Reys, et. al. 1979). There is research evidence to suggest that varied approaches to the same concept using perceptually different models (multiple embodiment) not only increase the opportunity for children to learn but also actually enhance the concept development (Suydam and Higgins 1976). It is in this spirit, along with bridging from the concrete to the abstract, that a Popsicle-stick model is demonstrated.

Popsicle-Stick Models

The Popsicle-stick models are made by writing numbers on the sticks with a dark, permanent-ink marker and then covering the sticks with transparent tape to prevent them from soiling. The transparent tape also allows the children to write on the sticks with a water-soluble-ink pen. Figure 2 shows a beginning set of Popsicle sticks for children to use. Some are filled completely with numbers, a few are partially filled, and others are blank. Each stick has a front and a back. A fine red border on the front side helps distinguish it from the back of the stick, which has no border. The difference between the front and back is that the front is completely filled whereas the back of the stick uses the same pattern but is only partially completed. The fronts can be used in activities in which the principal task is identifying the rule or pattern. The backs can be used to test rules.

To introduce the use of the sticks, choose the stick with the red dot and another stick, say A. Place them beside one another in a vertical position as shown in figure 3. The child then looks for a pattern relating the two lists of numbers, determines the solution for a number missing on A, and writes conjectures or predictions in the blanks on the back of stick A.

If a written record of the child's work on a series of problems is desired, it can be obtained in several ways. Figure 4 shows a self-directed activity card to be used in conjunction with the sticks. It has been laminated so that children can record solutions directly on it with a water-soluble-ink pen. Figure 5 provides a series of four activity cards that are designed for second and third graders as they use the sticks.

There are a variety of ways to use these sticks to develop problem-solving skills through patterns. Some suggestions for tasks involving functions with one operation, two operations, and inverse operations are described in the sections that follow.

One Operation

Four basic types of problems fall in the category of one operation. For the first type, the materials needed are two sticks, both complete. (See fig. 6) The problem is to find the rule that relates the numbers on the two sticks. The rule is "add 4," which can be written as follows:

$$\xrightarrow{+4}$$

Thus

$$\bullet \xrightarrow{+4} D.$$

A more complex, but certainly acceptable, solution would be the following:

$$\bullet \xrightarrow{+1} C \xrightarrow{+3} D$$

In this case, you could say, "Add one, then add three." (See fig. 7) Thus pupils quickly learn that solutions with sticks are not unique. In fact, one of the most challenging aspects is searching for "other" solutions.

In the second type of task, the materials needed are two sticks, one complete and the second only partially filled. The problem is to find the rule and then complete the missing data on the stick. (See fig. 8) Once the rule,

$$E \xrightarrow{-4} L$$

is found and the missing blanks are filled, the pupil can turn the stick over for a check.

For the third type of task, the pupil starts with one stick and the rule. (See fig. 9) The task is to find a second stick

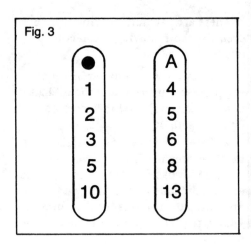

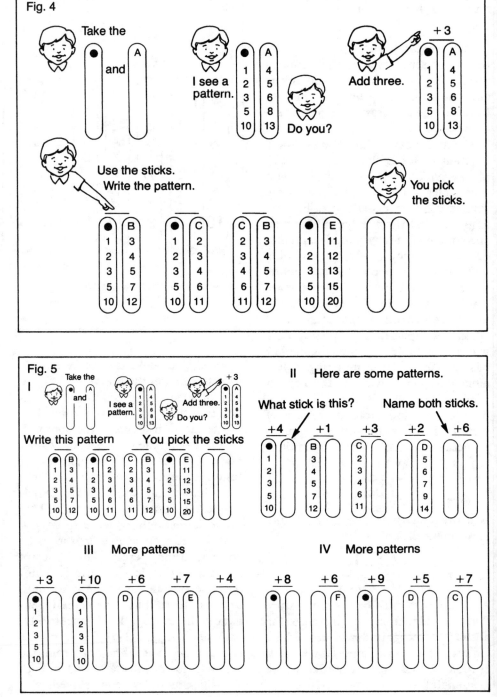

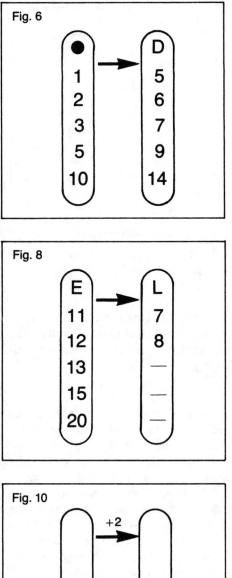

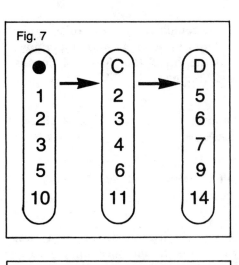

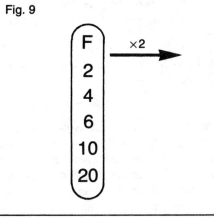

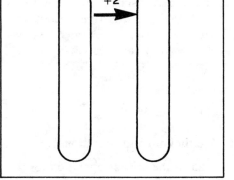

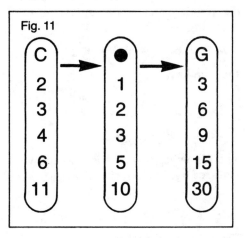

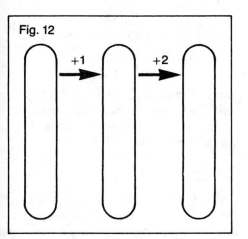

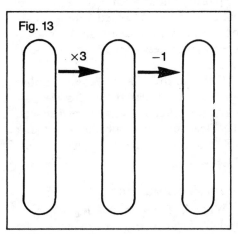

that fits the rule or to take a blank stick and make the missing stick.

For the fourth type of activity, the rule is given and the task is to find two sticks that satisfy the rule. For the example shown in figure 10, several pairs are possible. Sticks "red dot" and B, C and A, and B and D would all fit the rule.

Two operations

As with one operation, with two operations several types of activities are possible. For one type, the materials needed are three sticks, each complete. The problem is to find the rules that related these. For example, the following would relate the sticks in figure 11:

$$\xrightarrow{-1}, \xrightarrow{\times 3}$$

New problems can be made by simply reordering the sticks. For example, the following rule provides a challenging problem and increases pupils' a awareness of the role of different operations, as well as the importance of their order:

$$G \xrightarrow{} \bullet \xrightarrow{} C$$

In another type, two rules are given and the problem is to find the sticks that fit those rules. (See fig. 12) For example, the combined rules

$$\xrightarrow{+1}, \xrightarrow{+2}$$

could be solved by starting with the stick with the red dot. Then the following would satisfy the problem:

$$\bullet \xrightarrow{+1} C \xrightarrow{+2} A$$

If a different starting stick had been chosen, the result would be a different set of sticks, but the problem-solving process would have been the same.

For the preceding example, some pupils would find that the two operations

$$\xrightarrow{+1}, \xrightarrow{+2}$$

is equivalent to

$$\xrightarrow{+3}$$

For the preceding example, some pupils would find that the two operations could be combined. Thus

$$\xrightarrow{+1}, \xrightarrow{+2}$$

is equivalent to

$$\xrightarrow{+3}.$$

Fig. 14

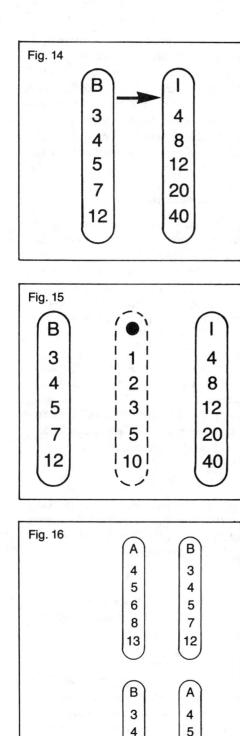

Fig. 15

Fig. 16

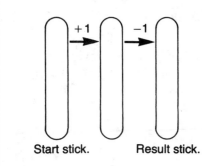

Start stick.   Result stick.

The combination of two rules can be explored in other ways. For example, find the sticks that fit the following rules (see fig. 13):

$$\xrightarrow{\times 3}, \xrightarrow{-1}$$

Suppose the red-dot stick is chosen. Then

$$\bullet \xrightarrow{+3} G$$

but a new stick will need to be made to show

$$\xrightarrow{-1}.$$

Pupils will learn that they can start with any stick, but sticks may need to be made to show the results.

Choose the red-dot stick again. will

$$\xrightarrow{-1}, \xrightarrow{\times 3}$$

result in the same stick? Is the following true?

$$\bullet \xrightarrow{\times 3} \xrightarrow{-1} = \bullet \xrightarrow{-1} \xrightarrow{\times 3}$$

In another type of two-operation problem, the pupil starts with two sticks, each complete. (See fig. 14) The task is to find the rule(s) that relate the two sticks. If the child is unable to find a rule or pattern, a clue may be provided by adding an intermediary stick, the red-dot stick. Once rules for the following have been found

$$B \xrightarrow{\quad} \bullet \text{ and } \bullet \xrightarrow{\quad} I$$

then we have

$$B \xrightarrow{-2} \bullet \xrightarrow{\times 4} I$$

or

$$B \xrightarrow{-2, \times 4} I.$$

The following sentence is also equivalent (see fig. 15), but the relationship is not obvious:

$$B \xrightarrow{\times 4 \quad -8} I.$$

Exploring under what conditions these rules may be combined into a single operation will greatly increase children's awareness of the order of operations.

Once children have become familiar with the sticks, ask them to make patterns for other classmates to discover. The teacher need only supply blank sticks and offer the necessary encouragement.

Inverse operations

What is the rule relating sticks A and B? In answer to the question, the

Fig. 17

child describes the rule as "subtract one" and records the following:

$$A \xrightarrow{-1} B$$

How will the rule change if the sticks are reversed? The child describes the rule as "add one" and records the following:

$$B \xrightarrow{+1} A$$

Now, let's chain these rules together and find the new stick. In figure 16, for example, filling in the values shows that if the "start" stick is A then the third stick is also A. "Subtract one" and "add one" are inverse operations. It is important to realize that regardless of the chosen "start" stick, if inverse operations are involved then the "start" and "result" stick must be identical. Here are some follow-up activities (see fig. 17):

What is the rule?

For $F \xrightarrow{\quad} I$?
For $I \xrightarrow{\quad} F$?

Are they inverse operations?

What is the inverse operation for the following:

$$J \xrightarrow{\quad} G?$$

What is the last stick for the following?

$$J \xrightarrow{\div 3}, \xrightarrow{\times 3} ?$$

For the last example, check to see if the child must use the intermediate stick, or does he or she quickly realize that the result will also be J?

Conclusion

A variety of comparable follow-up activities with these modified Popsicle sticks will provide some unique opportunities to introduce and develop the idea of functions. Such active involvement in searching for and making patterns will provide pupils with many new insights.

Let's get on the sticks and try it!

Author's note. The author gratefully acknowledges the suggestions received from Barbara J. Bestgen and J. Wendell Wyatt in the preparation of this article. Thanks also are due to Dorothy Hawkins, Gundlach School, St. Louis, and to Sheryl McGruder, Fairview School, Columbia, Missouri, for trying these ideas and providing valuable feedback.

References

Frederique. *Mathematics and the Child.* New Rochelle, New York: Cuisenaire Company of America, Inc., 1968.

Reys, Robert E., Barbara J. Bestgen, Terrance G. Coburn, Harold L. Schoen, Richard J. Shumway, Charlotte L. Wheatley, Grayson H. Wheatley, and Arthur L. White. *Keystrokes: Calculator Activities for Young Students: Addition and Subtraction.* Palo Alto, Calif.: Creative Publications, 1979.

Suydam, Marilyn N. and Jon L. Higgins. *Review and Synthesis of Studies of Activity-Based Approaches to Mathematics Teaching.* Final Report to the National Institute of Education, 1976. ♣

Let's Do It

Many of the best problem-solving situations in primary schools come from everyday situations: "How many more chairs will we need if we are having five visitors and two children are absent?" "How many cookies will we need if everyone has two?" However, these situations do not always arise at the appropriate time, nor do we always have time to take advantage of them when such situations do arise. There is a need for a set of problems that can be used at any time and the problems selected for this article are of this type. They require a minimum amount of computation but, often, a maximum amount of thinking.

All the problems use a set of geometric pieces. The problems involve not only geometry, including area, but also logic, combinations, division, and money. None of these topics is dealt with formally; all are presented in the form of a puzzle or problem.

The pattern for the five easy pieces is shown in figure 1. There are four *A*s, four *E*s, one *I*, two *O*s, and one *U*, or twelve pieces altogether. The problems are written for yellow and blue pieces. If you are making classroom sets, make a duplicating master and run off copies on yellow and blue construction paper. If you want more durable sets, use heavy tagboard. You might also want to make and use only one complete yellow and one complete blue set with a class.

Fig. 1

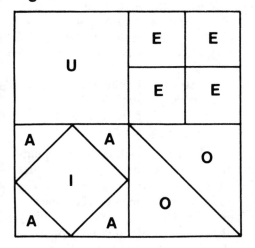

The problems can be put on four-by-six-inch index cards from which you can make up sets suitable for your children. Or you may wish to use the problems in other ways—oral directions to

Problem Solving With Five Easy Pieces

By **Mary Montgomery Lindquist**
National College of Education
Evanston, Illinois

the children or a problem each week posted on the board. The pieces that are needed for each problem are indicated; "one complete set" refers to either one yellow or one blue set. The answers to the problems are included.

As you and the children work with these activities, you will see other problems or questions. For younger children, you may want to make more of the problems they find within reach (probably the simpler puzzles, patterns, and cost cards) and for older children you will want to extend the problems.

Basic Relationships

In these three sets of problems, the children are asked to investigate the area relationships among the pieces. Doing these problems, especially those in Basics 1, should help the children do the later logic and cost problems.

In Basics 1, most children will have no difficulty seeing that two *A*s cover an *E*; more children will have trouble seeing that four *A*s cover an *I* as well as an *O*. There are not enough *A*s to completely make a *U*, but with a little ingenuity, children should be able to see that it takes eight *A*s. Notice how the children solve the problems. Do any cover as much as they can with *A*s and see that half of *U* is covered? Do any of the children use *E*s to help to solve the problem? Do any use *O* to help?

Basics 1
Take: One complete set
How many *A*s does it take to cover

an *E*?
I?
O?
U?
Answers: *E*, 2; *I*, 4; *O*, 4; *U*, 8

Since the *E*s will not completely cover *I* or *O*, the problems in Basics 2 are more difficult than those in Basics 1. The children will either have to imagine cutting up piece *E* or use the relationship they found in Basics 1—since two *A*s cover an *E*, and four *A*s cover an *I*, it would take two *E*s (if they were cut) to cover *I*.

Basics 2
Take: One complete set
How many *E*s does it take to cover an *I*?
O?
U?
Hint: You may have to pretend to cut piece *E*. Use *A* to help you.
Answers: *I*, 2; *O*, 2; *U*, 4

The problems in Basics 3 reinforce the relationship that *I* and *O* are the same in area, and *U* is twice as large as *I* and twice as large as *O*.

Basics 3
Take: One complete set
1. If you could cut up piece *I*, would it cover piece *O*?
2. How many *O*s does it take to cover *U*?
3. How many *I*s (pretend that you could cut an *I*) does it take to cover *U*?
Answers: 1, yes; 2, 2; 3, 2

Puzzles

Do not expect all children to come up with all the variations on Puzzles 1. As the children find them, you may want to put the possible arrangements on the bulletin board.

Puzzles 1
Take: One complete set
How many different ways can you make a copy of the square *U*?
Example:

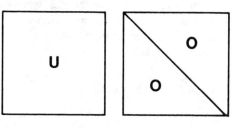

Answers:

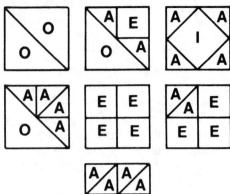

Other arrangements of the pieces are possible in some of these squares.

Only one solution for Puzzles 2 is given here; other solutions are possible. You may vary this puzzle by asking the children to make one triangle, one rectangle, or one parallelogram.

Puzzles 2
Take: One complete set
Take all the pieces. Can you make one large square?
Answer:

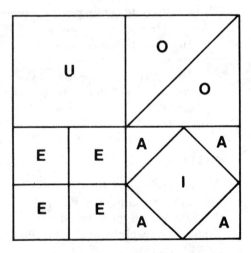

One solution. Others are possible.

Let children experiment with Puzzles 3 through 6 and make up other puzzles. For young children, put only one question on a card. Be sure children understand that in all these puzzles, when two pieces are fit together, sides of equal length must be matched. For example,

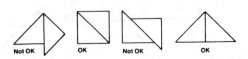

Puzzles 3
Take: Two *A*s
1. Can you make a triangle?
2. Can you make a square?
3. Can you make a four-sided figure that is not a square?
Answers:

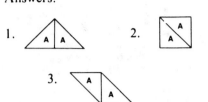

Puzzles 4
Take: Three *A*s
1. Can you make a four-sided figure?
2. Can you make a five-sided figure?
Answers:

Puzzles 5
Take: Four *A*s
1. Can you make a triangle?
2. Can you make a square?
3. Can you make a rectangle that is not a square?
4. Can you make a four-sided figure that is not a rectangle?
5. Can you make a five-sided figure?
6. Can you make a six-sided figure?
Answers:

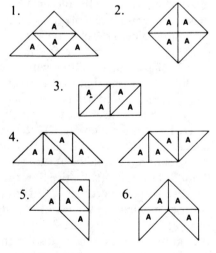

Puzzles 6
Take: Four *E*s
1. Can you make a four-sided figure?

2. Can you make a five-sided figure?
3. Can you make a six-sided figure?
4. Can you make an eight-sided figure?
Answers:

2. not possible

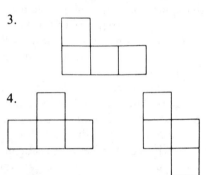

Patterns

In the pattern-making problems, children may come up with answers different from those given. Ask children to explain their patterns—their patterns, though different, may be legitimate. Also ask the children who come up with the given solutions to explain the patterns—they may be seeing a pattern in a different way.

Patterns 1
Take: Yellow and blue *A*s and *E*s
Put in a line:
1. yellow *A*, yellow *A*, blue *A*, yellow *E*.
What would be the next two pieces?
2. yellow *A*, blue *E*, blue *A*, blue *E*.
What would be the next two pieces?
3. yellow *A*, yellow *A*, yellow *E*, blue *A*.
What would be the next two pieces?
Possible solutions:
1. yellow *E*, blue *E*; 2. *A*, *E* (either color); 3. blue *A*, blue *E*

As with the puzzles, the rule of putting pieces together by matching sides of equal length must be followed. The restriction that one side of one piece must be placed on a given line limits the endless possibilities of "tipping." The further restriction that the pattern must be above the line or, if problems are written on the cards, "on the card" is optional. Either eliminates the possibility of flipping the pieces over the line—getting a mirror image, in other words. Feel free to omit these restrictions, but if you do, you can expect many other possible results.

Patterns 2

Take: Two blue *A*s and two yellow *A*s

Using two pieces, how many different figures can you make? (One triangle must be on the line and the figure should be above the line.)
Example:

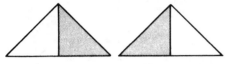

Answer:

Each shape can be varied four ways with the color changes.

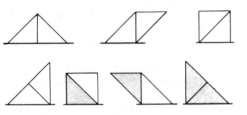

Patterns 3

Take: Three yellow *E*s and three blue *E*s

Using three pieces, how many different patterns can you make? (One square must be on the line and the pattern should be above the line.)
Example:

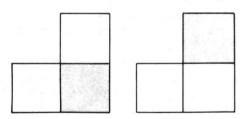

There are eight color variations of this shape.

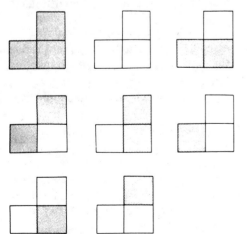

There are five other shapes. Each can be varied eight ways with color.

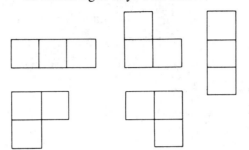

Patterns 4

Take: Four yellow *A*s and four blue *A*s

Take any four pieces and make a shape. How many variations of your shape can you make by changing colors?
Answer: Suppose the shape is

There are sixteen color variations

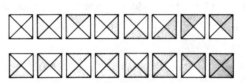

Some children may realize that once they specify a shape on Patterns 2, there are four ways to vary the color. Patterns 4 is a variation of the ideas begun on Patterns 2 and 3. If there are children who see that there are sixteen ways to vary the colors, you may want to look at Patterns 2, 3, and 4 with them. There are four ways to vary the colors with two pieces, eight ways with three pieces, sixteen ways with four pieces. What would you expect with five pieces?

Do not expect many children at this level to see the numerical pattern. You can be satisfied if they begin by moving the pieces to see the variety of possibilities. You can help those children who are ready to organize their work by asking questions like the following: How many variations can you make if no triangles are blue? If only one triangle is blue? If two triangles are blue? If three triangles are blue? If four triangles are blue?

Logic

The logic cards progress in difficulty from 1 to 6. It may help some children to write the new names for the pieces on slips of paper so they can move the names around to match the clues.

Logic 1

Take: One *E*, one *I*, one *U*

These three squares renamed themselves—Ali, Bet, and Tim.

Ali said, "I'm bigger than Tim."

Bet said, "I'm bigger than Ali."

Who's who?

Answers: Tim is *E*, Ali is *I*, Bet is *U*.

Logic 2

Take: One *A*, one *E*, one *O*

These three pieces renamed themselves—Bill, Jill, and Lil.

Bill said, "I'm twice as large as Jill."

Jill said, "I'm the same shape as Lil."

Who's who?

Answers: Jill is *A*, Bill is *E*, Lil is *O*.

Logic 3

Take: One *A*, one *E*, one *O*, one *U*

These four pieces renamed themselves—Mary, Larry, Harry, and Cary.

Mary said, "I'm a fourth as large as Harry."

Larry said, "I'm bigger than Harry."

Who's who?

Answers: Mary is *A*, Cary is *E*, Harry is *O*, Larry is *U*.

Logic 4

Take: One *A*, one *I*, one *O*, one *U*

These four pieces renamed themselves—Floe, Joe, Moe, and Woe.

Joe said, "I'm twice as large as Moe."

Floe said, "I'm the same shape as Woe."

Woe said, "I'm smaller than Moe."

Who's who?

Answers: Woe is *A*, Moe is *I*, Floe is *O*, and Joe is *U*.

Logic 5

Take: One *A*, one *E*, one *I*, one *O*, one *U*

These five pieces renamed themselves—Dan, Nan, Stan, Ann, and Fran.

Fran said, "I'm the same size as Dan, but larger than Stan."

Dan said, "I'm larger than Nan, but smaller than Ann."

Nan said, "I'm smaller than Fran,

but larger than Stan."
Fran said, "I'm the same shape as Nan."
Who's who?
Answers: *A* is Stan, *E* is Nan, *I* is Fran, *O* is Dan, *U* is Ann.

Logic 6
Take: One *A*, one *E*, one *I*, one *O*, and one *U*
These five pieces renamed themselves—Al, Cal, Mal, Pal, and Sal.
Pal said, "I'm twice as large as Sal."
Mal said, "I'm four times as large as Al and the same shape."
Pal said, "I'm larger than Mal."
Who's who?
Answers: *A* is Al, *E* is Cal, *I* is Sal, *O* is Mal, *U* is Pal.

Areas

Instead of having the children cover the figures with other pieces to find the area of the figures, they are given the results of someone's covering. The children then have to determine what units were used. If the children enjoy this challenge, make up some larger shapes that permit more possibilities.

Areas 1
Take: One complete set

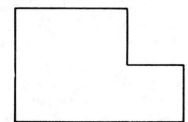

1. Bob covered this figure with pieces. He took 4 of one kind and 3 of another. What pieces did he use?
2. Karen covered this with pieces. She took 2 of one kind and 2 of another. What pieces did she use?
Answers: 1. four *A*s and three *E*s
2. two *O*s and two *A*s

Areas 2
Take: One complete set

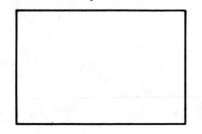

1. Hal covered this rectangle with pieces. He took 4 of one kind, 1 of another, and 1 of another. What pieces did he use?
2. Sue covered this with pieces. She took 2 of one kind, 2 of another, and 1 of another. What pieces did she use?
Answers: 1. one *O*, one *I*, four *A*s
2. two *O*s, two *A*s, one *E*

Costs

Costs 1 depends on the children seeing the basic area relationships between the pieces. It may help younger children to work with pennies (or chips).

Costs 1
Take: One complete set
1. If *U* costs 12¢, how much does
   E cost?
   A cost?
2. If *I* costs 8¢, how much does
   E cost?
   U cost?
Answers: (1) 3¢, 1½¢, (2) 4¢, 16¢
It may help in question 2 of Costs 2 to have the children paper clip the price on each of the four pieces.

Costs 2
Take: One *A*, one *E*, one *O*, and one *U*
1. If *A* cost 1¢, how much would each of the other pieces cost?
2. Using just these 4 pieces, how would you pay a bill for each of the following:
   1¢, 2¢, 3¢, 4¢,
   5¢, 6¢, 7¢, 8¢,
   9¢, 10¢, 11¢, 12¢,
   13¢, 14¢, 15¢
Answers: 1. *E*, 2¢; *O*, 4¢; *U*, 8¢
2. 1¢, *A*; 2¢, *E*; 3¢, *A* and *E*; 4¢, *O*; 5¢, *O* and *A*; 6¢, *O* and *E*; 7¢, *O*, *A*, and *E*; 8¢, *U*; 9¢, *U* and *A*; 10¢, *U* and *E*; 11¢, *U*, *E*, and *A*; 12¢, *U* and *O*; 13¢, *U*, *O*, and *A*; 14¢, *U*, *O*, and *E*; 15¢, *U*, *O*, *E*, and *A*.

Costs 3 is similar to the puzzles and the rule of fitting sides together applies. Again, for younger children you may want to separate the questions, one question to a card. For children who find these problems easy, change the price of *A* to 3¢, or make up cost varia-

tions for Puzzles 3 through 7.

Costs 3
Take: Four *A*s. Each *A* costs 1¢.
1. Can you make a four-sided figure that costs 3¢?
2. Can you make a three-sided figure that costs 4¢?
3. Can you make a five-sided figure that costs 3¢?
4. Can you make a five-sided figure that costs 4¢?
Answers:

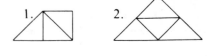

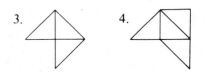

On Costs 4, the children have to focus on both the total number of pieces and the total cost.

Costs 4
Take: One complete set
1. If *A* costs 1¢, what would each of the other pieces cost?
2. Can you sell the pieces to two people so that each person gets the same number of pieces and each person would have to pay the same amount?
Answers:
1. *E* costs 2¢, *I* costs 4¢, *O* costs 4¢, and *U* costs 8¢
2. First person: one *U*, three *E*s, two *A*s
   Second person: two *O*s, one *I*, one *E*, two *A*s
   (Each person gets six pieces that cost 16¢.)

The ideas for many of the problems that have been described here come from *Developing Mathematical Processes* (DMP). Acknowledgement is due the many writers of DMP who inspired these problems and the many teachers and children who have tried similar problems. □

Everyday Applications

The Big Pumpkin Count

By Lenny Coplestone-Loomis

Halloween isn't just a time for ghosts, goblins, and Jack-o-lanterns in my second-grade classroom at Rosemary Hills Primary School. It's also a great time to introduce counting by tens above one hundred. What do we count? Pumpkin seeds, of course!

About two weeks before Halloween, three pumpkins are purchased—a large one, a middle-sized one, and a small one. The students are then asked to guess how many seeds each of the pumpkins has. The children write their guesses on slips of paper, one for each pumpkin, and place them in the containers beside each pumpkin.

When it is time to make the jack-o-lanterns, six volunteers serve as "pumpkin-seed scoopers." They carefully remove the seeds from the pumpkins, keeping the seeds from each pumpkin separated from those of the others. Immature seeds are kept with the mature ones.

Other volunteers help clean the seeds, which are placed in large foil pie pans, one for the large pumpkin, one for the middle-sized pumpkin, and one for the small pumpkin. To get the seeds thoroughly dried out, they are placed in a 250 degree oven for 30 minutes. Then they are put on a shelf to cool, in preparation for the next day's lesson. In the meantime, I have prepared strips of black construction paper, each measuring 5 cm by 15 cm.

The time for counting comes next. Starting with the small pumpkin, the entire class begins to count pumpkin seeds. The seeds are grouped into sets of ten and each student is given a strip and ten seeds. The students in turn glue their pumpkin seeds in a row on their strip of black construction paper (fig. 1).

After the students have completed their gluing, the seeds from the pumpkin are counted in sets of ten—ten, twenty, thirty, . . . The total number of seeds in the smallest pumpkin is 331.

On the second counting day, the seeds of the middle-sized pumpkin are counted in the same manner that the seeds had been counted the day before. This time there are 336 seeds.

On the final counting day, the seeds of the largest pumpkin are counted and

Fig. 1

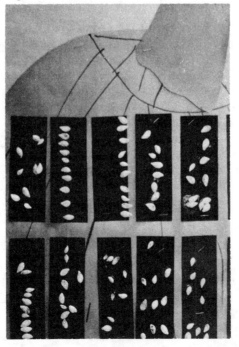

sets of ten seeds are glued to the strips of paper. We find that the largest pumpkin has 334 seeds when we count them by tens.

When the counting, grouping, and gluing is completed, we make a display of our project. This takes the shape of three very large paper pumpkins on which the seeds for each pumpkin are displayed in groups of ten (fig. 2). There are more than one thousand seeds in our three pumpkins!

On the final day of our pumpkin project, we gather in the hall in front of our bulletin board to count again and record all the sets of ten.

This unit helps the children attain growth toward many objectives. Not only do they learn to count by tens, they also learn to make estimates; but also they have constructed a visual representation of one thousand. They have learned to count by tens beyond one hundred, to cooperate in a group project, and that Halloween is more than ghosts and goblins.

They also learned that the largest pumpkin doesn't always have the most seeds. ▼

Fig. 2

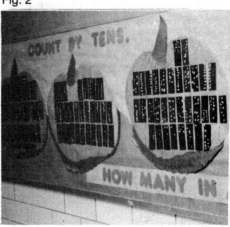

Lenny Loomis is a graduate of San Francisco State University. At the time this article was written, she was teaching second grade at the Rosemary Hills Primary School in Montgomery County (Maryland) Public Schools.

From the File

Problem Solving

ORANGE SECTIONS (a kindergarten activity)

Problem to be investigated: Does an orange always have the same number of sections?

Procedure: Let the children work in pairs. Hand out oranges, paper towels, and pieces of string.

Questions to be answered:
1. Will your piece of string go completely around your orange? Is the string too long, too short, or just right? (Record the answers.)
2. How many pieces of peeling are you going to get when you peel your orange? (Record answers.) Find the largest and smallest pieces.
3. Estimate the number of sections your orange will have. (Record the estimates by tallies on the chalkboard.)
4. Pull the sections apart, count them, and record the number.
5. Divide the sections into two equal piles. Was everyone able to do this?
6. Eat and enjoy.

Extensions: Children may ask questions like—
• Are there more sections in a seedless orange than in an orange with seeds?
• Do tangerines have more sections?
• Do oranges from Florida have more sections than oranges from California?
• Do big oranges have more sections than little oranges?
• Which oranges peel easier, those with seeds or those without?

From the file of
Eunice Neidhold, kindergarten teacher, Spokane Lutheran School, Spokane, Washington.

AT-10-81

Sweeten Mathematics with M & M's

By **Henry M. Lunde**

Are you still searching for ideas for presenting different mathematical concepts with concrete and semiconcrete materials and ways that will capture the children's attention? Try M & M's. Children like the candy and are intrigued with the idea of using them for mathematics.

The day before the M & M's lesson, announce to the children that they must come to class the next day with clean hands. (You might have a package of Wet Ones on hand, in case someone forgets.) You will need a supply of paper plates or paper napkins—the children can put their M & M's on these as they do the mathematics. And you need a supply of small packages of M & M's, one for each child. Each child will also need paper and pencil.

Activity

First activity

Distribute a bag of M & M's to each child. Then ask the children to try and figure out, without opening the bag,

---

Henry Lunde is an elementary mathematics teacher in the Burlington (Iowa) Community Schools. He works with nine and ten-year-old children in a departmentalized program at Washington School. The idea for this activity was given to him by Sally Allen, a Title I teacher, who got it from her daughter, a student at the University of Iowa.

---

how many M & M's are in their packages. After recording their guesses, the children open their packages, count the M & M's, and record the actual number.

Number of M & M's

My guess ____

Actual number ____

How far off is the guess? ____

How many guessed too many? How many guessed too few? Did anyone guess the right number?

Second activity

Separate your M & M's into sets by color. Let G equal the number of green M & M's, R the number of red ones, O the number of orange ones, Y the number of yellow ones, L the number of light brown ones, and D the number of dark brown ones. Record the number in each set.

$G =$ ___	$Y =$ ___
$R =$ ___	$L =$ ___
$O =$ ___	$D =$ ___

Use the symbols $>$, $<$, or $=$ to show the relationships between the numbers of M & M's of each color.

(1) G	R	(5) Y	R
(2) G	L	(6) O	L
(3) G	Y	(7) O	G
(4) Y	D	(8) O	Y

Solve the following mathematical problems.

(1) $L + D =$ ___

(2) $R \times Y =$ ___

(3) $R \times (O + G) =$ ___

(4) $Y + (G + R) =$ ___

(5) $(O + L) \times D =$ ___

(6) $G + R + D =$ ___

Solve the following mathematical problems.

(1) $D + O =$ ___   (7) $R \times D =$ ___

(2) $R + L =$ ___   (8) $Y \times D =$ ___

(3) $Y + G =$ ___   (9) $L \times Y =$ ___

(4) $G + L =$ ___   (10) $D \times L =$ ___

(5) $R + D =$ ___   (11) $O \times Y =$ ___

(6) $Y + D =$ ___   (12) $G \times L =$ ___

Third activity

Count out fifteen M & M's and put them in a pile in front of you. Answer the questions.

(1) Into how many groups of four can you separate the M & M's? ___ How many remain? ___

(2) Into how many groups of seven can you separate them? ___ How many remain? ___

(3) Into how many groups of five can you separate them? ___ How many remain? ___

(4) Can you rewrite questions 1, 2, and 3 using mathematical symbols? The first one is done for you.

$$15 \div 4 = ?$$

_____

_____

(5) Put two M & M's in your mouth. How many are left? ___ Write a mathematical sentence telling what you have done. _____

(6) Put four more M & M's in your mouth. How many are left now? Write a mathematical sentence telling what you have done. _____

(7) Put all of your remaining M & M's in one pile. How many groups of six can you make? Write the mathematical sentence telling what you have just done. _____ Complete the problem below to show what you have just done.

$$\sqrt{} \quad \text{remainder} \ \_\_$$

Fourth activity

Using all your remaining M & M's, try to arrange them in a rectangular or square array. Can you do this? ___ If you can, what multiplication fact is suggested by this arrangement? _____

Using different numbers of M & M's, try making other rectangular or square arrays.

(1) Can you see something special about the numbers of M & M's that can be put in rectangular or square arrays? _____

(2) What do the number that cannot be made into rectangles or squares have in common? _____

Fifth activity

How many M & M's did each person in your row, including yourself, have in her or his package? Record the numbers.

1st person ___
2nd person ___
3rd person ___
4th person ___
5th person ___
6th person ___
7th person ___

Using these numbers, find the average number of M & M's in a package. ___ What was the greatest number? ___ the least number? ___

Final activity

Put $3 \times (2 + 2) - 5$ M & M's in your mouth. How many are left now? ___ Put $(4 \times 5) - (5 \times 3)$ more in your mouth. How many are left now? ___ Subtract the rest of your M & M's, using the same method as you have before.

Conclusion

As you can see, these activities are very enriching. They are lots of fun, but they are also meaningful. They can have far-reaching effects as the children progress in school. Very basic, rudimentary concepts such as these are critical and stepping stones to more sophisticated mathematics later on. The number of these activities and the kind that you use in one class period or in one lesson will depend on the individual situation. ◆

8

Multipurpose Aids

Let's Do It

Punchy Mathematics

By **Jean M. Shaw**, *University of Mississippi, University, MS 38677*

Let's Do It—activity approaches to teaching and learning mathematics in the primary grades, with extensions through grade six.

Is there a paper punch lurking in the corner of your desk drawer? Could you muster another two or three paper punches? If so, they can be put to good use teaching and reinforcing mathematical concepts. Perhaps paper punches are appealing to children because punches have traditionally been the province of adults. Perhaps their neatness, efficiency, and the activity they offer make the use of paper punches attractive to children. Whatever the reason, children can use them to discover, illustrate, and extend their knowledge about a wide range of mathematical ideas.

The activities outlined in this article can be carried out by individual children or in small groups. If each child or pair of children has a paper punch, the activities can be done by the entire class as the children follow the teacher's directions.

The activities are also well suited for use in a mathematics center. They can be explained by the teacher or written up on task cards for the children to use independently. The activities involve a process as well as a product. Learning results from carrying out the process; a sense of pride and accomplishment is fostered in the making and displaying of the materials, the verbal sharing of ideas, and taking the products home.

The only necessary supplies are paper punches, paper, and crayons or pencils. The use of variety of types of paper adds interest and tactile appeal. Scraps of construction and notebook paper can be recycled in paper-punching activities. Adding-machine tape, newsprint, newspaper, and old computer printout sheets are also appropriate because they are thin and readily available. Encourage children to do their punching over a piece of paper, pie pan, or tray and to save the punched-out dots for other uses. Dots can be neatly and attractively stored in plastic bags, plastic film cans, or baby food jars.

Fig. 1 The holes can be connected in many ways.

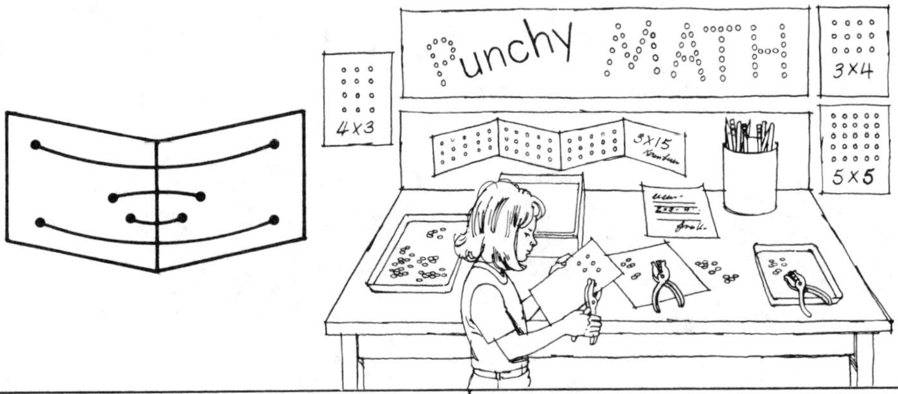

Fig. 2 Which side has more holes?

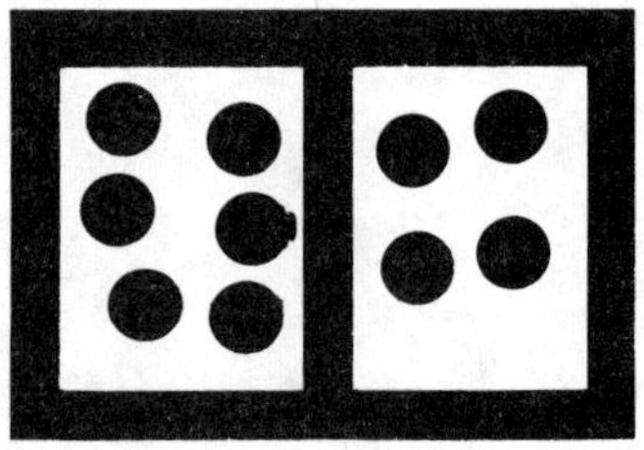

"Punchy" Math Activities

One-to-one correspondence and the meaning of numbers

Have children fold a small piece of paper in half. They should punch four holes in both layers of paper, then open the folded paper and place it on their table. Help the children see that each hole has a "partner." Have them draw lines from the holes in one half of the paper to the holes in the other half (fig. 1). Have children show you different ways that the holes can be joined. Repeat the process working with other numbers of holes. Children enjoy punching holes, then exchanging papers and completing this exercise.

Have the children use two pieces of paper. They should punch holes in one piece, then in the other. Next they glue the pieces on another piece of paper or place them side by side on

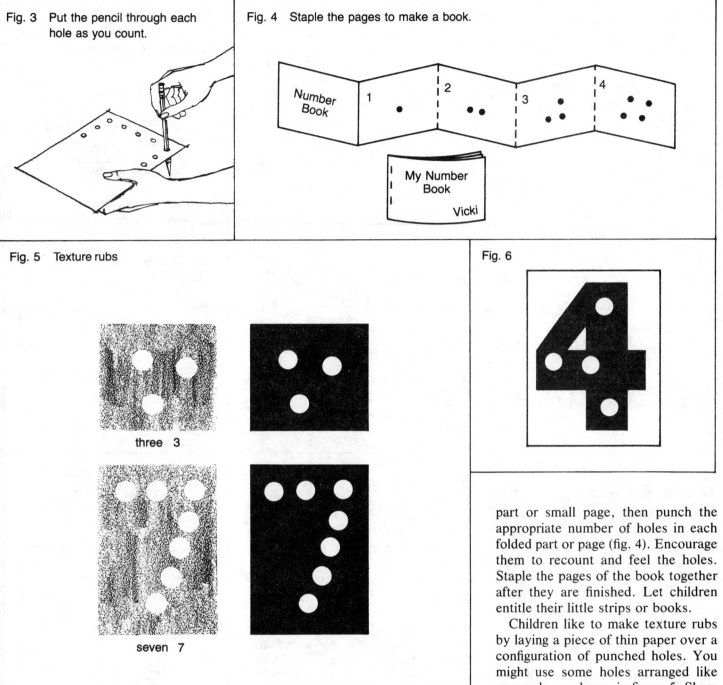

Fig. 3 Put the pencil through each hole as you count.

Fig. 4 Staple the pages to make a book.

Number Book 1 2 3 4

My Number Book

Vicki

Fig. 5 Texture rubs

three 3

seven 7

Fig. 6

the desk (fig. 2). The children should join as many holes in one piece of paper with holes in the other piece of paper as possible. Let them see which paper has more and fewer holes or whether they both have the same number of holes. Have children write the numeral for the number of holes on each piece of paper.

Meaningful counting is easy for young children when they use a paper punch. No holes are present until the paper punch is used to make them, so children can be encouraged to count the holes one by one. Punching holes is a sensory experience. Children hear, see, and feel the holes as they punch them. Children can recount the holes after they are finished punching. Show the children how to insert a crayon or pencil in each hole as it is counted to add meaning to the counting process (fig. 3).

Help children make a number strip or book by folding a long strip of paper or by cutting small rectangular pieces of paper for the pages. Have them write a numeral on each folded part or small page, then punch the appropriate number of holes in each folded part or page (fig. 4). Encourage them to recount and feel the holes. Staple the pages of the book together after they are finished. Let children entitle their little strips or books.

Children like to make texture rubs by laying a piece of thin paper over a configuration of punched holes. You might use some holes arranged like numerals, as shown in figure 5. Show the children how to hold the paper in place and rub across it with the side of an old crayon from which the paper wrapper has been removed. Let children display both the rubbing and the punched design from which it was made. Children should write the appropriate numeral and number word on or below the texture rub.

Reproduce large, thick numerals on worksheets. Have the children cut out the numerals, punch the appropriate number of dots in each, and then paste them onto colored paper or newspaper (fig. 6).

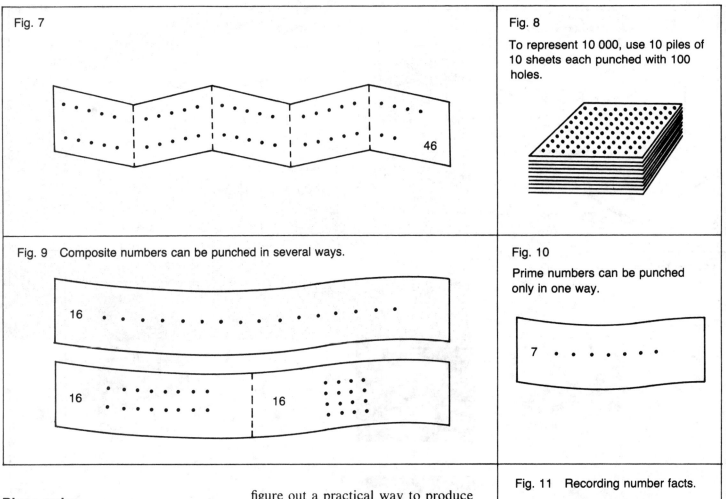

Fig. 7

Fig. 8

To represent 10 000, use 10 piles of 10 sheets each punched with 100 holes.

Fig. 9   Composite numbers can be punched in several ways.

16

16   16

Fig. 10

Prime numbers can be punched only in one way.

7

Fig. 11   Recording number facts.

...   .
3   +   4   =   7

Place value

As children begin to study place value and grouping by tens and ones, let them punch holes to develop the meanings of numbers less than 100. To show 46, have the children fold a long strip of paper over 5 times. Through 4 layers they should punch 10 holes. These 10 holes can be arranged in any pattern, although it is easiest for most children to use 2 rows of 5 holes each to represent 10. Next have children punch 6 holes in the last layer. When they unfold the paper, the children will see 4 groups of 10 holes and 6 single holes. Have them write the numeral on the paper (fig. 7). Encourage children to punch and display examples of other two-digit numbers.

Large numbers

Groups of students can work together to illustrate large numbers with punched holes. Assign groups of students to punch numbers of holes such as 10 000, 4242, or 999. Have students

figure out a practical way to produce the assigned number of holes. The group assigned 10 000 holes may see that they need 100 groups of 100 holes each. They may be able to punch through only 10 layers of adding-machine tape at a time, and so they may approach the problem by making 10 groups of 10 piles of grids of 100 holes each (fig. 8). If the groups display their punched paper on a bulletin board with a contrasting background, they are sure to be impressed with actually seeing their large numbers of holes.

Prime and composite numbers

Students can explore prime and composite numbers by punching various rectangular arrays of holes in long strips of paper. For composite numbers, they will find various arrays. For example, 16 could be represented as 1 by 16, 8 by 2, or 4 by 4 (fig. 9). Prime numbers, such as 7, will have only one arrangement—1 by 7 (fig. 10).

Operations and the properties of numbers

Have children punch holes to represent two addends. Children will enjoy suggesting addends for each other to show with punched holes. Have children count the holes and write the appropriate number sentence (fig. 11). To illustrate the commutative property of addition, have children fold their papers in half and then punch 2 ad-

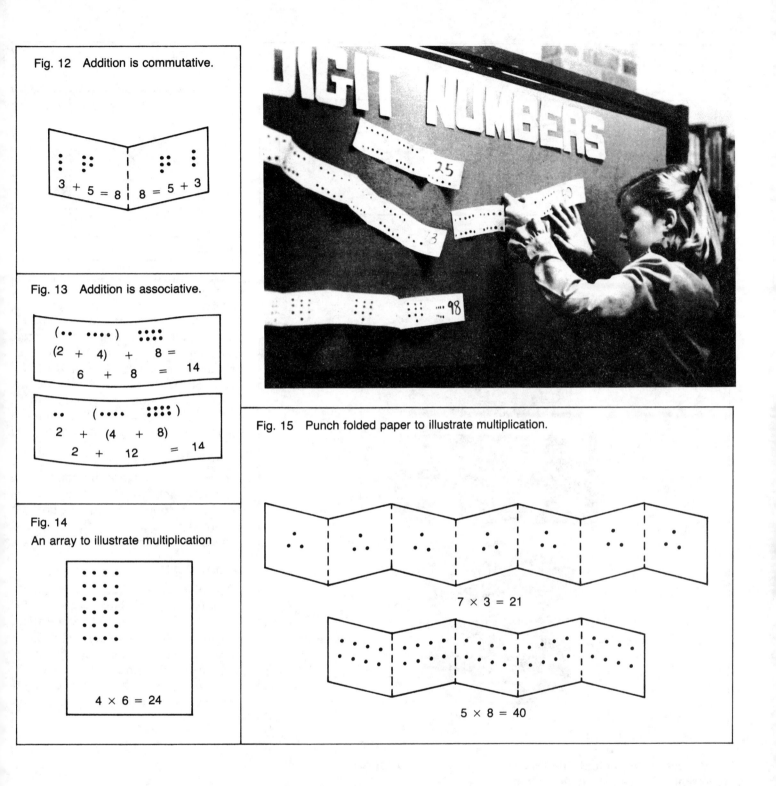

Fig. 12 Addition is commutative.

3 + 5 = 8   8 = 5 + 3

Fig. 13 Addition is associative.

(2 + 4) + 8 =
6 + 8 = 14

2 + (4 + 8)
2 + 12 = 14

Fig. 14
An array to illustrate multiplication

4 × 6 = 24

Fig. 15 Punch folded paper to illustrate multiplication.

7 × 3 = 21

5 × 8 = 40

dends. They should then unfold the paper, examine the arrangements of holes, and write the appropriate number sentence (fig. 12). After several examples, encourage the children to make conclusions about the order of addends in addition problems.

For examples of the associative property, have students punch holes to represent 3 addends in 2 layers of paper. They should lay one paper above the other, and then draw paren-

theses around the holes to illustrate the associative property. Last, they write number sentences to go with the examples (fig. 13).

To illustrate multiplication, have children punch rectangular arrays of dots into small pieces of paper. They then count the dots and write the appropriate number sentence (fig. 14).

Paper punching lets children easily illustrate multiplication as repeated addition. For example, to illustrate

7 × 3, have children fold paper over 7 times, then punch 3 holes through all the layers of paper to represent the other factor. They can then unfold the paper and write the appropriate number sentences (fig. 15).

To illustrate the distributive property vividly, students can fold paper and punch several holes through all layers. They should then unfold the paper and draw a dark line segment between any two of the sections.

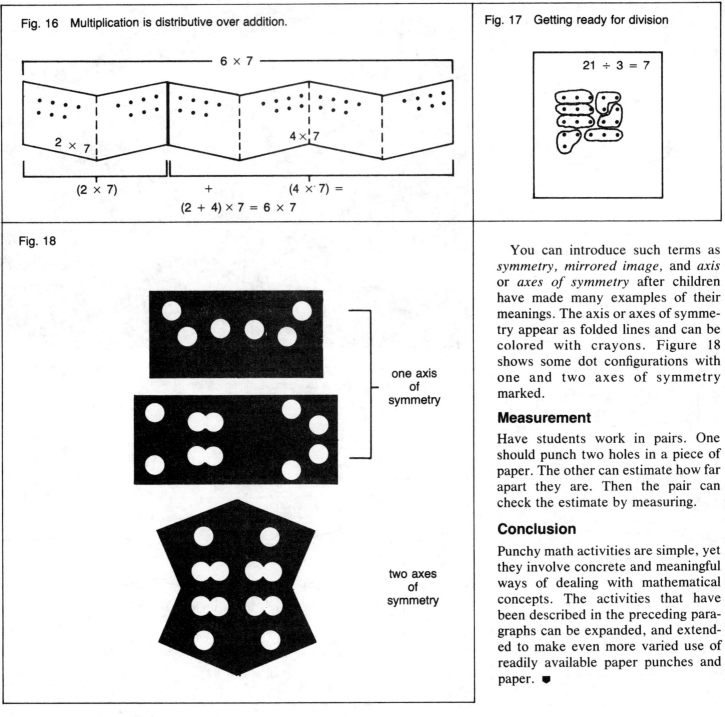

Fig. 16 Multiplication is distributive over addition.

6×7

2×7

4×7

(2×7) + $(4 \times 7) =$

$(2 + 4) \times 7 = 6 \times 7$

Fig. 17 Getting ready for division

$21 \div 3 = 7$

Fig. 18

one axis of symmetry

two axes of symmetry

You can introduce such terms as *symmetry*, *mirrored image*, and *axis* or *axes of symmetry* after children have made many examples of their meanings. The axis or axes of symmetry appear as folded lines and can be colored with crayons. Figure 18 shows some dot configurations with one and two axes of symmetry marked.

Measurement

Have students work in pairs. One should punch two holes in a piece of paper. The other can estimate how far apart they are. Then the pair can check the estimate by measuring.

Conclusion

Punchy math activities are simple, yet they involve concrete and meaningful ways of dealing with mathematical concepts. The activities that have been described in the preceding paragraphs can be expanded, and extended to make even more varied use of readily available paper punches and paper. ◗

Next, record the multiplication facts represented by the dots in the sections divided by the line and have children write an appropriate number sentence (fig. 16).

To promote readiness for division, have students punch a number of holes in paper to represent the dividend in a problem. Have students draw around groups of holes determined by the divisor. The number of groups is the quotient. Students should write the appropriate number sentence on each example (fig. 17).

Geometric shapes

Students can show examples of symmetry by folding a small sheet of paper in half. Have them punch holes, in any pattern, through both layers of paper. Next they unfold the paper and examine the pattern. Have students see if both halves are the same. Have students fold another sheet of paper in another way and repeat the process. Students should try this several times, making folds in the paper in many different places.

> **Editor's note:** This activity would be excellent for the learning-disabled student who needs tactile reinforcement for learning numbers. When the children do the punching, they actually get a feel for the numbers.

Let's Do It

That's Eggzactly Right!

By **Rosalie Jensen** *and* **David R. O'Neil,** *Georgia State University, Atlanta, Georgia*

Have you been saving styrofoam egg cartons? Do you have empty hosiery containers or some of the brightly colored plastic eggs that are available at this time of year for filling with goodies? Have you wondered how you could use these abundant and inexpensive items to enhance your mathematics teaching? If your answers are yes, read further and discover how to develop a variety of concepts and skills in your classroom.

Using Eggs Labeled with Dots

In order to do these activities, you need plastic eggs and small objects that fit inside the eggs, such as pieces of felt or cork, plastic chips, lima beans, or small plastic animals (for large eggs). On the outside of each egg, glue a certain number of dots removed from a hole punch or stick on gummed dots available at office and educational supply stores (fig. 1).

The range of numbers depends on the level of the children. You may wish to start with sets of up to 5 or 6 dots and extend the numbers up to 10 or 12. The number of small objects needed depends on the number of eggs to be filled. You might have several eggs for each number.

Matching sets

Give each child several eggs and a collection of objects. Have the children fill each egg with as many objects as there are dots on the outside of the egg. The children may exchange eggs and check the work of others by matching or by counting. Explain that if they have one object for each dot

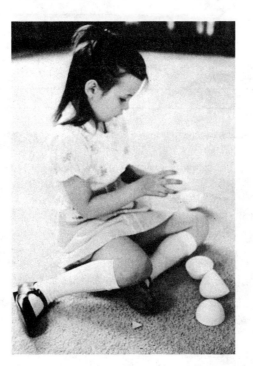

we say that the two sets have the *same number* of things.

Have a variety of small objects in your mathematics center with which children can fill the eggs. In this way they will develop the notion that the type of object in each set is not important to matching sets by number. Allow small groups of children to work at the mathematics center, filling the eggs and checking each other's work.

Once the eggs are filled properly, disconnect the upper and lower portions and scramble the order of the tops of the eggs. Then ask children to put the parts of the eggs back together by matching upper and lower portions.

Comparing sets

Give each child two empty eggs, with

a different number of dots on each egg, and some objects. Have the children fill the eggs with objects, matching the number of objects to the number of dots. Then tell them to remove the objects from each egg and to line up the two sets of objects in rows next to each other. For each pair of sets of objects, have the children decide which has *more* members and which has *fewer* members.

At some point in the development ask children to count the number of objects in each egg and to make an oral statement concerning the comparison of the two numbers. Decide ahead of time whether you wish the statements to say that one number is *greater than* the other number or *less than* the other number. Ask the children if they can make the same statements by comparing the dots rather than the objects.

Put the objects in the eggs in such a way that in some the number of objects and the number of dots are the same and in others the numbers are not the same (fig. 2). Give each child several eggs and ask them whether each egg has matching sets of dots and objects. Whenever sets do not match, discuss whether there are more objects or more dots.

Ordering sets

Remove the tops from the eggs. Have the children sort the tops into groups so that the tops in each group have the same number of dots on them.

Choose one egg top from each set of tops. With the help of the children arrange them in order from the small-

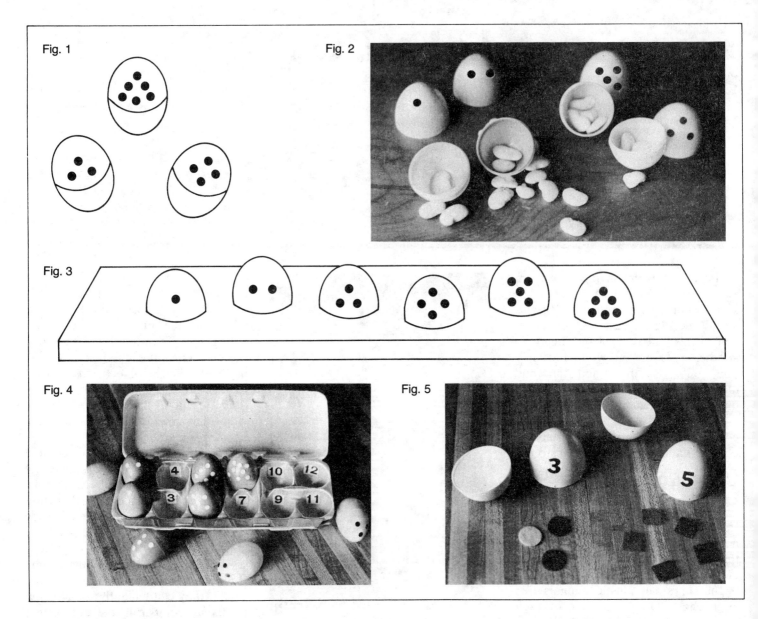

Fig. 1

Fig. 2

Fig. 3

Fig. 4

Fig. 5

est to the largest number of dots (fig. 3).

Matching sets of dots with numerals

You will need some styrofoam egg cartons and some numerals. The numerals may be cut from old calendars or purchased on sheets, along with stick-on letters, at stationery departments in drug and variety stores. Secure the numerals in the cups of the egg cartons. Have the children place the small plastic eggs in the cartons by matching the dots on the eggs with the appropriate numerals (fig. 4). Later, children may be asked to place small objects, rather than eggs, in the cups of the prepared egg cartons.

If you have large plastic eggs that will not fit in the cartons, have chil- dren place numerals made of card- board, wood, or plastic inside each egg or next to each egg top to indicate the number of dots.

Using Eggs Labeled with Numerals

Place a stick-on vinyl numeral on each egg top. Check to be sure that the children can recognize each numeral that is on an egg.

Matching sets of objects and numerals

Have each child fill several eggs with the number of objects indicated by the numeral on each egg. Children may exchange eggs and check each other's work; or they may open their eggs and take out the objects one by one as the other children count them.

Comparing numbers

Give each child two eggs filled with objects. Have them remove the ob- jects from the eggs and then compare the two sets of objects by attempting to match them, one to one. If the two sets match, the child should be able to say that the sets have the same num- ber of objects. Then they should check that the numerals on the two eggs name the right number of objects in each.

If the two sets do not match, the child should be able to say which set has more (or less) objects and make a "greater than" (or "less than") state- ment about the two numbers (fig. 5).

Ordering numbers

After children have had practice with

Fig. 6

Fig. 7

+	0	1	2	3	4	5	6	7	8	9
0	0	1	2	3	4	5	6	7	8	9
1	1	2	3	4	5	6	7	8	9	10
2	2	3	4	5	6	7	8	9	10	11
3	3	4	5							
4	4	5	6							
5	5	6	7							
6	6	7	8							
7	7	8	9							
8	8	9	10							
9	9	10	11							

missing number. When the children close their eyes this time, remove an egg and scramble the order of the remaining eggs. Who can be the first to discover the missing number?

Introducing zero

Label an egg with 0 and ask children how many things should be placed in this egg. Discuss the fact that an egg labeled with 0 should be left empty.

Where should this egg be placed in the line of eggs that are arranged in order? Can we compare 0 to the numbers on the other eggs? Yes, 0 is less than each of the other numbers. This fact can be established by comparing an empty set of objects to any set with a given number of objects in it. Therefore, the egg with 0 on it should be placed to the left of the egg with a 1 on it.

Developing basic facts of addition

Use two sets of eggs labeled with the numerals 0 through 9 to develop the basic facts of addition. Fill the eggs with objects. A record of the facts that are developed each day may be kept on a bulletin board or pegboard.

In order to establish a basic fact, such as $2 + 3$, remove the objects from an egg labeled "2" and an egg labeled "3." How many objects do we have if we push the two sets of objects together to make one set?

Beginning with the "easy" facts involving addition with 0, 1, and 2, children can begin to construct an addition table. After several days the partial table might look like figure 7.

In developing the addition table, you should help children see that changing the order of the addends does not change the sum. One way to do this is by exchanging the position of the eggs. The position of the eggs in figure 8a, for example, indicates that we are finding the sum of 3 and 5. In figure 8b, we are adding 5 and 3. In either case, the number of objects is 8 when the sets are combined.

As children begin to work with larger numbers, you may wish to teach them to group objects into a set of ten and a certain number more. For example, in adding 8 and 5 the objects

the concepts of "less than" and "greater than," they should be ready to arrange the egg tops in order from one to a given number. In figure 6, the numbers 1 through 9 are shown in order.

Objects may also be placed under each egg top for use in comparing sets. Using the objects, children can check to see that any number is less than the number to its right (or greater than the number to its left) when the numbers are arranged in order.

Display the eggs in order in front of the children and ask them to close their eyes. Remove an egg and then have the children open their eyes. Call on a child to name the missing number. If the child is correct, replace the egg and allow her or him to come up and remove an egg while the other children have their eyes closed. Continue the game until all children have had an opportunity to name the missing number and to remove an egg.

Play the "missing number" game with a new twist after the children have become proficient in naming the from the two eggs are pushed together and then separated into a set of ten and a set of three (fig. 9). Therefore, the sum of 8 and 5 can be thought of as 10 + 3, which is a name for 13.

Developing the concept of subtraction through comparison

Children need to use several models for solving problems that involve subtraction. One of the patterns, the comparison model, can be well illustrated using the eggs filled with objects.

Consider the following problem: Larry and Toby are playing checkers. Larry has taken 9 checkers and Toby has taken 6. How many more checkers does Larry have than Toby has? To solve the problem, a child would compare objects from an egg labeled "9" with objects from an egg labeled "6" to determine that Larry has 3 more checkers than Toby has (fig. 10).

Using Egg Cartons

Practicing basic facts

Egg cartons with a numeral in each cup can be used for games that provide practice in the basic facts of addition, subtraction, and multiplication. For practice in the basic facts involving a particular addend, such as 8, write an "8" on a Ping-Pong ball (fig. 11). Have the child toss the ball into an egg carton. Each time the ball lands in a cup the child tossing the ball should name the sum (or the product) of 8 and the number in the cup.

To practice subtraction facts involving 8, each participant should toss the ball and decide whether the number in the cup is less than 8 or greater than 8. The smaller of the two numbers should then be subtracted from the larger.

In order to practice all of the basic facts of addition, children should toss two objects (for example, pennies or washers) into the egg carton. The numbers in the cups should then be added. If a child fails to get the object into a cup, he or she may retrieve the object and toss again.

Figure 12 shows an egg carton that provides subtraction practice for minuends from 1 through 12. In the example

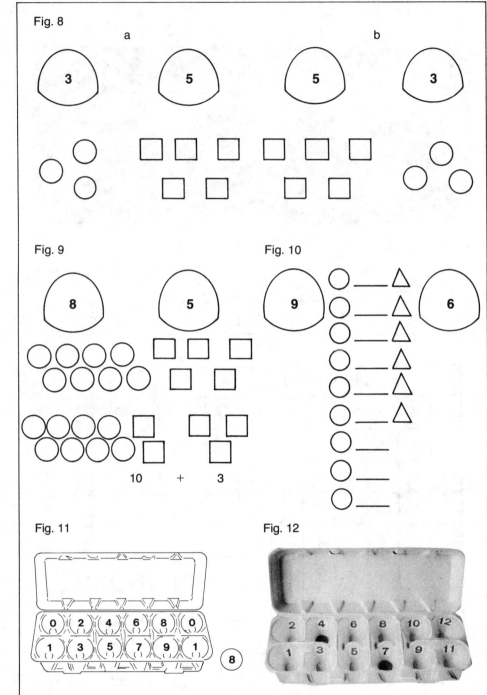

Fig. 8

Fig. 9

Fig. 10

10 + 3

Fig. 11

Fig. 12

ple illustrated, the child would decide that 7 is greater than 4 and find the difference between 7 and 4.

Developing place-value concepts

Cut egg cartons of two different colors so ten cups remain in each carton. Label one carton "ones" and the other carton "tens." Use beans or other objects to represent tens and ones.

Since children are familiar with the notion of having "rules" in games,

they can relate this idea to the idea of having rules in working with numbers. The rules to establish in working with the egg cartons and beans are as follows:

1. The small beans are placed only in the carton labeled "ones," and the large beans are placed only in the carton labeled "tens."

2. Only one bean is placed in each cup.

3. Whenever a "ones" carton is

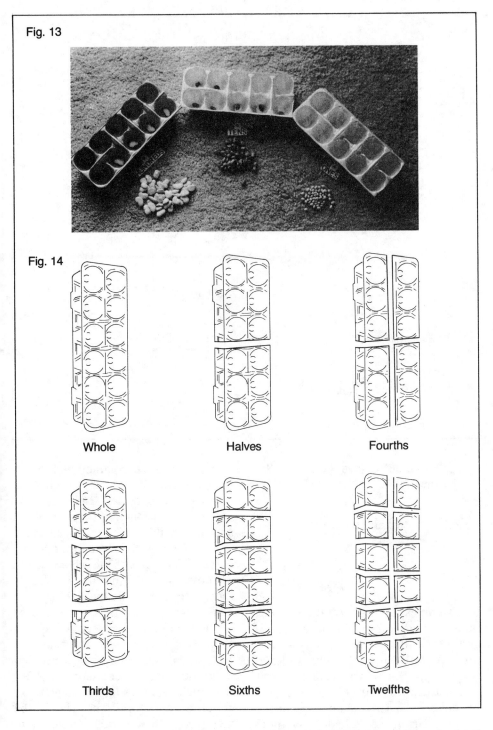

Fig. 13

Fig. 14

Whole   Halves   Fourths

Thirds   Sixths   Twelfths

many small beans in the "ones" carton. Whenever ten beans are accumulated in a carton, they must be traded for a larger bean for the tens carton or the hundreds carton. The game continues until one child has beans representing an agreed upon number, such as 100 or 200.

Naming and comparing fractions

Egg cartons can be cut apart to represent fractions for the various denominators that are factors of 12. Using cartons of different colors, cut one carton to represent each of these fractional parts: halves, thirds, fourths, sixths, and twelfths (fig. 14). If cartons of different colors are not available in your community, collect egg cartons and get spray paint to make the cartons different colors—halves one color, thirds another color, and so on.

Have children put like parts together to make whole cartons. Discuss the fact that a whole can be separated into 2 halves, 3 thirds, and so on.

Introduce symbols for the fractions 1/2, 1/3, 1/4, 1/6, and 1/12 by naming individual pieces, like the ones in figure 14. Then develop the notion that two 1/3-pieces put together can be called 2/3. Have children help you decide how to represent other fractions, such as 3/4, 4/6, and 5/12. What do we notice about the pieces that represent fractions like 2/2, 3/3, and 4/4? Can we put these pieces together to make a whole carton?

Children can begin to compare fractions by referring to the egg-carton model. Which is greater, 1/3 or 2/3? 2/3 or 3/4? By visual inspection or by counting the individual cups in the pieces that represent each fraction, children can compare any two proper fractions with denominators of 2, 3, 4, 6, or 12 using the egg-carton model. Later they will learn to compare fractions with the same denominator by comparing their numerators, and to compare fractions with different denominators by using a common denominator method (fig. 15).

Every fraction has many names. Some different names for 1/2 can be found by using the egg-carton pieces. Children can place two 1/4-pieces,

full (there is one bean in each cup), the ten small beans must be traded for a large bean, which is placed in the "tens" carton.

Using these rules children may represent any number between 0 and 100 by placing a certain number of beans in each carton.

By cutting another egg carton and providing beans of a third size, you can offer children a model for numbers between 0 and 1000. In figure 13, the egg cartons and beans are used to

show 472 in the form of 4 hundreds, 7 tens, and 2 ones.

The materials in figure 13 can also be used to play a "trading" game. Each participant needs three cartons and a supply of beans of each size to play. (An alternative is to let a "banker" have the beans to distribute as needed.) A chance device, such as a spinner, a die or dice, or a set of flash cards, is needed for each group of children. On each child's turn, he or she uses the chance device to obtain a number. The player then places that

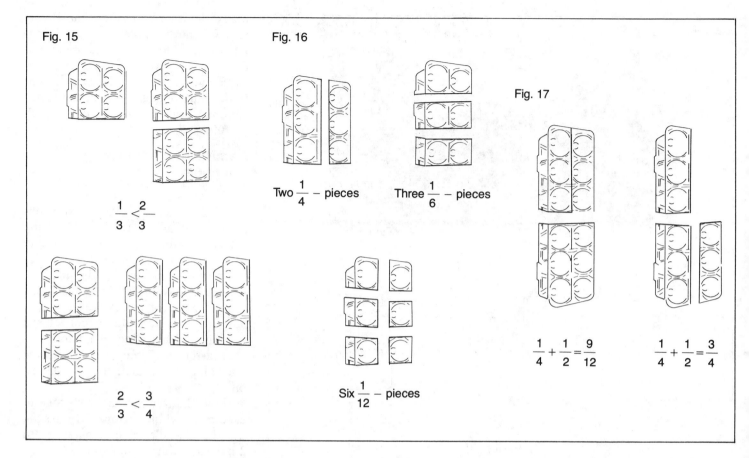

Fig. 15

$$\frac{1}{3} < \frac{2}{3}$$

$$\frac{2}{3} < \frac{3}{4}$$

Fig. 16

Two $\frac{1}{4}$ – pieces

Three $\frac{1}{6}$ – pieces

Six $\frac{1}{12}$ – pieces

Fig. 17

$$\frac{1}{4} + \frac{1}{2} = \frac{9}{12}$$

$$\frac{1}{4} + \frac{1}{2} = \frac{3}{4}$$

three 1/6-pieces, or six 1/12-pieces in a 1/2-piece in order to fill all of its cups. Therefore, 2/4, 3/6, and 6/12 are names for 1/2 (fig. 16).

Using the egg-carton model, what names can we find for 1/3? 1/4? 1/6? 2/3? 3/4?

Adding fractions

A well-developed sequence of addition of fractions includes the following steps:

1. Adding fractions with like denominators.

    Examples: $\frac{1}{4} + \frac{2}{4}$

    $\frac{2}{6} + \frac{3}{6}$

2. Adding fractions where one fraction has a denominator that is a factor of the other.

    Examples: $\frac{1}{4} + \frac{1}{2}$

    $\frac{2}{3} + \frac{1}{6}$

3. Adding fractions where neither

denominator is a factor of the other.

Examples: $\frac{1}{2} + \frac{1}{3}$

$\frac{1}{6} + \frac{3}{4}$

Examples of each of these types may be worked by using the appropriate pieces. For example, you can find the sum of 1/4 and 1/2 in either of two ways (fig. 17). One way is to put a 1/4-piece together with a 1/2-piece in a whole carton. How many cups of the whole carton are filled (covered)? Since 9 of the cups are covered, the answer is 9/12. On the other hand, you can put the 1/2-piece next to the 1/4-piece and fill the 1/2-piece with two 1/4-pieces. The resulting configuration represents an answer of 3/4.

Notice that it is possible to obtain an answer of 9/12 or an answer of 3/4, depending on the method used to solve the problem. Initially, you may allow children to give either answer. Eventually, as children work toward finding a least common denominator to solve problems, you can illustrate

that 4 is the least common multiple in the problem 1/4 + 1/2 by placing the two 1/4-pieces in the 1/2-piece.

Likewise, in finding the sum of 1/2 and 1/3, children might first place a 1/2-piece and a 1/3-piece in the whole carton. Ten cups of the whole carton are covered; thus, the sum is 10/12. Is there a simpler name for 10/12 that we could find by using the carton pieces? Since five of the 1/6-pieces occupy the same space, 5/6 is another name for 10/12 and it is simpler in the sense that it has a smaller denominator. After working several examples using these concrete aids, children should be more ready to approach computational methods for solving such problems.

In Closing

There are many ways to use familiar materials in teaching mathematics. Plastic eggs and styrofoam egg cartons are inexpensive, colorful, and easy to obtain. They can be used at the concrete level to teach many concepts related to whole numbers and fractions. You and your pupils will probably think of many ways to use them once they are introduced in the mathematics classroom. ◆

Let's Do It

We've Got You Pegged!

By **Rosalie Jensen** *and* **David R. O'Neil,** *Georgia State University, Atlanta, Georgia*

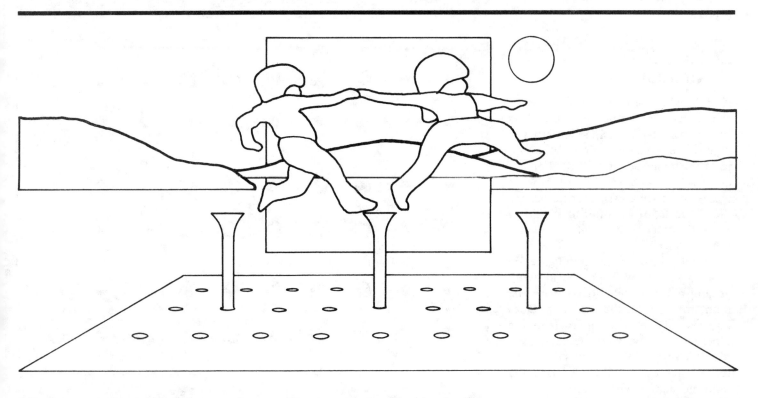

Preschool and elementary-school teachers are always searching for inexpensive, versatile manipulative teaching aids. Ordinary pegboard, used with such common items as pegs or golf tees, can be such an aid. Pegboards of several types and wooden golf tees will be used in illustrations throughout this article. Golf tees were selected because they are colorful and easy for children to handle.

Figure 1 shows some different ways of making pegboards for children to use on a flat surface—a desk, a table, or the floor. Two of the boards are constructed of pegboard cut from larger sheets purchased in the home-improvement section of a discount store. One of these was made by attaching strips of wood on four sides of a 12-hole-by-12-hole piece of board in order to leave

Fig. 1

a 10-by-10 section of holes free for use. The other was made by attaching spools to the four corners of a 10-hole-by-10-hole board. The corner holes fit over the holes in the spools so that golf tees or pegs will fit in these holes as

well as in all others. The round pegboard was made by drilling holes in a wooden cheese-box cover. The box itself is used to store pegs, golf tees, hooks, small pictures, numeral cards, and other items needed to do the activities.

Sorting According to Color

Young children enjoy sorting objects with respect to some attribute. Classification activities can contribute to reading readiness if containers for sorted objects bear a label indicating the class of objects to be placed inside. Suggested containers for small objects include empty boxes, cosmetic jars, egg carton sections, styrofoam meat and vegetable trays, and plastic margarine tubs. In figure 2, golf tees have been sorted according to color and placed in clear, plastic cups labeled with the name of the color. The words are spelled with vinyl peel-off letters (available in stationery sections of department stores and drugstores) with a piece of clear tape across each word. The children can see the color of the tees inside the cup and the word for the color at the same time. At the end of any activity the golf tees should be sorted by the children into the appropriate containers.

Developing the Concept of Conservation of Number

A child who conserves number understands that the number of objects does not change if the arrangement of the objects is altered (assuming that no objects are removed or added). For example, the teacher can place five or six tees of one color on the pegboard as indicated in figure 3a and ask a child to place the same number of tees of another color below your line. The child will likely place the tees as in figure 3b. Rearrange the child's pegs as in figure 3c and ask the child to compare the number of tees in the two rows. Does one row of tees have more than the other or do they have the same number of tees? The child who can say consistently that the number remains the same no matter what changes in configuration are made is said to conserve number or to have the concept of conservation of number. In order to develop this concept, some children need a great deal of experience with manipulating objects. The pegboard and golf tees offer opportunities for making many different configurations with the same set of tees.

Copying and Making Patterns

The ability to perceive patterns is an asset in learning mathematics as well as in other areas such as science, reading, art, and music. Interesting patterns, both simple and complex, can be made on the pegboard. The teacher can make row patterns with different colors as in figure 4 and ask children to copy the patterns on the pegboard.

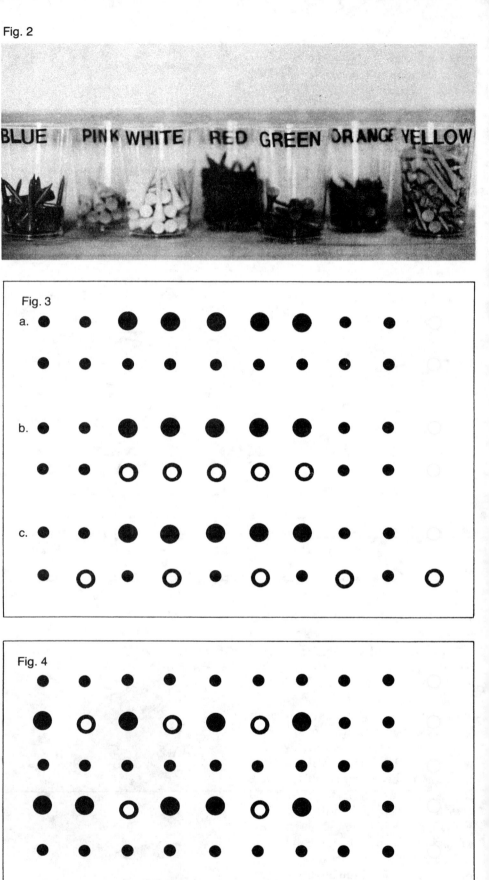

Fig. 2

Fig. 3

a.

b.

c.

Fig. 4

Fig. 5

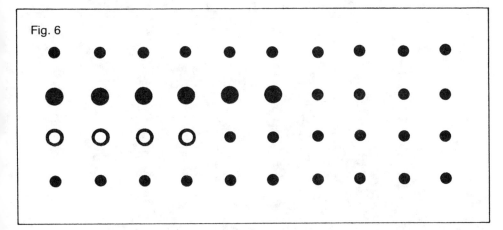

After children can copy a pattern made by the teacher they should be led into extending or completing a pattern. Using patterns such as the ones in figure 4, the teacher might ask the child to copy the pattern and then to place one, two, or three pegs at the end of the row by following the same pattern. Children at an appropriate stage of development may be asked to verbalize a pattern, such as "two blue, one red" or "one yellow, two red, three green."

Pattern copying should not be limited to items in a row. Children may also be asked to duplicate two-dimensional designs like the ones in figure 5, using the correct number, arrangement, and color of pegs.

Counting and Comparing Small Numbers

Give each child a small number of golf tees (less than ten) in two different colors. Ask the children to put all the tees of one color in one row (starting at the edge of the board and skipping no holes) and to put the tees of the other color in the row directly below (fig. 6). Which row has more tees? How can we tell which row has more? Which row has fewer tees? How can we tell?

Young children are able to count objects more easily if the things to be counted are in a row. Give children less than ten golf tees of the same color and ask them to put the tees all in one row on their pegboards, counting as the pegs are placed in the holes. If the children are working in a small group, the group may count with the child as he or she puts the tees in place or touches the tees one by one. As the children become proficient at counting and are ready to associate numerals with the number of objects, they can choose the correct numeral card and place it beside the objects they have counted. (Numeral cards can be made from numerals cut from old calendars.) Once children can count and read numerals the teacher might hand each child several numeral cards. The children then select the correct number of pegs to go with each card and display the card along with the pegs on the pegboard. Children will enjoy placing

Fig. 6

Fig. 7

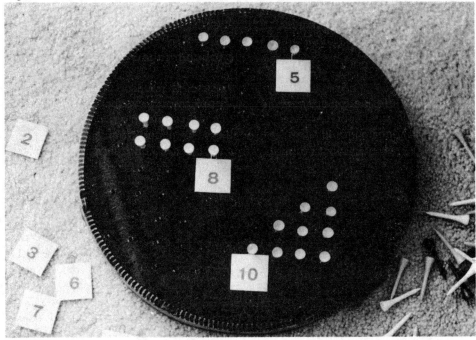

their pegs in different configurations rather than always in rows (fig. 7).

Ordering Small Numbers

Children can use a "stair" like the one in figure 8 to investigate the "greater than" and "less than" relations for numbers 1 through 10. Since no holes are empty within a given row, two numbers can be compared by comparing the lengths of the rows representing these numbers. Assuming that children can conserve number, there should be no confusion between this activity of comparing lengths or rows and the rearrangements in the previously described conservation activity.

Grouping by Tens and Ones

Ask the children, "How many golf tees can you hold in one hand?" Then have children in turn reach into a container, bring out as many tees as possible in one hand, and place their tees in a row on a 10-hole-by-10-hole pegboard. Does anyone have so many pegs that that they cannot be put in one row? How many do you have? Next look at examples of larger numbers of tees, enough tees to fill more than one or two rows. How many rows of ten are there in each case? How many tees are in the row with less than ten? Emphasize the notion that numbers greater than ten can be thought of as so many tens and ones because the tees representing such numbers can be arranged in rows of ten or as rows of ten and a row of less than ten. Provide practice in naming numbers by counting the rows of ten and the number of ones. Introduce two-digit numerals when children are comfortable with the practice of grouping by tens and ones.

A slightly more abstract model for place value than grouping in rows of tens and ones can be developed by assigning different colors to 1, 10, 100, and so forth, depending on the size of the numbers that the children are working with. Figure 9 pictures a pegboard on which cards for ones and tens are held in place by white tees. Directly above each card are nine holes.

Fig. 8

Fig. 9

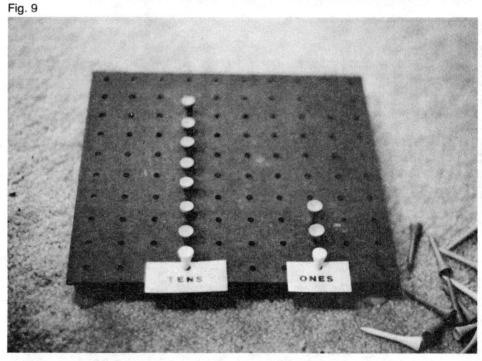

The tees for tens are a different color from the tees for ones. The number indicated on the board in figure 9 can be thought of as 7 tens and 2 ones, or 72.

In order to understand that a tens-tee represents the same number as 10 ones-tees, the children need practice in exchanging 10 ones-tees for 1 tens-tee. One way to practice is through playing a trading game. In addition to pegboards and golf tees, each small group of children participating needs a chance device—a deck of numeral cards, a spinner, or a pair of dice. Sup-

pose that the group has a set of cards with numerals from 1 to 9. As players in turn draw a card, they receive the indicated number of ones-tees from the person designated as the banker. Any time that a child accumulates 10 or more ones-tees, he or she must trade 10 ones-tees for a tens-tee. As soon as a player has accumulated 10 tens-tees, he or she trades them to the banker for a hundreds-tee. The first player to get a hundreds-tee is the winnner.

Students can use additional colors and words cards to display numbers in

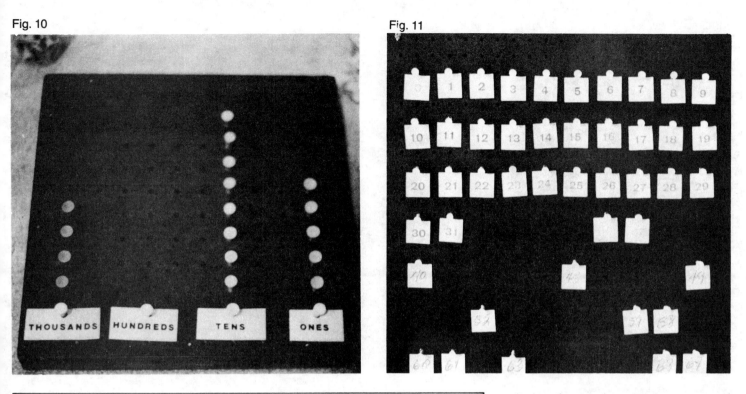

Fig. 10

Fig. 11

THOUSANDS   HUNDREDS   TENS   ONES

Fig. 12

the hundreds and thousands. Figure 10 illustrates 4 thousands, 0 hundreds, 8 tens, and 5 ones, or 4085. The pegboard and golf tees used in this way function much like an open-end abacus.

Making Charts and Tables

A large piece of pegboard nailed on the wall can be used to display charts and operation tables. (Allow space behind the board so that tees or pegs will fit in

the holes.) Figure 11 shows a partially completed hundreds chart. As they place the numeral cards on the chart, children learn that the one-digit numbers are in the top row and that in each other row the numerals have the same digit in the tens place. They can also discover that the numerals in each column have the same digit in the ones place.

Addition and multiplication tables can be made in a similar way. The teacher begins the process of making an addition or multiplication table by

placing the numbers 0-9 in a row and in a column as in figure 12 and by placing string or yarn to form the lines separating these numbers from the body of the table. As each new fact is discovered or demonstrated through materials, the resulting sum or product is placed on the board.

Making Block Graphs

A pegboard and golf tees can be used in several different ways to display information graphically. The most appropriate graphs for young children are the block or picture graphs, where each block or picture represents one object.

Begin graphing experiences with some items that can be separated into two categories. For example, figure 13 shows a pan of water and some small objects. Which of these objects will float and which will sink when placed in the water? Before placing each object in the water, ask the children to make a conjecture—Will it sink or will it float? Sort the objects on the basis of the actual experiment—those that sink in one pile, those that float in another. Have children draw pictures of the objects on cards (or have the names of the objects printed on cards). The children can then make a graph that will compare the numbers of objects in each category. Each picture is held in place

Fig. 13

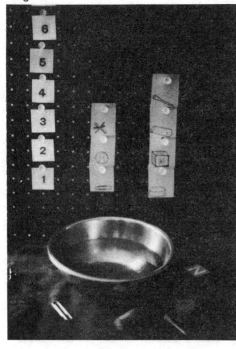

Fig. 14

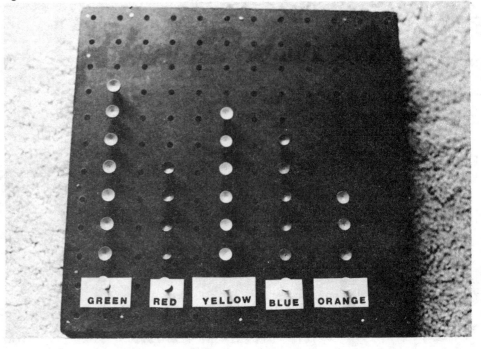

Fig. 15

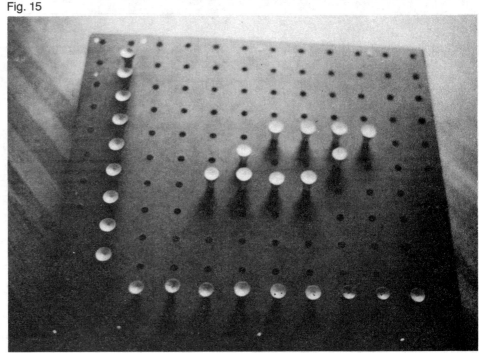

by a tee. Children can determine how many objects sink and how many float by counting the objects or by reading the numerals put along the side of the board. The words *sink* and *float* can be placed below the columns.

Using Pegs to Represent Items on a Graph

Children enjoy displaying information about themselves. Almost everyone has a favorite animal, mode of transportation, ice-cream flavor, or television program. Any of these subjects can be used as the basis of a graph. The graph in figure 14 was constructed after the teacher had asked each child to choose a golf tee in her or his favorite color.

Once the graph is made, you can ask children questions like these concerning the information pictured on the graph:

Which color is the most popular?
How many people like red best?
How many more people like yellow than like orange?

Each child can make a permanent record of the graph by putting colored dots on a piece of paper.

Using Ordered Pairs of Numbers to Make Pictures

To introduce children to the idea of

points located by ordered pairs of numbers, have the children line up a row of pegs of one color at the lower edge of a 10-hole-by-10-hole board and a column of pegs of another color at the left-hand edge. By following directions given as ordered pairs of numbers, children can produce a design such as the one illustrated in figure 15. The directions for this graph would indicate a certain number of yellow tees (across) followed by a certain number of pink tees (up). Using Y for yellow and P for pink, the set of ordered pairs

for this graph would contain these pairs:

(Y3, P4), (Y4, P5), (Y5, P6), (Y6, P6), (Y7, P6), (Y8, P6), (Y7, P5), (Y6, P4), (Y5, P4), (Y4, P4)

Another way of writing these directions is:

Y (across)	3	4	5	6	7	8	7	6	5	4
P (up)	4	5	6	6	6	6	5	4	4	4

178   TEACHER-MADE AIDS

Fig. 16

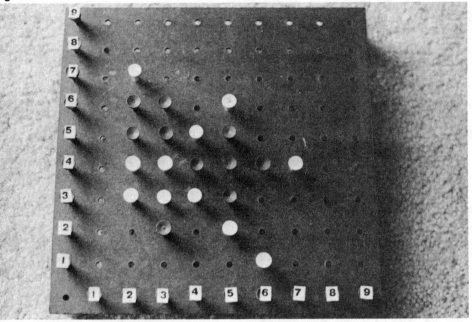

Playing "Four in a Row"

The lower row and left-hand row of tees in figure 15 can be replaced by tees with numerals glued to them, as in figure 16. Using this arrangement children may make graphs and play games such as "Four in a Row." The object of this game is for one of two players to place four of her or his tees in a row ei-

ther vertically, horizontally, or diagonally. To begin the game each player takes all the tees of one color. In turn each player calls an ordered pair of numbers, such as "over 3, up 2" or simply "3, 2", and places a tee of her or his color in the hole corresponding to the ordered pair (3, 2). Figure 16 shows a board on which one player has just won the game with a slanting row on the points (3, 4), (4, 3), (5, 2), and (6, 1).

Summing Up

Teaching aids that are versatile, attractive, and sturdy are not necessarily expensive. The truth of this statement is demonstrated through the many interesting activities that can be pursued using a pegboard and golf tees or pegs. Try some of these ideas and let your children create their own activities and games. If you do, we think you will agree when we say "we've got you pegged." ♥

Let's Do It

Wallpaper Caper

By **Mary Montgomery Lindquist**
National College of Education
Evanston, Illinois
and **Marcia E. Dana**
Spring Harbor Elementary School
Madison, Wisconsin

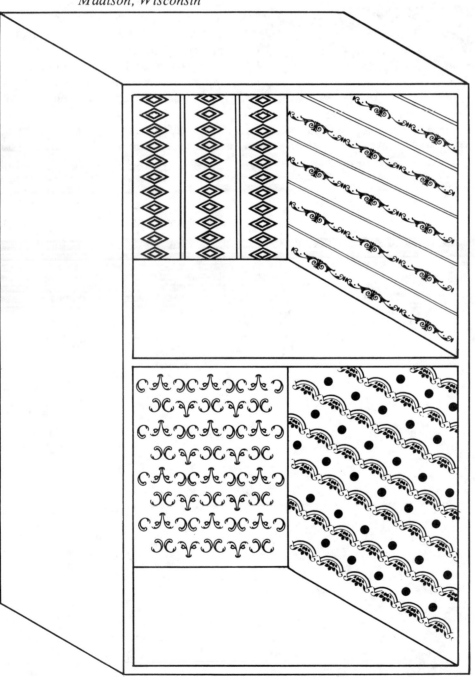

Get a sample wallpaper book or some old pieces of wallpaper and come wallpaper capering! Wallpaper is a fantastic source for many problems involving geometry, statistics, measurement, and estimation. The capers we have suggested involve these types of problems, but you may think of capers that involve computation, probability, or other topics in a comprehensive mathematics program.

We have included examples of questions that can be asked about wallpaper. The specific questions that you use, however, will depend on your samples of wallpaper and, of course, on your class. We found that when we picked a piece of paper, it helped us to ask ourselves questions like the following: Does this sheet have a lot of shapes? Does it have figures that are symmetric? Are there a lot of things pictured in the design so that it would be fun to guess how many? Is there something obvious to measure? (When you come across a sheet with no design, it is rather difficult to think of any mathematics questions, but such sheets are good for other things in the classroom.) The other approach that we found helpful was to think of a topic. For example, if we choose symmetry as a topic, then we find wallpaper samples that have many types of symmetric figures as well as some with no symmetric figures.

It also helps to think in terms of how to organize your class. You may, for example, want to set up centers or a wallpaper center. A card with appropriate questions could be attached to each wallpaper sample. Questions like those suggested later in the measurement section would be appropriate for this type of organization. Or you may want a large group activity, with each child having a different sample. Many of the questions in the statistics section lend themselves to this organization. At times you can find duplicate samples in a wallpaper book that differ only in color. If the pattern is small you can often cut enough pieces so that each child in your group has a piece of the same sample. The coordinate capers in the geometry section are based on this last organization. We have also suggested some games for pairs. So, almost any type of class organization is appropriate for some caper.

Although we have written about wallpaper, you may find that cloth samples, tiling samples, or wrapping paper are more readily available. Any of these materials could be used in the same ways.

Geometry

As you are well aware, many pieces of wallpaper are full of geometric shapes. Even if you don't see a geometric shape at first glance, you can create shapes by connecting a point on one figure to the corresponding point on a repetition of that figure (See figure 1.) Line symmetries also are often present in wallpaper. Wallpaper can be classified according to the design repeats (tiling). Some wallpaper lends itself to coordinate systems. The capers suggested in this section look at these aspects of geometry. Other topics that you may wish to investigate are parallel and perpendicular lines; tracing networks; and flip, slide, and turn symmetries.

Line symmetry capers

1. Either give each child in the group a piece of wallpaper or have a set of wallpaper sheets at a center. Have the children find pieces of papers that satisfy each of the following descriptions. (Use the word *figure* to mean either a single entity or a grouping in a design.)

The sample has at least one figure with two lines of symmetry.
The whole sample has at least one line of symmetry.
The sample has a figure with four lines of symmetry.
The sample has no figures with lines of symmetry.
The sample has a figure with one line of symmetry and another with two lines of symmetry.

2. Draw lines of symmetry on figures and lines that are not lines of symmetry. Label the lines *a, b, c. . . .* Have children tell which are lines and which are not lines of symmetry.

Fig. 1

Fig. 2

diamond

rectangular

stripe

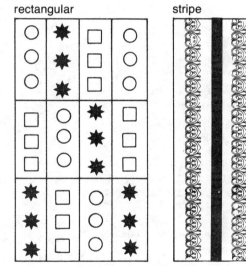

Shape capers

1. Give every child a sheet of wallpaper, then have the children identify the shapes—circles, equilateral triangles, triangles, parallelograms, and so on. For older children, have them connect corresponding points, as shown in figure 1, and then identify the resulting shapes.

2. Make a bulletin board of the shapes. As children find a shape on a sheet of wallpaper, have them cut it out and add it to the collection.

Tiling capers

Have the children decide what kind of design covers a sheet of paper. (See figure 2.) Again, you may have to connect corresponding points as in figure 1. Older children may find other tiling

patterns, such as hexagons or other parallelograms. After tiling patterns have been identified, you may investigate the size of the tile. Are all the diamond tiles the same size? Can you find a sheet with a larger rectangular tiling pattern than this one?

Coordinate capers

Many wallpaper sample books have patterns similar to the one in figure 3. Such patterns can be used as geoboards. In figure 3, for example, if you call the figure marked by X an apple, look at how the apples are arranged on the sheet (in alternating rows). If you cannot find a wallpaper pattern like this, you could draw a simplified version of such a pattern. If you can find one, cut out portions of the pattern, about the size shown in figure 3, for each child. Have children put a plastic sheet on the portion and use a grease pen to do these capers.

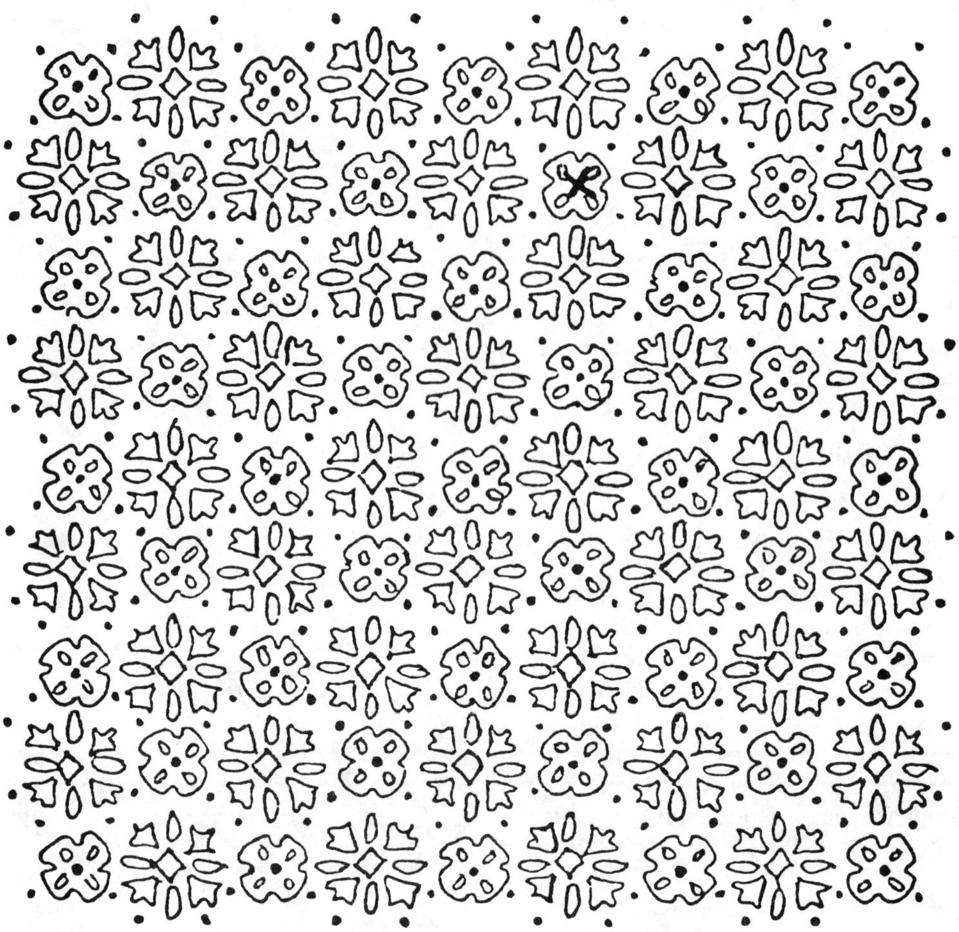

1. If you connect only the centers of the apples with straight lines, what geometric shapes can you make?

Can you make a square? Can you make a square in more than one way?

Can you make a triangle? What kind of a triangle? Can you make a triangle in more than one way? Can you make more than one kind of triangle?

2. Make some designs, using the following symbols for directions:

U   up
D   down
R   right
L   left
↗   move diagonally up,
         to the right
↖   move diagonally up,
         to the left
↘   move diagonally down,
         to the right
↙   move diagonally down,
         to the left

Combine these so that a direction such as 3D, 2↘, means to move down three apples and then diagonally down and to the right two apples.

3. Using figure 3, have children do the following problem:

Begin at the upper right hand apple. Move to other apples according to the directions that follow. Place an X after each move—the first X is placed for you. Connect the Xs in order.

Move 1: 1L, 1↙   Move 5: 3L
Move 2: 2D, 1↘   Move 6: 1↖
Move 3: 1R   Move 7: 1R
Move 4: 1↙   Move 8: ?

Move 8 should get you back to the original X. Write a move that will do this. When you have connected the Xs, what do you see? (Note: There are several moves that can be used; for example, 1 ∪ 3↗ or 1 ↖4↗)

Statistics

Children need skill in classifying data before they can develop skill in pro-

Fig. 3

cessing data. The first capers look at ways to have young children classify wallpaper. The other capers suggest ways to graph information about wallpaper.

Classifying capers

1. Cut pairs of pieces from wallpaper sheets, mix them, and then have children match the pairs. You could put one piece of each pair on the bulletin board or on a large sheet of paper and have the children match their pieces to the displayed pieces. (Fig. 4) Or you could just mix the pairs up and let the children sort them.

2. Display three sheets of wallpaper at a time (two could be the same pattern but different colors), and ask children how the patterns are alike or different.

3. Give everyone in the class a piece of wallpaper. Then have the children group themselves in various ways. For

example, everyone that has a plaid piece gets in one group; a striped piece, in another, and so on. They might also sort by color, by shapes within the designs, or by texture.

Graphing capers

1. Let the children, during their free time, each choose a favorite sheet of wallpaper. With young children, make a graph of the set of samples chosen that tells about the set. For example, as in figure 5, graph the dominant color or the type of design. With older children, let a group of children decide how they are going to classify the set. Then, they should graph how many are in each subset. After one group has classified the patterns and graphed their results, let other groups do the same. When all groups have had an opportunity to do this, display the various graphs and talk about how the different groups categorized the patterns.

Fig. 4

Find my match

Fig. 5

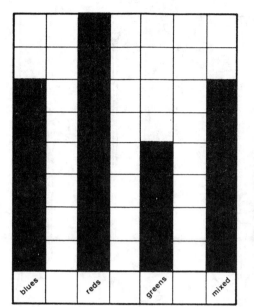

blues | reds | greens | mixed

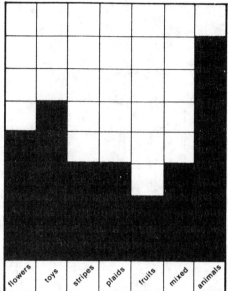

flowers | toys | stripes | plaids | fruits | mixed | animals

2. Select wallpaper patterns that have several different objects or designs in them. Give each child one of these, then have each child decide how to present the information—objects and numbers—on a graph. When you have a set of about ten graphs, see if the other children can match each graph with its sheet of wallpaper.

Measurement

Almost any piece of wallpaper lends itself to measurement questions—How long is this flower stem? What is the perimeter of the rectangle containing the frog? What is the radius of the smallest circle you can draw to enclose the monkey? What is the area of the smallest diamond? Or, what is the size of the largest angle of the hexagon?

The capers that follow are written for older children and focus only on striped paper. Many problems that are suitable for any age, however, could be written about almost any sheet.

Take a striped sheet like the one in figure 6. Pieces of any size will do, but cut the pieces of wallpaper so that their dimensions are a whole number of centimeters. If the sample has too many stripes, you can group the stripes into sections, or cut off a piece of the pattern that has only six to eight stripes on it. Draw a diagonal line across the stripes as shown in figure 6 and label the stripes (or sections) with letters for ease of communication.

Fig. 6

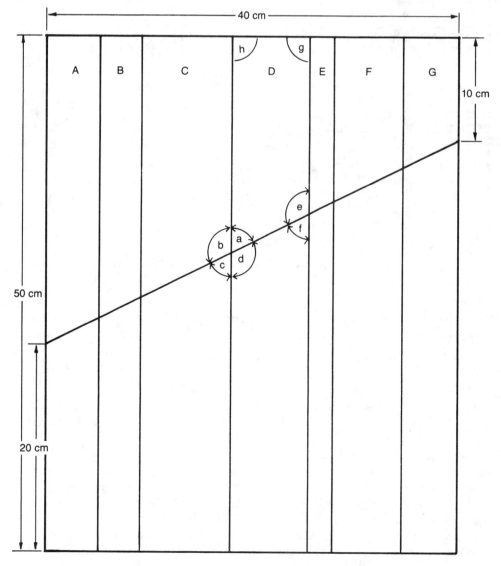

Fig. 7

they need to know how to find the area of a trapezoid. See "Problem Solving with Trapezoids in the Middle School" by Thomas in this issue for ways to present this.

3. In how many stripes is the top part (as cut by the diagonal line) larger in area than the corresponding bottom part?

Angle capers

Label angles $a, b, \ldots, h$ as shown in figure 6.

1. Which angles are larger than a right angle?

2. Measure each angle with a protractor.

3. How many different sizes of angles are formed by the diagonal line and the edges of the stripes? (2)

4. What is the sum of the measures of angles $a, e, g,$ and h? Find the sum of the measures of the angles in another four-sided figure.

5. Have pairs of children play a game. Cut out eight small pieces of paper, about the size of half of a 3-by-5 card for each pair of children. Label two of them with the measure of angle a, two with the measure of angle b, and the rest with 90°. The children, in turn, draw a card and claim, by making it in the same way, an angle of that size on the striped paper. When all four angles of a quadrilateral (treat the bottom and the top of each stripe, as defined by the diagonal line, as a separate quadrilateral) are claimed by one person, it is his or her quadrilateral. Keep shuffling cards and drawing until all angles are claimed. If a card is drawn and there is no angle left of that size the turn is lost. The winner is the one with the most quadrilaterals, which is not necessarily the one with the most angles.

Estimation

One of the questions, How many? How long? Or, How large? can often be asked about a sheet of paper. To encourage the children to estimate, two types of capers are suggested. The first estimating caper is a contest about *How many*?; the second caper is a game for two about *How long*? or *How large*? (in area). The group caper is suggested for *How many* so that you can assist in developing more sophisticated ways of

Length capers

1. What is the width of each stripe? Which stripe is the widest; the narrowest?

2. What is the distance across each stripe on the diagonal line? For which stripe is the distance the longest?

3. What is the perimeter of the largest four-sided figure formed by the diagonal line, the sides of a stripe, and the edge of the paper?

4. What is the shortest path (staying on the edges of the paper, on the edges of the stripes, or on the diagonal line) you can take to get from the top right corner to the bottom left corner? From the top left corner to the bottom right corner?

Area capers

1. How much more is the area of the largest stripe than the area of the smallest stripe?

2. The diagonal line divides the paper into a top part and a bottom part. Which area is larger? How much larger? (Children could answer which area is larger by tracing a piece the size of one part and placing it directly on the other. To find out how much larger,

counting. The group can be large or small. The game is suggested for two so that individual children will have more practice in measuring to check their estimates.

How many? capers

Have a contest each day for a week. For each contest choose a different piece of wallpaper. Each piece of wallpaper should have a number of objects on it in the range of numbers your students are familiar with. Have a contest to see who can make the best guess as to how many objects are on the piece of wallpaper. Show the paper long enough for a reasonable guess to be made, but not long enough for the children to count the objects. After each child has had an opportunity to guess, count the objects (or establish a reasonable approximation) together.

Younger children may need help organizing their counting. For example, suppose that the wallpaper has houses with different numbers of windows, and you want the number of windows. Then it could help to tally the windows in a house and check that house off on the sheet. After tallying the windows in each house, the count of houses could be made. If the pattern of objects is regular in any way, adding or multiplying may assist in the counting. For example, suppose the sheet has rows of flowers, each of which has six petals, and you are counting the number of petals, then, multiplying will help. If the pattern of objects appears to be random but fairly evenly spaced and the number of objects is large, then you might count them in one-tenth or one-sixteenth of the piece of paper. Or, if the design is small enough, you might find the repeat pattern to assist in the approximating. Unless the guesses are very close, an approximate answer will often suffice.

Once you have introduced some counting techniques, you may want small groups of children to do their own sheet. Another worthwhile variation is to begin with the question about a smaller part of the sheet and then extend it to the whole sheet. For example, suppose you have a sheet of paper with about fifteen flowers, each of which has approximately the same number of petals. First ask, "How many petals are on a flower?" Have the children guess and check. Then pose the problem about how many petals are on the entire sheet. This encourages children to break the problem into smaller parts when they are estimating.

How long? capers

Give each pair of children a sheet of wallpaper with several obvious lengths to measure. For illustration, let us say the sheet of paper has flower stems of various lengths, as in figure 7. You may need to mark, or have each pair of children mark, about ten lengths on a piece of wallpaper and label the lengths with letters A, B, C.... Each child guesses the length of A, then measures it. The child whose guess is closer receives a point. Knowing the length of stem A can often help a child make a better guess for the length of stem B. The child with the most points, after all the guessing and measuring, is the winner.

This game can be made more challenging for older children by choosing curved lines or open or closed figures. A piece of string can help in the measuring of curved lines. Or, if a sheet contains many rectangles, children could estimate the areas.

Closing

You will think of many other capers as you try some of the suggested capers. The following are some variations that you might keep in mind: estimating how many rolls of paper are needed to paper a room of a given size, (keep the rooms simple); finding the length of the repeat (the answer to this is often given on the back of a sample piece); or finding how much wallpaper would be needed to cover the top of a table wider than one strip (be sure the patterns match when put together). Some children may be interested in reproducing the designs, especially if the designs are geometric. Other children may wish to design their own paper.

As the children become familiar with questions about wallpaper, turn the questioning over to them. By asking them to list the mathematics questions they could ask about one or more sample pieces, children will participate in important aspects of problem solving—asking appropriate questions and seeing if they can be answered.□